VOICES OF COURAGE

THE BATTLE FOR KHE SANH, VIETNAM

VOICES OF COURAGE

THE BATTLE FOR KHE SANH, VIETNAM

Ronald J. Drez and Douglas Brinkley

Bulfinch Press

New York · Boston

Bulfinch Press

Time Warner Book Group
1271 Avenue of the Americas
New York, NY 10020
Visit our Web site at www.bulfinchpress.com

First Edition: September 2005

ISBN 0-8212-6196-7

Library of Congress Control Number: 2005921959

Voices of Courage: The Battle for Khe Sanh, Vietnam is produced
by becker&mayer!, Bellevue, Washington.
www.beckermayer.com

Design by Todd Bates

Printed in China

Voices of Courage *is dedicated to all who fought in our nation's longest, most controversial war, and never lost a battle.*

CONTENTS

FOREWORD

At night in Khe Sanh, waiting there, thinking about all of them (40,000 some said), thinking
that they might really try it, could keep you up. If they did, when they did, it might not
matter that you were in the best bunker in the DMZ, wouldn't matter that you were young
and had plans, that you were loved, that you were a noncombatant, an observer. Because if
it came, it would be a bloodswarm of killing, and credentials would not be examined.
   —Michael Herr, *Dispatches* (1977)

Back in 1967 Michael Herr—an ace reporter with a counterculture demeanor—went to Vietnam for
Esquire magazine. His first article for editor Harold Hayes from the war zone was titled "Hell Sucks;" it
was greeted as a brazen triumph of the so-called New Journalism, the voguish New York publishing trend
where writers injected a fiercely subjective viewpoint into their colorful nonfiction copy. Unlike Ernie Pyle
or Edward R. Murrow during the Second World War, the twenty-seven-year-old Herr was essentially an
anti-war correspondent. His riveting, horrific, and at times hallucinatory prose expressed disrespect for
President Lyndon B. Johnson and a loathing for General William Westmoreland, the commander of U.S.
Forces in Vietnam from 1965 to 1968. In 1977—two years after the dramatic U.S. evacuation of Saigon—
Herr published his acclaimed Vietnam journalistic novel titled *Dispatches* to laudatory reviews. He had
become, through his graphic depictions of battlefield agony, a literary star. "Michael Herr has so often been
called the Stephen Crane of our age," Gloria Emerson enthused, "but I think he is a finer writer and that
Dispatches will endure as a remarkable classic."

  The centerpiece of *Dispatches* was the Battle for Khe Sanh—located on a highland plateau near
Highway 9, which links Vietnam with southern Laos. The showdown took place during seventy-seven
bloody days in early 1968, closely intertwined with the Tet Offensive. A gifted prose-stylist, Herr did a fine
job, in *Dispatches*, of explaining the strategic importance of Khe Sanh to both Washington, D.C., and Hanoi
policymakers. His impressionistic prose perfectly captured the surreal eeriness of the isolated, besieged
U.S. Marine base. "When I think of it quickly, just seeing the name somewhere or being asked what it was
like, I see a flat, dun stretch of ground running out in an even plain until the rim or the middle distance
takes on the shapes and colors of jungled hills," Herr wrote. "I had the strangest, most thrilling kind of
illusion there."

  Back in Washington, D.C., President Lyndon Johnson was having illusions of his own. As Herr recounts,
President Johnson, worried that a loss at Khe Sanh on the heels of Tet would doom his presidency,

ordered the Joint Chiefs of Staff to assure the public that the fortified outpost be held at all costs. He was worried that he had another Dien Bien Phu (1954)—or "Dinbinfoo," as the Texas wheeler-dealer called the Eisenhower-era Vietnam turning point—on his hands. Unlike the French Army, however, Johnson didn't plan on having American troops decimated, or giving up Southeast Asia's version of "The Alamo" without a kinghell fight. Since July 1962, Khe Sanh had been an important U.S. Special Forces base. It was first hit by North Vietnamese mortar rounds in 1966. Within a year somewhere between 30,000 to 40,000 communist troops started encircling the U.S. compound run by Colonel David Lownds. Of the 6,808 Americans huddled together at Khe Sanh, refusing to give ground, 5,905 were stalwart Marines.

As the U.S. Marines and the North Vietnamese Army squared off in the northwestern corner of South Vietnam, President Johnson was understandably anxious. Less understandable was the way he dissembled. General Maxwell Taylor later recalled that an "air of gloom" permeated the Johnson Administration in the grim days following the Tet Offensive. Desperately LBJ tried to micro-manage Khe Sanh from the White House, pacing around a terrain map in the "war room" as if he were a field general. Just as Johnson strong-armed legislators on passing sweeping Civil Rights bills, he tried *willing* an American victory at Khe Sanh by not sleeping. Exhausted, and in questionable mental health, Johnson feared humiliation in Southeast Asia more than anything he ever encountered. From January 21, 1968 (when the NVA attacked Hill 861) until April 14, 1968 (when the U.S. Marines broke out of siege and took Hill 881N) Khe Sanh dominated international news coverage. Death tolls and bomb droppings were reported with daily regularity. It was a "set-piece" military showdown, with the concerned eyes of the world watching on television. The result? The U.S. won the battle but lost the spin.

Khe Sanh, as a special place in a tumultuous time, has not been entirely forgotten in U.S. history. (The same, unfortunately, can't be said for An Khe, Qui Nhon, Bong Son, An Lao, Dak To, Mang Buk, Polei Klang, and Kontum.) Which is a good thing. But a grievous misperception of Khe Sanh has taken root since 1968. Viewing Khe Sanh as directly connected to Tet, most Johnson-era reporters based in Saigon—like Herr—were seemingly influenced by their staunch anti-war beliefs. They were, in essence, pulling for "doves" back home—like Senators Eugene McCarthy of Minnnesota or Robert F. Kennedy of New York—to prevail. Nineteen sixty-eight was, after all, an election year. In print, reporters, with a few rare exceptions, never gave the Marines and Air Force heroics at Khe Sanh just coverage. For liberals it was essential not to be perceived as being too "pro-Vietnam." Too often, as in *Dispatches*, the Marines were portrayed in cartoonish fashion, as alienated, pot-smoking, hippie-dippie Jimi Hendrix freaks who had death in their red eyes and a joint in their puckered lips. It was as if Khe Sanh were a street in the Haight-Ashbury district of San Francisco. Certainly drugs were a problem in Vietnam, but not on the front lines, and certainly not at a besieged Khe Sanh.

One of the primary reasons we wrote *Voices of Courage* was to spotlight the raw heroism with which the U.S. Armed Forces—the Marines in particular—performed at Khe Sanh. We wanted to dispel the *Dispatches* notion that U.S. Marines resembled Wavy Gravy more than Chesty Puller. It is also our conclusion, as military historians, that General Westmoreland—the commanding officer—actually *won* the Battle of Khe Sanh. (It's also true, however, that he misread Tet). The Vietnamese communists boldly claimed that Khe Sanh was "America's Dien Bien Phu"—our Waterloo, of sorts. North Vietnamese General Vo Nguyen Giap, in fact, clearly outmaneuvered the Johnson Administration on the PR front—*bigtime*. That fact, however, does not change the reality that Giap was full of unadulterated communist propaganda regarding the so-declared North Vietnamese victory at Khe Sanh. All one has to do is count. The U.S. had approximately 730 KIAs, 2,598 wounded, and 7 MIAs. Tough numbers. But this toll was miniscule compared to the one that the communists paid. While *exact* North Vietnamese casualty statistics at Khe Sanh are impossible to authoritatively declare, it has been estimated that over 10,000 to 15,000 soldiers were killed.

Some might argue that KIAs or who "won" Khe Sanh doesn't matter, that the carnage happened four decades ago. But to the men who fought there, and sacrificed, it matters a great deal. The Marine Corps veterans of Vietnam we interviewed believe *deeply* that their very honor is at stake over this contentious historical issue. They claim confusion over victory arose in 1968 because of LBJ's shocking decision not to seek re-election and the cold fact that the U.S. withdrew from Khe Sanh on July 6. Marines, even to this day, have never forgiven Johnson for bailing out of Khe Sanh once victory had been achieved. It is a bone, which, nearly forty years later, is still stuck in their craw. In fact, Vietnam scholar Ronald Spector, a history professor at George Washington University, calculated that in the first six months of 1968, the deaths the Marines suffered exceeded the casualty rates in World War II and the Korean War. They wished LBJ would have respected their gallant effort and, at the very least, held onto Khe Sanh until the U.S. election was over in November.

Vietnam veterans remain baffled about Johnson's rationale for abandoning Khe Sanh. Like a choir they ask: Was Johnson nuts? "The decision to abandon Khe Sanh is better described as a tactical withdrawal rather than a forced retreat," Peter Brush correctly explained in *Vietnam Magazine*. "The Marines on the ground were willing to maintain their positions at Khe Sanh if ordered to do so. I was at Khe Sanh from December 1967, before the fighting began, until April 1968, when the siege was officially declared ended. There was no sense that we were a defeated force, and I had no idea the base was scheduled for closing. My Marine unit was told that we would remain at Khe Sanh until another mortar battery could replace us. When that happened we relocated to the east and continued operations against the North Vietnamese."

The dozens of Marines interviewed for this book don't resemble the druggie, acid-tinged characters in *Dispatches*. They are pure, patriotic fighting men. Ferocious defenders. America's best. They feel—in their hearts—that they truly defeated General Giap's army on those terrifying hills near Laos. While set-backs are admitted—like on January 21, 1968, when a Vietnamese rocket destroyed the principle Marine ammunition dump, blowing up fifteen hundred tons of high explosives, catching them off-guard—the brave initiative of American forces comes bursting through the oral histories we've relied upon in writing *Voices of Courage*. Put more succinctly, American-style revenge was soon inflicted: massive retaliation. The U.S. troops, Marines in particular, with heavy Air Force bombardment support—persevered. General

Westmoreland's Operation Niagara—a component of which was B-52s dropping over fifty-nine thousand tons of bombs from the sky—devastated the enemy. The net effect of the bombing—from the enemy's perspective—was complete disaster. Khe Sanh became a burial ground for the North Vietnamese dead.

Unlike most books and articles about Khe Sanh, we don't focus solely on the mistakes made by LBJ and Secretary of Defense Robert McNamara—although they take their well-deserved licks. Or on the drug use on the battlefield, which, due to books like *Dispatches*, has been exaggerated. (Herr was also a screenplay writer for "Apocalypse Now" and "Full Metal Jacket"). We instead have interviewed true blue American heroes, men like Charles Rushforth and Bill Dabney and Earl Breeding. Up until now, they have kept their stories of Khe Sanh largely to themselves. And, in large part, the reputation of General Westmoreland, long a scapegoat for Johnson Administration failures in Vietnam, is somewhat redeemed in this narrative. Whatever his shortcomings, he led his entrenched troops well in battle, thwarting the North Vietnamese back into the hinterland.

Still, the controversy over Khe Sanh continues. It is historian/journalist Stanley Karnow, author of *Vietnam: A History*, who offers the best critique of why Khe Sanh was, in his opinion, a full-fledged American disaster. He feels that Westmoreland had swallowed an "enemy ruse" by placing such a high priority on Khe Sanh. "His exaggerated focus on Khe Sanh was finally punctured a few days after he ended his tour in Vietnam in June, when the fortress was abandoned," Karnow wrote. "A withdrawal conducted in secret to avoid jarring the American people, who had been told that the U.S. Marines were trying to secure the 'crucial anchor' of the defense chain in the sector." To a degree we concur with Karnow's assertion. By giving up Khe Sanh after winning it, the Johnson Administration killed Marine morale and confused the public as to why a strategic location so vital in April was suddenly devalued in July. Beat poet Allen Ginsberg had a point when he asked that summer in Chicago, "All the Khe Sanh carnage for what?" But, unfortunately, Karnow skips over the battlefield analysis of Khe Sanh. We don't. Far from being a failure, Khe Sanh—from Marine and Air Force perspectives—was an undeniable win. Chalk it up for G. I. Joe.

Today you can go to Khe Sanh and tour a small museum. You can hear birds sing outside instead of bombs dropping. It's a communist victory memorial. But the real story of Khe Sanh is—in our opinion—best told by the surviving Marines and Air Force pilots who won the high-stakes showdown. This book is an opportunity for their valorous voices to be heard. Honest people can debate whether U.S. involvement in Vietnam was moral or just or noble, but nobody who knows what happened at that remote highlands can claim that our Cold War soldiers didn't perform with stunning fortitude.

INTRODUCTION

....

After World War II, the United States found itself in a quandary. It had promised France that it could reacquire its colonial possessions in Indochina,* but had also committed to the Atlantic Charter in 1941, espousing the right of national self-determination. President Franklin D. Roosevelt had personally advocated independence for Indochina, but at war's end, Roosevelt was dead and political realities had changed.

In 1947 President Harry S. Truman initiated the Truman Doctrine, designed to confront Communist expansionist aims worldwide. The threat of global communism prompted the American government to take a hands-off policy in the Indochinese war that pitted French colonial forces against the rebellious Viet Minh forces. Washington saw the war as necessary to stop the fall of Vietnam into Communist hands.

By 1948 President Truman was forced to confront the Communists on a more significant battlefield when the Soviets tried to take over Berlin by blockading the city. The Berlin airlift defeated those expansionist goals, but the victory was short-lived.

The 1949 collapse of the Chinese National Government and emergence of the Communist People's Republic of China—recognized immediately by the Soviet government as an ally—sharpened American apprehension of Red expansion, and one year later, the Soviets and the Chinese recognized the rebellious Ho Chi Minh's claim to govern Vietnam. This new stroke prompted the Truman administration to declare Ho Chi Minh the mortal enemy of a free and independent Indochina.

In the span of two years, the United States had gone from a hands-off policy to a full-fledged commitment to assist France in defeating Ho Chi Minh and his Viet Minh army.

In 1950 Communist forces invaded South Korea, shattering whatever remained of the original U.S. hands-off policies, and by 1954, the Americans were paying for 80 percent of France's war in Vietnam. The American government had given France more than two billion of the five billion dollars that nation had spent to keep Vietnam as a colony and out of Communist hands.

But the French forces blundered onto the wrong battlefield in 1954, and were decisively defeated at Dien Bien Phu after a fifty-seven-day siege by the Viet Minh forces under General Vo Nguyen Giap. Nagged by this humiliating defeat and protests of the war at home, the French forces abandoned Vietnam. After seven years of war, they dug up their dead and left—lock, stock, and barrel. Vietnam was partitioned at the 17th parallel: the country to the north under Communist control; the country to the south still free.

The Communist threat of world domination reinforced the wisdom of the Truman Doctrine to Presidents Eisenhower, Kennedy, and Johnson, who embraced it and expanded on its dictums. Eisenhower formed his

*Indochina, also called French Indochina, was a collection of French colonies in Southeast Asia. The Annam, Cochin China, and Tonkin territories now form Vietnam.

"domino theory" regarding the threat of a Communist takeover of Southeast Asia. He announced a policy of "massive retaliation" against any Communist attack on America or its allies.

In 1962 President John F. Kennedy brought the United States to the brink of war over missiles in Cuba, and faced down Soviet premier Nikita Khrushchev, forcing him to order their removal. The young president also focused world attention on the American–Soviet face-off in Berlin* and committed advisory forces to South Vietnam.

Five days after Kennedy's assassination, President Lyndon Johnson embraced the Truman Doctrine and pledged that he would "keep our commitments from South Vietnam to West Berlin." But by 1965, South Vietnam's Army of the Republic of Vietnam (ARVN) was losing its war, and Johnson committed United States forces to prevent the collapse of the country to the invading forces from the north.

At the end of 1967, after almost three years of American armed intervention in South Vietnam, the United States found itself in a position to possibly complete the military turn-around it had sought. There now appeared a light at the end of the tunnel. The South Vietnamese army was no longer losing the war. The North Vietnamese commanders saw their military advantage slipping away. In an attempt to stop this turn-around, they planned a daring strategy that called for the defeat of a major American force.

This decisive battle was to duplicate the 1954 showdown at Dien Bien Phu and force the Americans to withdraw as the French had. Gen Giap would initiate the battle on the ground chosen by the Americans in the far northwestern corner of South Vietnam at the Marine combat base at Khe Sanh. To many observers, this remote geographical spot seemed unimportant, but so had the remote battlefield of Dien Bien Phu.

In the early days of 1968 this seemingly insignificant outpost became important. The battle would be fought for the highest of stakes: the Communist goal to defeat the United States Marines and conquer and reunite Vietnam under the Communist flag, and the American determination to stop the spread of communism and defeat a major portion of the North Vietnamese Army. It would draw news reporters, television cameras, writers, and pundits to it like moths to a flame. It would turn President Lyndon Johnson into an insomniac pacing the inner sanctum of the White House, wondering if he was not witnessing a reenactment of the 1836 attack on the Alamo. It would hold the world on the edge of its seat for seventy-seven days and would command headline news coverage. It would bring the opposing warriors face-to-face in a grim test of nerves and endurance. The battle for Khe Sanh would be the showdown.

*In October 1961 Soviet and American tanks squared off on opposite sides of Checkpoint Charlie, which separated East and West Berlin, because of a decree published by the Soviets stating that foreign civilians were required to show identification at the checkpoint. The situation escalated. President Kennedy forced Krushchev to withdraw the decree and his tanks.

A welcome sign at Khe Sanh Combat Base.

CHAPTER 1

THE ROAD TO THE SHOWDOWN

Marines land on the beach at Da Nang, March 8, 1965.

	APRIL 24, 1967	MAY 13, 1967	DECEMBER 1967	JANUARY 21, 1968	JANUARY 31, 1968
TIMELINE	Hill Fights begin at Khe Sanh	Hill Fights end. Marines fought off elements of the 325C NVA Division in a two-week battle that cost the enemy 824 KIA. 168 Marines were killed and 443 wounded in the struggle.	General Westmoreland decides to reinforce Khe Sanh in the face of enemy buildup.	NVA attack hill 861 and bombard combat base exploding ammo dump, and attack Khe Sanh village. Siege begins.	NVA launch countrywide Tet Offensive.

In January 1967, as the people of Vietnam prepared to usher in the Year of the Goat, elements of the 3rd Marine Division faced increasing enemy buildup along the Demilitarized Zone (DMZ) in Quang Tri Province, the northernmost province in South Vietnam. The North Vietnamese Army (NVA) had thrust portions of two divisions into the area and now threatened the western approaches to the heavily populated coastal regions.[1]

Twenty months had passed since Marines first landed on the beaches at Da Nang on March 8, 1965. They were the first United States ground combat troops introduced into the Vietnam War, but instead of engaging a well-entrenched enemy force on the beach, the Marines were greeted by giggling, bouncing girls from the Central Vietnam schools, who wrapped garlands around the Americans' necks.[2]

Four months later, the Marines met and defeated the 1st Viet Cong (VC) Regiment in an amphibious and helicopter action called Operation Starlite, and at the beginning of 1966, U.S. troop strength was up to 184,000 men.

The enemy strength also increased from five VC maneuver regiments to twelve, and intelligence detected nine NVA regiments inside South Vietnam.[3] The Marines reasoned that the success of their "pacification program," meant to expel the VC from all populated areas, had forced the enemy to try to draw American forces away from those locales and into the northern provinces of Quang Tri and Thua Thien, south of the DMZ.

Gen William C. Westmoreland, Commander of U.S. forces in South Vietnam, reacted to the enemy troop movements and saw an opportunity to meet and defeat a large enemy force. "I saw no alternative to sending American troops to oppose the new threat," said the general.[4]

The enemy buildup in the north was especially frustrating to President Johnson, who had ordered the bombing of North Vietnam in the early days of the war, hoping to bring the foe to the bargaining table. But Operation Rolling Thunder—a bombing campaign of fits and starts, stand-downs, cancellations, and target

DISK 1, TRACKS 4-6: Arriving at Khe Sanh and the Hill Fights.

FEBRUARY 5-8, 1968	FEBRUARY 23, 1968	FEBRUARY 29, 1968	APRIL 14, 1968	JUNE 19-JULY 5, 1968
NVA attack Hill 861 Alpha, Lang Vei, and Hill 64.	Enemy gunners bombard base with more than 1,300 rounds in heaviest attack.	NVA launch regimental size attack against base.	Marines break out of siege and attack and seize Hill 881N.	Khe Sanh Combat Base is destroyed and abandoned by American forces.

denial—was a total tactical failure. It was better described as an attempt at political arm-twisting than as a dedicated military offensive.

On orders from the White House the air forces were not allowed to bomb ninety-four targets they considered important. The "arm-twisting" Johnson thought he was applying was as ineffective as Rolling Thunder, and the enemy moved reinforcements with virtual impunity from North Vietnam into South Vietnam.

By June 1966 the office of the Commander in Chief Pacific (CINCPAC) disclosed that North Vietnam was capable of infiltrating fifteen battalions (nine thousand men) per month into South Vietnam. In July Gen Westmoreland ordered the Marines to move to the north. Recon teams that had met no resistance in the past now could not stay in the field for more than a few hours before they were forced to call for extraction because of heavy enemy contact.[5]

On July 18, the Marines launched Operation Hastings in a remote northern area just two miles below the DMZ. The area was a hornets' nest. Eight thousand Marines and three thousand South Vietnamese soldiers engaged an equal number of NVA soldiers from the 324B Division. The action was savage and became the most violent operation of the war to that time. In a two-week running gunfight, the Marines killed 700 enemy soldiers while losing 126 of their own killed and 448 wounded. The South Vietnamese suffered an additional 60 casualties.[6]

The NVA infiltration of the DMZ continued. An estimated sixty thousand enemy soldiers poured into South Vietnam in 1966, and as these soldiers flooded across the border, the military and political leaders proposed their own solutions. Westmoreland advocated forming an allied multinational force to block the infiltration routes. This multinational force of Korean, Australian, New Zealand, and American soldiers would also lead to international recognition of the American claim that the North Vietnamese were indeed sending forbidden forces into South Vietnam. The North Vietnamese had consistently denied their presence in South Vietnam and maintained that the Viet Cong soldiers of the National Liberation Front (NLF) were doing all the fighting in the south.[7]

On August 16 Ambassador to Vietnam Henry Cabot Lodge forwarded to the secretary of state another proposal by Westmoreland to defoliate the terrain around the DMZ. Neither of these proposals was adopted. But on September 7, the Joint Chiefs sent to Admiral Ulysses S. Grant Sharp, CINCPAC, a truly bizarre idea. They planned to build an anti-infiltration barrier that would impede both foot and vehicle traffic.

The foot-traffic barrier would run inland from the coast along the southern edge of the DMZ to the Laotian border, then 25 miles into Laos, and then northwest for another 35 miles. The vehicle barrier would be farther west where roads were more numerous. Minefields with acoustical detectors and sensors would monitor the front twenty-four hours a day so that air strikes could be called against intruding NVA. This grandiose, high-tech plan was rejected by Sharp, but despite this rejection, Secretary of Defense Robert S. McNamara urged President Johnson to authorize installation of the barrier.[8]

The air portion of this barrier would be the responsibility of the Air Force while the ground responsibilities would fall to the Marines, who did not like the idea at all. They reluctantly stretched their defensive line across the width of northern South Vietnam just below the DMZ, paralleling Route 9. Their line ran from Dong Ha in the east to Khe Sanh in the extreme west, just 9 kilometers from the Laotian border.

The outer wall of a bunker at the combat base. **OPPOSITE ABOVE:** Gen William C. Westmoreland speaks at a press conference in 1967.
OPPOSITE BELOW: Secretary of Defense Robert S. McNamara at a press conference in 1967.

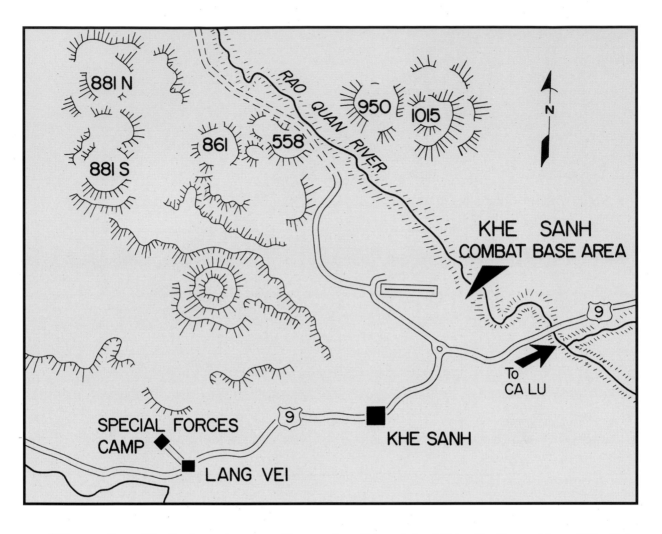

Khe Sanh and the surrounding hills.

"When you're at Khe Sanh, you're not really anywhere," complained Brigadier General Lowell English. "You could lose it and you really haven't lost anything."[9]

For the first two months of 1967, Marines sat in their stretched-out defensive positions, facing north to intercept the invading enemy. All was quiet until February 27, when the NVA attacked the strong points at Con Thien and Gio Linh. For the next month, the NVA hammered at these positions. On March 20, they bombarded the Marines with more than one thousand mortar and artillery rounds.[10]

Khe Sanh was a plateau sitting on the extreme northwestern tip of South Vietnam. Trees rose 60 feet high, and secondary growth of dense elephant grass obscured most of the trails. The tallest peak was Dong

Tri Mountain, rising 1,015 meters (3,330 feet). Four other hills dominated the avenues of approach to Khe Sanh and access to Route 9. These were Hills 950, 881N (North), 881S (South), and 861.

There were three natural avenues by which enemy forces might enter the northern province at Khe Sanh. The first was along the Rao Quan River that ran to the southeast and passed between Hill 950 and 861. The second was to follow the ridgeline that included 881N, 881S, and 861. And the third avenue was from the west along Route 9 through Laos and the Annamite mountain pass dominated by the Co Roc massif at the border. A strong force at Khe Sanh could interdict all three approaches.

The weather at Khe Sanh is quite different from that of most of South Vietnam. Between mid-October and mid-May, most of South Vietnam receives only moderate rain. But in the northern province, the northeast monsoon brings drizzling rain with low-hanging fog that the French nicknamed the *crachin.* It rolled in

> THE MARINES OPENED FIRE, KILLING THE NVA SOLDIERS, BUT A TRAILING ENEMY PLATOON OF FORTY MEN COUNTERATTACKED. THE MARINES SLUGGED IT OUT WITH THE SUPERIOR ENEMY FORCE FOR TWENTY MINUTES, BUT JUST AS IT APPEARED THAT THEY MIGHT EXTRICATE THEMSELVES FROM THE FIREFIGHT, AN EVEN LARGER ENEMY FORCE OF ONE HUNDRED FIFTY SOLDIERS SURROUNDED THEM.

and hung over the land like a shroud, obscuring visibility. Air operations during the *crachin* were virtually impossible, and the cover allowed the NVA to move with perfect concealment.

In February, four months after the Marines had reluctantly reinforced Khe Sanh with a battalion, they withdrew three-quarters of the force, leaving only one company to provide security for the airstrip and to patrol the surrounding area. There had been little contact, and most of the heavy action was farther to the east around Con Thien.

Although the action around Khe Sanh had been sparse, several recon patrols had made significant contact with the enemy. On January 26, 1967, Marine Force Recon inserted a patrol of six men and a dog on the Laotian border 12 miles to the northwest of the Khe Sanh Combat Base.

The men patrolled to the north in the dense terrain and after eight hours, they suddenly came upon an enemy patrol of ten men. The Marines opened fire, killing the NVA soldiers, but a trailing enemy platoon of forty men counterattacked. The Marines slugged it out with the superior enemy force for twenty minutes,

*This French slang term meant "spit," probably derived from the verb *cracher*, "to spit."

but just as it appeared that they might extricate themselves from the firefight, an even larger enemy force of one hundred fifty soldiers surrounded them. The patrol leader frantically requested air cover and a reaction force to come to their rescue.

Two helicopters of Marines, escorted by two gunships, scrambled to assist the beleaguered patrol. A seven-minute flight from the base brought the helos to the battle area, but from the air, the rescue force could see the patrol was hopelessly surrounded by the enemy force, some of the enemy only 30 meters (less than 100 feet) from the Marine lines.

The first UH-34 helicopter attempting to land and evacuate the patrol was driven off by fire. When a second approached from a different direction, hovered, and attempted to land, enemy fire ripped through the cockpit and sheared gas and oil lines. Other rounds cracked through the aircraft's skin. The pilot struggled to lift the wobbling, stricken helo from the hot zone, and retreated to Khe Sanh for an emergency landing.

The escorting Huey (UH-1E) gunships strafed and rocketed the encircling enemy positions to provide cover for two CH-46 aircraft, one carrying a reaction force. It was 1845 and daylight receded as a threatening weather front formed. The reaction force turned back while Captain Joseph Roman attempted to land the second helicopter to extract the recon team.

"One UH-34 had tried to make it into the zone and was hit twenty times," said Roman. "The zone was 2,500 feet high. I made my approach into the zone and was hit two or three times going in, and I could hear the fire going through the aircraft. I sat down right where the recon team marked it.

"At that time we were hit with what had to be heavy caliber automatic weapons and the aircraft was unflyable. I jettisoned my window and jumped into the elephant grass, which was 6 to 8 feet high. I looked to my left before I jumped, and saw that the recon team was in a firefight with four or five of the enemy. We made our way to the team and set up a 10-meter [about 33 feet] perimeter. I called for a reaction force to be put in. In about twenty-five minutes, a second helicopter attempted to come into the zone. He made his approach, and as he was setting down, he took fire. I saw the flames down over the hill in the direction from where he came. We started to holler quite a bit so they'd know our position, and they made it up the hill in five or ten minutes, and then we had thirty-one men in the zone."[11]

Throughout the night, Roman was able to direct supporting fire to hold off the enemy attacks; some of those rounds impacted only yards outside the Marine positions. In the morning, three helicopters rendezvoused

....

Capt Michael Sayers and Bravo, 1st Battalion, 9th Marines patrol on Hill 700 in April 1967. **OPPOSITE:** Two CH-46 helicopters on the ground at the combat base.

and successfully extracted the force.* The violent contact confirmed enemy infiltration from North Vietnam. But was it for an attack at Khe Sanh or were they just passing through and moving south?

The Marine company responsible for security and patrolling at Khe Sanh was Bravo, 1st Battalion, 9th Marines (B/1/9) commanded by Capt Michael W. Sayers. He had the unenviable task of achieving a level of security previously provided by an entire battalion. He shortened his perimeter and sent four patrols each day to screen the terrain to his front toward Hill 861. For night security, Sayers established listening posts and ambush sites. On February 25, a patrol made a heavy contact.

"My thirteen-man squad with a two-man gun team was assigned on a combat patrol in front of our perimeter," said Sergeant Donald Harper. "Corporal Wright spotted three people going up the trail to the hill, plus one man with a khaki shirt running through the brush away from us. We got on line and swept this area and a mama-san Montagnard† pointed out the ravine where the man had run. We proceeded to the very top of the hill and we just seemed to walk on top of them.

*For his heroic action, Capt Joseph Roman received the Silver Star.
†Montagnards are aboriginal tribespeople that inhabit the mountains of Indochina.

. . . .

Chaplain Ray W. Stubbe on patrol near Hill 861 with C Company, 1st Battalion, 26th Marines in 1968.

"They were three yards in front of us. Cpl Wright, with a 12-gauge shotgun, and the machine-gun team opened up on them, killing one instantly and wounding the others. Cpl Hughes shouted that he had shot a man running down the ravine to his front. We started receiving rounds, which apparently were from VC 50 yards to our front down the reverse slope. I pulled my people back and requested mortar fire. I was informed that a reinforced squad was coming up, and we all started up the hill again. Forty meters from the top of the hill, we were hit again. At this time we decided that there were a lot more up there than just a squad or two."[12]

When the Marines finally captured the hill, they found only nine enemy bodies, but they also discovered an enemy mortar, mortar rounds, and numerous backpacks.

In April, aerial reconnaissance detected enemy positions dug in the hills north of the Khe Sanh airstrip, and Sayers sent two platoons to sweep toward 861 to check out a series of caves. On April 24, the platoons followed parallel paths leading to 861 and were separated by 250 meters (a little more than 800 feet). As they approached the hill, the point man in the left column signaled to the front. Five NVA soldiers approached the column, moving along the same trail. The Marines quickly set up an ambush and opened fire, gaining the upper hand—but only for a moment. A superior enemy force soon engaged them.

"After 300 meters [about 328 yards], we received heavy fire from the right flank and we were pinned down," said Staff Sergeant Dennis W. Ritchie. "We had one man from 60mm mortars set up in the open area and deliver heavy, accurate mortar fire on the enemy position. We called for mortar rounds from the rest of the platoon. They were pinned down, but this man got up and exposed himself, and went after the mortar rounds and picked them up. He did this three times until he got all the mortar rounds and fired all of them on the enemy position."[13]

On Hill 700, one kilometer (0.6 miles) south of 861, Sayers had set up a mortar fire support team, led by Second Lieutenant Thomas G. King, that bombarded the enemy area with 81mm mortar fire. But observation of the target area was not possible from Hill 700, so King sent a forward observer (FO) team to 861 under the direction of First Lieutenant Phillip H. Sauer.

"I set up the tube and dispatched a five-man observation team to Hill 861 for better advantage so they could call fire missions," said King. "This OP [observation post] was ambushed, and they radioed back that they were taking heavy small-arms fire. I told them to pull back and I would throw 81s where they were ambushed. That was the last radio contact I had with this five-man OP. I tried for half an hour to make contact but had no luck."

Finally King spotted one man staggering back down the ridgeline. The surviving Marine, Private First Class William Marks, reported that NVA dug in near the top of 861 had ambushed them. Lt Sauer had ordered the FO team to withdraw, and stood firing his .45 pistol to provide cover, but only Marks managed to escape. King sent men to try to retrieve the casualties, but heavy fire pinned them. They found two bodies but did not see the other two and returned to Hill 700.

"I called artillery fire on Hill 861 where I assumed the NVA were dug in," said King. "Capt Sayers flew out in a helicopter and joined me. His helicopter came in and took fire from a machine gun from behind us.

I immediately turned the 81mm tube around and fired on the position. Three of my men said they saw one body fly into the air."

After more mortar and artillery fire, a patrol returned to the ambush site and retrieved the remaining two bodies. As the helicopter touched down on Hill 700 to evacuate the bodies, unseen NVA troops watched from the crest of 861.

"The helicopter's wheels had no more than touched the ground when the whole tree line on top of 861 opened up with heavy automatic-weapons fire," said King. "The helicopter took thirty-five hits. Two Huey gunships flying cover buzzed the tree line and opened up with machine guns and just tore the daylights out of that place. Again we fired support missions for the two platoons advancing in the sweep of the caves."[14]

Neither of the attacking platoons of Company B was able to gain the summit of 861. One platoon pulled back and dug in, and the other was tragically hit by a friendly air strike mistaking them for the enemy. The next day both platoons attempted to evacuate casualties, but were stymied by bad weather and fog.

Late in the afternoon on April 25, Company K, 3rd Marines, commanded by Capt Bayliss L. Spivey, attempted to relieve the pressure on Company B. By 1715 the Marines were 300 meters (about 325 yards) from the summit of 861 but heavily engaged, coming under withering fire from well-constructed enemy bunkers concealed and camouflaged in dense vegetation. Enemy mortars dug in on the reverse slope of the hill pounded the Marine lines with high-angled fire.

"I JUST DIDN'T HAVE THE HORSEPOWER TO TAKE THAT HILL," SAID SPIVEY. "I HAD NINETEEN KILLED AND FORTY WOUNDED."

"I received orders to take Hill 861 and be prepared to continue to the northwest to aid Bravo 1/9 and exploit their contact," said Capt Spivey. "Three-quarters of the way up, we deployed the company for the final attack. It was 1500 when the two attacking platoons separated to go up two ridgelines approaching the hill from the south. At 1600 we were in our final position 500 meters [about 550 yards] from the top. I was moving with the 1st Platoon up the ridgeline south of the summit of 861. My 3rd Platoon was moving on the ridgeline coming in from the east. At 1705 we made contact. We were 300 meters [about 325 yards] from the crest of the hill. I moved up with the 1st Platoon leading elements and advanced 200 meters [about 220 yards], all the time receiving sweeping automatic fire from the bunkers on the crest of the hill. At 1730 we were within 100 meters of the crest but had run out of troops. I had ten effective men remaining in the 1st Platoon."

Capt Spivey dug in for the night and brought up his reserve platoon. In the morning he continued the attack but could not budge the enemy off of 861.

"I just didn't have the horsepower to take that hill," said Spivey. "I had nineteen killed and forty wounded."[15]

Both Sayers's company and Spivey's company had been shattered on 861. Bogged down with casualties, the commanders had great difficulty disengaging from the enemy. Company K, 9th Marines was sent forward to help.

"Just as we reached the base of Hill 861, we noticed there was a lot of gear lying around and there were signs of pretty heavy fighting all up and down the side of the hill," said Lance Corporal Larry W. Umstead from K/1/9. "As we approached B/1/9 Headquarters, we could see them bringing down some of the wounded and dead. A lot of men were telling us not to go up, how bad it was up there—no water, no nothing, and how well the VC were dug in.*

"And then we moved up toward the top of 861 to pull them out. The closer we got, the heavier the volume of fire became. We got most of their wounded and dead and brought them back down. Kilo 3/3 was on the backside of 861, so we headed there. The fog came in about 5 o'clock. We reached

them about 1900, and we saw how bad off they were. We gave them all the water we had, and our corpsman got working right on their wounded. After we had their wounded and dead staged in one area, we started making litters. We moved all through the night through the rain, and it was pretty hard with the mud, and with the stretchers, we were slipping and sliding. We made an LZ [landing zone] and the choppers came in at 8 o'clock in the morning and medevaced all."[16]

Lieutenant Col Gary Wilder, who commanded 3rd Battalion, 3rd Marines, had moved his headquarters to a position just south of Hill 861. After the fierce action by both Sayers' and Spivey's companies, he concluded that the enemy forces were larger than originally thought. (In fact, the force arrayed against him

*The term "VC" was often used to refer to all enemy soldiers, including the NVA.

....

Members of B/1/9 carry a dead Marine to a helicopter on Hill 700, April 27, 1967.

was a regiment of the 325C NVA Division that had been moving into the Khe Sanh area along the ridgeline route from 881N, through 881S, to 861. The Marine patrols to locate caves had triggered a premature attack and exposed the massed effort.)

On April 26, a second Marine battalion was heli-lifted into Khe Sanh to reinforce Wilder's battalion. Three companies of 2nd Battalion, 3rd Marines commanded by LtCol Earl DeLong, linked up near Hill 861 to attack the entrenched NVA forces. During the next two days, the Marines directed massive artillery and air strikes against 861. Marine and Army artillery covered the crest with earth-shaking explosions. Two thousand rounds impacted the target. Marine aircraft battered the hill with 250 tons of bombs that stripped off the dense tree growth and exposed dozens of well-prepared bunkers and hundreds of fighting holes.

On April 28, just before 2nd Battalion's assault, two B-52 bomber strikes from Guam delivered successive strings of 500-pound bombs, further pulverizing the enemy position.

Looking west at a large bomb crater on the eastern face of Hill 861. **OPPOSITE:** A corpsman assists a wounded Marine at Khe Sanh.

"All of a sudden, the ground starts shaking," said Bob Maras with Company G, 3rd Marines. "And then you start hearing this *BOOOM, BOOOM,* and you're hearing each one of these bombs starting to hit, and you know that a B-52 raid has been conducted. You could feel the whole earth shaking and feel the concussion like a blast that's close up. I was wondering if they could feel this back in the world."[*17]

As the last bombs fell, DeLong's Marines stormed up the hill, overwhelming the remaining sporadic resistance, and Wilder's Marines turned to the west, occupying the ground between 861 and 881S. The maneuvering Marines could see NVA forces digging in and setting up mortars on the crest of 881S. Marine artillery engaged them, and at 0800 on April 30, Wilder's battalion attacked.

The summit of Hill 881S was distinguished by two adjacent knobs, each heavily fortified. The approaching Marines received only sporadic fire and could not see the enemy dug in on the twin knobs and the crest of the hill. The nature of the terrain restricted the Marine attack. Two companies assaulted, one behind the other. After a two-hour maneuver uphill, the lead elements reached the western edge of the crest.

Just as success seemed within the Marines' grasp, the NVA force struck back. Automatic-weapons fire and exploding mortars stunned the attackers and pinned them to the ground. The enemy lines were just 30 meters (less than 100 feet) from the Marines, and air strikes threaded their bombs into this narrow zone.

*American soldiers in Vietnam referred to home as "the world."

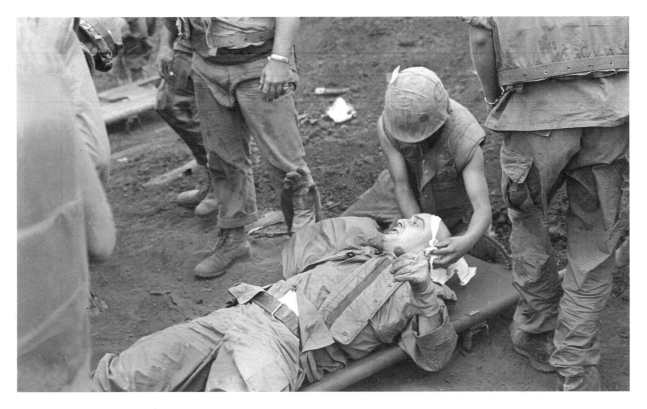

"There was supposed to be at least a company of enemy on 881 dug in and Mike 3/3 [Company M, 3rd Battalion, 3rd Marines] was up there trying to get them out," said LCpl Larry Umstead, who was in the second assaulting company, "and if they ran into any trouble, we were supposed to go up and help them. An hour later all hell broke loose up on top of the hill. You couldn't hear yourself think, there was so much fire and mortar fire going on. The captain came up and told us we were going to move out and take the hill, platoons on line."[18]

"2nd and 3rd platoons went up the left side to try to get to the top, and we went around on the flank on the right and halfway around the hill," said LCpl Terrence Walsh, a squad leader with Kilo Company, 9th Marines. "We got on a little knoll, and we were crossing in front of this knoll and got pinned down by a sniper who shot the rocket man. The corpsman was back working on the rocket man, and they called for him, and he jumped up and started to run across the hill, and was shot through the head.

A Navy corpsman dives for cover near a dead Marine solider that he was trying to save.

"One of the snipers ran across an opening on the top of the hill and tried to get up in a tree to get a better shot. One of our men shot him and knocked him out of the tree. Another North Vietnamese ran across the opening, and the squad opened up on him and just tore him apart."[19]

Two hours later, the Marines were forced to slip back down the fiercely defended hill. Casualties were severe: forty-three Marines killed and more than one hundred wounded.

Again artillery and air crushed the hilltop position. The massive bombardment flushed some NVA soldiers from their bunkers. Unable to endure the bombing, a platoon bolted from cover only to be discovered and engaged by the circling aircraft. On the morning of May 2, the Marines overran the hill, discovering more than two hundred fifty bunkers. Hills 861 and 881S were now in Marine hands. Only 881N remained occupied by the NVA.

On May 2, Earl DeLong's Marines attacked 881N from the south and the east. Company E smashed forward toward the crest, when a sudden storm with 40 mph winds and driving rain stalled the attack. With control lost, the company sought more defensible terrain on a hill to the south of 881N to regroup and prepare to continue the assault in the morning. At 0415 the NVA spoiled that plan by counterattacking with two companies, penetrating the Marines' lines from the northeast. In hand-to-hand combat, they overran a section of the line and occupied some old bunkers.

The Marines halted the penetration, but could not drive the NVA from their bunkered positions. The enemy massed for a new attack, but instead of being hidden by darkness, the new flanking maneuver was spotlighted by the brilliant light of two million-candlepower flares dropped by circling aircraft.

From Hill 881S, the Marines observed a two hundred–man force moving to attack Company E from the west in an attempt to encircle and overrun the hard-pressed Marines. Wilder's Marines quickly moved their 106mm recoilless rifles into position to support their fellow Marines. As the guns were positioned, the gunners focused through the sights and pulled on the firing handle to fire the .50-caliber spotting rifle. The red tracer streaked across the space between the two hills and pinpointed the spot of impact. Quickly adjusting for perfect aim, the gunners then pushed the handle and unleashed the 106mm round.

With blinding back-blasts, the guns fired their rounds, which smashed into the target area with thunderous explosions. The ranks of the attacking NVA first wavered and then broke. Like the guns of a great battleship, the recoilless rifles fired one hundred rounds point-blank into the enemy's flank, repelling the attack, while artillery pounded the retreat routes. At first light, reinforcing Marines attacked and sealed off the breach.[20] Twenty-seven Marines were killed, but the Communist forces were wiped out, leaving one hundred thirty-seven bodies on the hill. Three prisoners warned of further attacks to come the next night, and the Marines dug in for the onslaught.

The assault did not fall on the Marines' positions, however. Instead, the enemy attacked and overran the Army Special Forces camp at Lang Vei, 6 miles to the southeast along Route 9. The swiftness of the successful attack was due in part to the recent removal of the camp's protecting minefield. But the camp had had a small warning.

A long-range patrol under the command of Sgt William Steptoe had returned from a weeklong patrol on May 3—the day before the enemy would attack—and reported to Capt William Crenshaw that the patrol had been in constant contact with Communist forces.

"I told him that we needed to stand-to because we were being followed. I'd been in contact all the way back."

Steptoe's warning went unheeded, and the attack came at 0415 May 4, passing through the old minefield area and into the compound.

"I heard the first rounds come," said Steptoe. "I ran down the teamhouse steps, and mortars were coming in, and rockets. As I hit the main bunker, a mortar hit and blew off a finger as I dove through the door. I had my back to the bunker, and I told Crenshaw that people were in the camp, and at that time a burst from an AK-47 got me in the left arm and shoulder. The same bullets killed Crenshaw."[21]

At dawn, the attackers were gone, retreating to the west from whence they had come. Capt Crenshaw was dead, as was his executive officer. Twenty men of the ARVN force were also dead, and thirty-nine wounded, but the enemy attack down Route 9 had been stopped. Had their plan been to link up with the force attacking from the north through the hills?

At 0850 the next day, May 5, the Marines of 2nd Battalion attacked 881N in a final assault. They met only scattered fire, and at 1445 secured the hill. At the summit Marines found out the extent of the NVA defenses.

"Once we got up there, we found the bunkers were made out of logs 7 to 8 inches in diameter and stacked four high," said PFC Anthony Bruno. "Two-fifties just didn't do any good and napalm didn't hit good enough."[22]

The Marines were not content simply to kick the enemy off the hills. They immediately began to patrol to the northwest to locate the fleeing enemy forces. Aerial observers finally spotted the soldiers of the 325C NVA Division retreating toward North Vietnam and Laos. On May 9 Company D engaged elements of the force 3,000 meters (about 3,300 yards) northwest of the 881N battleground. After a fierce firefight with heavy casualties on both sides, the Marines, with superior supporting arms, drove off the NVA. A search of the area revealed thirty-one NVA killed and two hundred freshly dug graves.

"In some of the packs we found clean utilities, uniforms," said 2Lt Terry Weber, a forward observer with Company F. "They were in very good shape. It seemed like they had just come across the Laotian border to come back to gather their dead and bury them."[23]

To continue to screen and search for the enemy, 3rd Reconnaissance Battalion inserted Team Breaker to the northwest of 881N at 1650 on May 9. The seven-man recon team found an enemy base camp and moved into the bunkers in the center of the position.

"After the choppers left, we noticed that the area was heavily dug in with bunkers and heavily fortified positions," said Cpl Steven Lopez. "At 10 p.m. it seemed to be at least a company of NVA returned to their fortified position, and they walked right up to us and we cut a few of them down. They pulled back and

threw grenades and fired sniper rounds at us all night long. By midnight we had two men remaining in the patrol and the third man was unconscious."

Between 0220 and 0630 three attempts were made to extract the team, but the helicopters were driven off by fire. Lopez called in artillery dangerously close to himself to keep the enemy away.

"There was a time I thought I was the only man left in the patrol. I was on the radio and could hear the enemy in the bush. I thought they were going to walk in on us in the morning at dawn and finish us off, and I kept calling in the Hueys, the gunships, for ground cover, and they strafed right next to us because the enemy was so close to us."[24]

After a fourth unsuccessful attempt to insert a reaction force, the three remaining members of the team were extracted by gunship.* The Hill Fights were finally over.

*For his heroic action, Cpl Steven Lopez was awarded the Navy Cross.

Marines sort through captured NVA equipment on Hill 861.

CHAPTER 2

BOMBING AND THE BARRIER

A B-52 Stratofortress releases its deadly cargo over South Vietnam.

TIMELINE	APRIL 24, 1967	MAY 13, 1967	DECEMBER 1967	JANUARY 21, 1968	JANUARY 31, 1968
	Hill Fights begin at Khe Sanh	Hill Fights end. Marines fought off elements of the 325C NVA Division in a two-week battle that cost the enemy 824 KIA. 168 Marines were killed and 443 wounded in the struggle.	General Westmoreland decides to reinforce Khe Sanh in the face of enemy buildup.	NVA attack hill 861 and bombard combat base exploding ammo dump, and attack Khe Sanh village. Siege begins.	NVA launch countrywide Tet Offensive.

As the Hill Fights ended, the NVA retreated to their sanctuaries in Laos and North Vietnam. Although they had abandoned the battlefield, they remained close by to refurbish and refit, confident they would not be attacked or pursued because of the United States' strict adherence to its own self-imposed Rules of Engagement.

These "rules" were developed during the early stages of American military assistance to South Vietnam in 1962, while U.S. advisors were training Vietnamese air forces to perform combat and ground-support missions. Until those air forces could be properly trained, the American air forces flew "immediate response" missions to enemy attacks. To avoid embarrassing border violations and possibly firing on friendly targets, the Military Assistance Command Vietnam (MACV) established operational restraints on United States aircraft.

While good intentions might have initially motivated the creation of these "rules," it was not long before the rules took on a life of their own, expanded bureaucratically, and became an exacerbating obstacle to military strategy and planning. The very fact that in 1967 the NVA could invade South Vietnam, participate in a major attack like the Hill Fights, inflict casualties on American forces, and then, after being defeated, retreat to sanctuaries across the borders to lick their wounds and rearm indicates the level of absurdity to which the restrictions had risen. Still, restricted bombing was the pursued policy of Secretary of Defense Robert S. McNamara, who had full approval from President Lyndon B. Johnson. And few eyebrows were raised in Washington or the international community when the NVA continued to deny their presence in South Vietnam.

Rules restricting B-52 strikes against hostile targets moving in Laos were easily translated by the enemy into an advantage. No shrines, temples, national monuments, places of worship, or inhabited huts and villages could be within the target area. The enemy could keep his troops and vehicles close to these forbidden areas. If the military identified a lucrative target, the average time to clear and authorize an attack on it was 15.5 *days*.[1]

Hot aerial pursuit of enemy vehicles entering or leaving a battle area was similarly handcuffed. High performance aircraft could not attack vehicles unless they were first identified and cleared by a forward air controller (FAC). The element of surprise was lost, and enemy drivers knew the rules. Roaring American jets

 DISK 1, TRACK 7: Assault on Hill 950.

FEBRUARY 5-8, 1968	FEBRUARY 23, 1968	FEBRUARY 29, 1968	APRIL 14, 1968	JUNE 19-JULY 5, 1968
NVA attack Hill 861 Alpha, Lang Vei, and Hill 64.	Enemy gunners bombard base with more than 1,300 rounds in heaviest attack.	NVA launch regimental size attack against base.	Marines break out of siege and attack and seize Hill 881N.	Khe Sanh Combat Base is destroyed and abandoned by American forces.

posed no threat to them as long as the small FAC aircraft was not circling overhead. Upon spotting the FAC plane, drivers simply drove off the road for cover. And aircraft could not attack any target more than 200 yards off of a "motorable" roadway. When military commanders opined that FAC approval was unnecessary since "the only ones running around [were] North Vietnamese," their objections fell on deaf ears.[2]

In the beginning of 1967, Adm Ulysses S. Grant Sharp, CINCPAC, briefed Gen Earle Wheeler, Chairman of the Joint Chiefs of Staff, on his assessment of Operation Rolling Thunder. Sharp felt that to make the air offensive successful, the United States needed to apply pressure without respite. That meant no fruitless bombing pauses or stand-downs.

From the beginning the military had opposed the administration's assertion that a pause in the bombing campaign would lead to peace negotiations. Westmoreland, Sharp, and the Joint Chiefs were against it. They told President Johnson the extended pauses undid all that had been done. But Secretary McNamara's response to their complaints was "That's baloney."[3]

So the restrictions remained, and during the year there were eight more pauses and stand-downs, lasting a total of 137 days.[4] Bombing lucrative targets in the north at supply staging areas, bombing airfields

....

President Lyndon B. Johnson's (right) and Robert McNamara's insistence on bombing pauses and stand-downs frustrated the military throughout the Vietnam War.

bristling with antiaircraft guns and surface-to-air missiles, and mining the main port of North Vietnam, Haiphong Harbor, to stem the flow of war matériel were not options. Rolling Thunder was a paper tiger, and Secretary McNamara treated the military's recommendations for the conduct of the air campaign just as he had treated their recommendations against his proposed barrier plan. He ignored both.

President Johnson trusted McNamara's opinions in deference to his military generals and advisors. Outwardly the president liked to compare himself to the rough-and-tumble Texans of an earlier age who were his heroes. He could recite from memory the first two stanzas of a poem about the Alamo and had once told the National Security Council, "Hell, Vietnam is just like the Alamo."[5] He had also once publicly suggested that the United States would "fight to its last soldier."[6]

And the Texas Rangers were all heroes to him. "When you shoot a Ranger," Johnson said, "he just keeps comin' on."[7] From earliest childhood, Lyndon Johnson had been taught the values of courage, honor, loyalty, conviction, leadership, bravery, and sacrifice—and of heroes who fought for liberty, who did not retreat, and who died for their beliefs.

But inwardly those ideals faded, and he was a person with little in common with the defenders of the Alamo. In a 1965 phone call to Georgia senator Richard Russell, Johnson was candid in his assessment of his advisors and told Russell he favored Robert McNamara over his generals. "He is very conservative notwithstanding what people think," Johnson said, referring to a perception that McNamara was a hawk, "and he holds down the military a good deal." In the same conversation Johnson referred to Gen Westmoreland as a "far-sider," and other of his top military advisors as "irresponsible."[8]

FROM THE BEGINNING THE MILITARY HAD OPPOSED THE ADMINISTRATION'S ASSERTION THAT A PAUSE IN THE BOMBING CAMPAIGN WOULD LEAD TO PEACE NEGOTIATIONS. WESTMORELAND, SHARP, AND THE JOINT CHIEFS WERE AGAINST IT.

So the halfhearted pursuit of the war and the "holding down [of] the military" allowed the NVA to carve out sanctuaries close to its military objectives. And in 1967 its military objective was Khe Sanh and the area of South Vietnam along Route 9, south of the DMZ.

As the wounded elements of the NVA 325C Division departed the Hill Fights battlefield, other elements of the same division entered the same theater after a three-month trek from the north. Their objective was Hill 950, directly north of Khe Sanh Combat Base across the Rao Quan River. Sheer sides to the north, west, and south provided the position excellent protection, and the steep east face offered the only approach to the small crest.

The crest was tiny, only 50 feet by 100 feet, but the tall hill was ideal for a radio relay station and had been invested by the Marines since 1966. Both 26th Marines and 3rd Force Recon set up their antennas on this pinnacle. On a clear day, the operators could see the South China Sea to the east and into Laos to the west.

But Hill 950 was not without its drawbacks. First, there were not many clear days. The peak was often shrouded in clouds and fog, and the rains made the tiny outpost difficult to resupply. Because of the crest's small dimensions, there was not room for a substantial defensive force and barely enough room to carve out a landing zone for helicopters. A chopper "landing" was usually not a landing at all. The aircraft hovered or was negotiated with most of its wheels off the ground.

Secondly, the remote hilltop was far removed from the camaraderie and creature comforts that kept up morale. Horseshoes, card games, writing letters, and re-reading ones from home were all that separated the eighteen Marines from complete boredom. Resupply was always iffy, and sometimes the crest of Hill 950 did not come out of the clouds for a week at a time, leaving the Marines scrounging for previously discarded cans of cheese or peanut butter, thrown away when rations had been plentiful. Although the hilltop outpost seemed unassailable because of its steep sides, in the back of each Marine's mind was the knowledge that should the improbable happen, eighteen men were a small force indeed to deal with a concerted enemy attack.

....

A Marine sentry sits in a burnt tree atop Hill 950 on July 31, 1967. **OPPOSITE:** Aerial view of the outpost on Hill 950.

On June 4 approximately forty NVA soldiers began a three-day ascent up the daunting hill to attack the crest. They wore green uniforms and carried AK-47 assault rifles, RPGs (rocket propelled grenades), and light machine guns. They packed small blocks of explosives to employ as hand grenades.[9]

On the summit, Sgt Richard Baskins commanded eight men forming the security force of 26th Marines along with six radio operators. 3rd Force Recon also had three operators manning the second relay station.

Shortly after midnight, June 6, LCpl Charles R. Castillo stood watch on the western edge of the perimeter. The sky was clear, and he could see the combat base far below. From his perch his eye caught flashes below, and he watched as suddenly enemy rockets streaked across the sky and impacted on the base. Twenty-five rockets and mortars exploded on the Marines below. Sgt Baskins was asleep in his bunker when Castillo alerted him that the base was under mortar and rocket attack.

Before Baskins could stumble outside, a flare tripped on the east side of the crest. A moment later, an RPG whooshed overhead and set off another flare on the opposite side of the perimeter.

"I ran out and heard Castillo holler 'incoming grenades,'" said Baskins. "Before anyone knew it, there were NVA swarming up the eastern side of 950 and grenades were going off all over the place. I could hear people screaming and hollering, and there was a lot of confusion. I screamed to him, 'Bring in artillery on this side' and to make it close to our perimeter.

"There was a lot of fire, and I grabbed my M-16, and there were NVA on our right flank swinging around to our right, and they were penetrating right up through the center. I had Castillo and Green come up on my right, and Balzano concentrated fire right down the center of this avenue of approach."[10]

A second RPG slammed through the opening of the Force Recon bunker killing the three occupants. Four NVA soldiers mounted the bunker and began rearranging sandbags to form a fighting position on the top. LCpl William Balzano's machine gun disrupted the NVA plans as he cut two of them down. PFC Steven Arnold and LCpl Richard Green shot the other two.[11]

Supporting arms from the combat base ringed Hill 950 with fire, and they brought the deadly projectiles in as close as possible to Baskins' beleaguered Marines. At 0230, the base read the last transmission from 950, and it was dire indeed. The 950 operator called for fire *on top* of his own position, a request usually indicating being overrun. Artillery fired the last-ditch mission, and then there were no more transmissions. The combat base feared the worst.

But the fight on top of the mountain was far from over. Baskins marshaled his few remaining men and set up a tiny defensive perimeter on the southwest edge of the crest. Arrayed against the Marines were at least twenty-five enemy soldiers occupying the rest of the hilltop, and they fired steadily and threw grenades and explosives. The NVA soldiers tried to encircle the defending Marines, but the steep drop-offs and the American fire stopped them cold.

"The gun at the forward position where the NVA infiltrated was out of commission," said Baskins. "There was lead flying all around. There were grenades, and you could hear rockets to the northwest over our heads heading toward Khe Sanh. At the same time we could hear artillery pounding from Khe Sanh over our heads and then eventually coming right down on top of us. We had everything but the kitchen sink thrown at us in support."

Then there was more bad news. "Balzano hollered to me 'Sarge, my goddam gun is jammed. I can fire one round, but I can't get any sustained rate of fire out of it, no automatic fire.'

"We had one machine gun position and a small fighting hole in the center," said Baskins, "and we all got into these positions and stayed there, and these gooks crawling around to our left or right, we'd fire or throw grenades and chase them back. I could hear them dragging, and a lot of bushes moving, and I imagine they were taking their dead or wounded."[12]

....

The bunker on Hill 950. **OPPOSITE:** Chaplain Ray W. Stubbe conducts worship on Hill 950.

As the night wore on, Baskins knew that his only hope was to get to the bunker that contained the three radios, but the NVA were also there. In a bold move, he, Castillo, and Green approached from the right. "I could see two of them sitting behind this gun and I took aim," said the sergeant. "I had it on automatic. I squeezed the trigger, and the next thing I saw, these guys slumped back on the sandbags."

The Marines threw a smoke grenade to try to cover their final assault, but it was a dud, and Castillo in a moment of gallows humor shouted to the enemy in French to throw down their arms. A fusillade of return fire answered him, and then the Marines threw their last grenades and charged. The shock of their attack broke the enemy, and they abandoned their toehold on Hill 950.

"We could see the NVA diddy-bopping down the hill," said Baskins. "They took off!" Only two of the eighteen Marine defenders were unwounded. Six had been killed, and the enemy left behind ten dead within the perimeter. Baskins' force had seen several others, after being shot, fall off the steep hill.*

The attack on 950 was over, but the contacts and sightings with enemy forces all across the DMZ increased during the summer, including a shoot-down of an armed Huey gunship. But it was not the enemy that occupied most of the Marines' time during the summer. It was the installation of the hated barrier—code-named Operation Dyemarker—that had been instituted by Secretary McNamara, who demanded completion by November 1967.

*For his heroic action, Sgt Richard Baskins was awarded the Silver Star.

The Marines complained that construction of their portion of the barrier would take them away from aggressive operations against the threatening enemy and consume the entire efforts of the 3rd Marine Division.

"There was one terrible inhibiting factor that ruled the 3rd Division's life," said Gen Rathvon McCall Tompkins, "and that was the bloody Dyemarker!"[13]

It consumed more than 750,000 man-days and 115,000 equipment hours, and elicited the howls and scorn of the Marines. Major General Raymond G. Davis, a Medal of Honor recipient in Korea, called it "a six billion dollar blunder. My concept of defending an area against major inroads by North Vietnamese is to

South of the DMZ, Marines crawl out of their foxholes after a night of fighting the NVA. The helicopter at left was shot down attempting to resupply the unit. **OPPOSITE:** A reconnaissance patrol from Company B, 3rd Reconnaissance Battalion on the airstrip at Khe Sanh Combat Base, August 1967.

maintain a mobile force and destroy his force, not set up some big defensive bastion."[14] Lieutenant General Robert Cushman, commander of all Marines in Vietnam, called it "the stupid barrier,"[15] and MajGen Louis Metzger called it "a Maginot Line."[16]

The sentiments of all Marines were perhaps best summed up by the remarks of one officer, who said, "With these bastards you'd have to build the zone all the way to India, and it would take the whole Marine Corps and half the Army to guard it; even then they'd probably burrow under it."[17]

There was another significant battle fought in the summer of 1967, but it was not in Vietnam. Starting on August 9, the Preparedness Subcommittee of the Armed Services Committee conducted hearings in the Old Senate Building in Washington, D.C. The hearings were to investigate and to receive testimony concerning the conduct of the air war against North Vietnam. The committee, chaired by Senator John Stennis of Mississippi, wanted to learn about target selection, about the effectiveness of the bombing, who decided which targets were approved and which targets were off-limits—in short, what was going on with Rolling Thunder.

Adm Ulysses S. Grant Sharp (CINCPAC) was the first to testify. He had been stymied since 1965 in his efforts to conduct an air war that would bring maximum pressure upon North Vietnam's ports and power and fuel facilities, and thereby hinder its ability to support its army attacking in the south. Particularly

galling to Sharp were the restrictions placed on striking numerous targets he considered essential. Included in that number were the port of Haiphong and the airfield at Phuc Yen, both off-limits despite repeated, unanimous recommendations by the Chiefs of Staff.

Sharp felt that with the recent enemy defeat around Khe Sanh, it was time to step up the offensive. "Now, when the enemy is hurting, we should increase our pressures," he said. As he began his testimony, he paused to announce to the senators on the committee that on that very morning a remarkable "coincidence" had occured.

"This morning," he said, "I received authority to strike certain lucrative targets that I had not been able to strike before, and permission to restrike some targets that I had wanted to restrike and had been held off on."[18] The members acknowledged that this was indeed a strange coincidence.

"There are many lucrative targets that have not been struck," the admiral continued. "We have a list of approximately one hundred targets that we consider important."[19]

Senator Margaret Chase Smith of Maine asked, "To what extent, if any, are you given the reasons for not being given authorization to strike the targets which you have recommended?"

"I am normally not given the reason for not striking,"[20] the admiral answered. A buzz went around the room.

Each senator was given time to ask questions concerning the air war. The "denied targets" became the hot subject, consuming most of the session's time.

"Have you been permitted to hit the Phuc Yen airfield?" asked Stuart Symington of Missouri. When Adm Sharp answered, "No," Symington asked why not.

The answer was the same. "I have not been given a reason," Sharp answered.[21]

"I talked to one pilot," Symington said later, "who said, 'Four of my last five missions have been flown over Phuc Yen airfield . . . . I have watched Communist jets wheel into line to take off to destroy me; but I was not allowed to touch them on that field.'"[22]

The answers to questions concerning the target restrictions became monotonous. Senator Smith finally could stand it no more.

"I have listened in the past months," she exclaimed, "and again listened today on this off-again, on-again bombing; off-again, on-again target cancellations. It seems to be somewhat of a nightmare."[23]

Senator Symington was incredulous. "It is rather amazing that the man directing the air war over North Vietnam doesn't know why, is given no reason for the disapproval of the target he and his staff recommended."[24]

Senator Strom Thurmond then asked if the port of Haiphong was a sanctuary and was informed that it was.

"You're not allowed to strike it at all?" he asked, and Sharp answered, "That's correct."

Thurmond continued. "Sixty percent of goods and equipment that enters North Vietnam comes in through a sanctuary. You can stand off and watch them haul it in, knowing it is going to be used to kill American boys, and you can't turn your hand?"

"Yes, sir," the admiral answered.[25]

Gen Wallace M. Green said that the Marine commander in Vietnam (Gen Lew Walt*) had testified that the reason he lost so many Marine dead around Hill 881 was because of the NVA men and matériel brought south during the bombing pause in observance of the four-day cease fire for Tet (Vietnam's New Year celebration) in 1967. Admiral Sharp said there were indications the NVA was bringing artillery and rockets to the DMZ.[26]

The conduct of the air war was not the only subject discussed. Senator Margaret Chase Smith was especially interested in the subject of the barrier. As each of the Chiefs testified, she wanted to know how Dyemarker was conceived. Did any service recommend it? Did anyone think it a substitute for bombing? Had it been directed by the Department of Defense, or adopted outside normal procedures and without military recommendation?

Adm Sharp answered, "It will never be a substitute for the bombing. It was not conceived in my theater."[27]

*Gen Lew Walt preceded LtGen Robert Cushman as the Marine commander in Vietnam.

....

Adm Ulysses S. Grant Sharp, Commander in Chief, Pacific. **OPPOSITE:** Defense Secretary Robert McNamara speaks with Senator John Stennis, Chairman of the Senate Preparedness Investigation subcommittee, on August 25, 1967, before testifying on administration bombing policies.

Gen Earle Wheeler (Chairman JCS) said, "I first heard of it when McNamara discussed it. The services had not proposed it."[28]

Gen McConnell (Air Force Chief of Staff) chimed in, "The Joint Chiefs were not enthusiastic. We didn't actually support it . . . until the Secretary of Defense stated that we were going to go into the project."[29]

"From the beginning I have been opposed to the project," said Gen Wallace M. Greene (Commandant Marine Corps), and Gen Harold K. Johnson (Army Chief of Staff) added, "I'm just suspicious of it, myself. It is like closing the window and leaving the door open."[30]

Finally, on August 25, it was time for Secretary of Defense Robert McNamara to appear. The questioning continued, and each senator bored in with the questions highlighting target denial. McNamara argued that he was not of the same opinion as the Chiefs on target importance and the effectiveness of striking targets such as Phuc Yen, or mining Haiphong harbor, or destroying important sources of war matériel in the North rather than trying to strike those supplies dispersed on remote trails as they traveled toward South Vietnam.

McNamara responded to the question of ignoring the advice of military commanders by pointing out that the Constitution made the president the commander in chief. "I am sure that it didn't intend that he would exercise that by blindly following the recommendations of his military advisors."[31]

Eventually Senator Margaret Chase Smith questioned McNamara on the barrier, and asked him the same questions she had asked the military officers as to whose idea this was. She concluded by telling the secretary politely that he didn't have to give an immediate answer if it would take too long.

But McNamara snapped back, "I can give you a 30-second answer. The Institute of Defense Analysis . . . came up with a proposal. I considered it. I asked the Chiefs their views. There was divided opinion."[32]

Finally, Senator Howard Cannon of Nevada asked Secretary McNamara the question begging to be asked. "Is it the policy, your policy, to simply reject these targets and give the Joint Chiefs no reasons at all, or is it your policy to discuss the reasons with them?"

"I do not remember witnesses addressing this with the exception of Adm Sharp," said McNamara. "I think it has not always been appropriate for the reasons to be passed on to the unified commanders."[33]

The secretary's testimony before the Preparedness Investigating Subcommittee was a game of cat-and-mouse, with McNamara talking around many hard questions, answering some in vague terms, calling upon mind-numbing statistics to distract the subcommittee, proclaiming conclusions that he needed to prove, and deftly employing a technique called ignoratio elenchi to present arguments that had nothing to do with the posed questions.

Senator Margaret Chase Smith asked him, "Isn't Cambodia . . . used as a sanctuary for the Viet Cong?"[34] McNamara began: "Instead of using the word 'sanctuary,' let me substitute for it these words: used as a source of supply for material required by the Viet Cong and North Vietnamese troops in South Vietnam; used . . . as an infiltration route . . . used as a portion of a supply route for the movement of matériel from the North to the South . . . used probably for base purposes. I think the North Vietnamese and the Viet Cong are using it for all the purposes."[35]

McNamara neatly buried the word "sanctuary" under a deluge of words, and with it went the obligation to explain to the senators why his Rules of Engagement for U.S. forces forbade attacking the enemy, violating the Cambodian border and invading South Vietnam. A few minutes later, Senator Smith's time was up, and the word "sanctuary" disappeared from the discussion.

But McNamara didn't win every skirmish. As the secretary persisted in his argument that bombing of supply and matériel sources would not be effective since the enemy forces in the south could exist on 15 tons a day, Senator Henry Jackson put his pencil to the pad and called the secretary's hand on his statistics.

"Now that would be about 2 ounces per man per day," said Jackson.

McNamara immediately retreated. "These are the estimates of the intelligence analysts," he explained, distancing himself from the statistics he had, moments before, been happy to quote. McNamara was the ultimate statistician, with a reputation for pouncing on inaccurate figures and those who circulated them, and now he was confronted by his acceptance of an absurd number that supposedly included the weight of ammunition.

> **FINALLY, SENATOR HOWARD CANNON OF NEVADA ASKED SECRETARY MCNAMARA THE QUESTION BEGGING TO BE ASKED. "IS IT THE POLICY, YOUR POLICY, TO SIMPLY REJECT THESE TARGETS AND GIVE THE JOINT CHIEFS NO REASONS AT ALL, OR IS IT YOUR POLICY TO DISCUSS THE REASONS WITH THEM?"**

"To a layman, as I am," he said, "they look very small. I am willing to consider a 500 percent increase . . ." But he was not off the hook.

"It would still be only 10 ounces per man," Senator Jackson proclaimed. "I don't see how these estimates add up to a sensible figure."[36]

But sensible or not, those were Secretary McNamara's answers to very important questions. They infuriated most of the commissioners, generals, and admirals, but they left no doubt that the war was being dictated and micromanaged from the White House.[37]

Some years later, Graham Martin, who had been ambassador to Thailand at the time, described McNamara's addiction to statistics.

"If you could not convert what you were talking about into binary nomials, he was not intellectually prepared to cope with it. It was his insistence on statistics, statistics, statistics that drove everybody nuts!"[38]

Senator Stuart Symington summed up his feelings and those of most of his fellow senators concerning statistical reliance.

"At times computers are all right," he observed. "But I think these fellows out there that are worried about these heavy shipments, the quantity, quality, and the size of the stuff that is hitting them . . . are experts also; and their opinions on this should be respected."

Perhaps the most disturbing statement made by McNamara came near the end of his testimony as he guaranteed the NVA freedom from air attack even when they were building up to threaten American forces. When asked if the flow of war matériel to the DMZ was an important objective in the air campaign, the secretary said, " . . . as long as the forces stay north of the DMZ, the extent to which they are supplied there is of little importance to us."[39]

The hearings went on for twenty days. As they came to an end, those who remembered the 1947 Senate hearings on the creation of the Department of Defense and the post of Secretary of Defense might have concluded that a prophecy uttered twenty years earlier had been fulfilled.

During those hearings, Senator Ev Robertson of Wyoming, very concerned about the vast power given this new secretary, reminded the committee of the close relationship between Franklin Roosevelt and his Chiefs of Staff, especially Gen George Marshall, that had been so important in World War II. Why fix something that is not broken?

Robertson saw that the traditional lines of communications that the Joint Chiefs had enjoyed between their own secretaries and the president were now all channeled to the "super secretary."

"You are cutting Army, Navy, and Air Force completely off from the Joint Chiefs. They have no connection with anyone,"[40] he complained.

His great fear was that the single secretary would override the decisions of the various secretaries (Army, Navy, and Air Force) and veto military judgments made upon the experiences of those in the Armed Forces.

Undersecretary of War Kenneth Royall sought to allay those fears by appealing to the committee's common sense, saying that he was certain that any orders from the Secretary of Defense would only be issued "after careful consideration of the views of each of the armed services involved. No sensible man would adopt any other course," he said, "and it seems inconceivable that any man who did so would be retained."[41]

Senator Millard Tydings from Maryland asked about just such a man.

"Let us suppose that we got a dumbbell in wartime as the Secretary of National Defense, who would insist upon policies that were inimical to the welfare of the country and to the services. I can see where a martinet . . . might do tremendous harm."[42]

In 1967, 8,000 miles from Washington, the Marines struggled to install "McNamara's Line" while they fought enemy soldiers all along the DMZ who were supplied with a lot more than "10 ounces a day." The enemy continued to move massive amounts of war matériel south through sanctuaries, virtually unimpeded.

Far from Washington, the enemy hierarchy was also in a quandary. In Hanoi, in July, as the argument about the barrier and the air war raged among American politicians and generals, the leaders of North Vietnam faced the

fact that their forces were being held up on all frontiers. The VC had been driven from the populated areas by the Allied forces, and the Communists estimated that they had lost control of a million of the rural population because of pacification and the slow emergence of a semi-effective government in South Vietnam.

Whereas a Communist victory had seemed on the horizon in 1965, it now had receded from view. Something had to be done. It was obvious that continued guerrilla tactics could not bring about the military victory they sought, so they planned to up the stakes and decided to resort to increased large-scale military tactics. The plan called for a significant defeat of American forces while simultaneously overwhelming the South Vietnamese in Quang Tri Province. Wresting this northern province from South Vietnam's hands would be a shocking event that the North Vietnamese anticipated would bring about a "general uprising" in the south and leave the Americans isolated and in a compromising position like the French in 1954. Hanoi would then graciously offer a red carpet out of the country to the Americans.

This go-for-broke plan was adopted. In order to achieve maximum surprise, the main attack was scheduled for the Tet holidays at the end of January 1968.

....

North Vietnamese Communist Party leaders including Gen Vo Nguyen Giap (far left) and President Ho Chi Minh (second from right) at a celebration in Hanoi.

CHAPTER 3

RUNNING THE GAUNTLET: ROUTE 9 TO KHE SANH

An American tank moves along Route 9.

TIMELINE	APRIL 24, 1967	MAY 13, 1967	DECEMBER 1967	JANUARY 21, 1968	JANUARY 31, 1968
	Hill Fights begin at Khe Sanh	Hill Fights end. Marines fought off elements of the 325C NVA Division in a two-week battle that cost the enemy 824 KIA. 168 Marines were killed and 443 wounded in the struggle.	General Westmoreland decides to reinforce Khe Sanh in the face of enemy buildup.	NVA attack hill 861 and bombard combat base exploding ammo dump, and attack Khe Sanh village. Siege begins.	NVA launch countrywide Tet Offensive.

T he main north-south roadway in South Vietnam was Highway 1, located along the eastern edge of the country adjacent to the South China Sea. It was along this narrow corridor of lowland that 90 percent of the population lived and farmed. To the north, Highway 1 intersected with Route 9 just south of the DMZ at Dong Ha. Route 9 then headed west toward the Laotian border, and this primitive track was the proverbial "40 miles of bad road."

This 42-mile road included forty-nine bridges and had been closed to vehicular traffic for three years due to washouts and enemy ambushes. Its closure had forced the Marines to resupply forces at Khe Sanh by air.

Eight miles to the west of Dong Ha was Cam Lo, and 10 miles further west, the road turned abruptly to the south at a prominent conical geological formation called "the Rockpile." Seven miles farther to the south was Ca Lu, and there the road again turned, this time to the west toward Khe Sanh, 11 air miles away. But that final leg to Khe Sanh was not a straight run. It twisted and turned, following the trace of the river. Five miles west of Ca Lu was a tortuous bend called "the Elbow."

In the spring of 1967, on the very day that Marine patrols precipitated the Hill Fights in April, the NVA invested the Elbow and pulled off the perfect ambush. It was "perfect" in that an engineer platoon, trying to repair and maintain several bridges along the narrow land artery, sustained 100 percent casualties, and all their vehicles were damaged or destroyed.

This engineering platoon went out every day to put the bridges into operation guarded by a security force consisting of an Ontos—a tracked vehicle mounting six 106mm recoilless rifles—and an Army Duster. The Duster boasted twin 40mm guns and was mounted on a tank chassis. The two vehicles could provide enormous firepower.

But on April 24, as the convoy proceeded to the Elbow to install a bridge, it entered the killing field of an L-shaped ambush set up by the NVA. The long axis of the "L" paralleled the killing zone, with machine guns placed along the short axis to deliver enfilading fire on the column. The machine guns fired head-on and the weapons along the long axis of the "L" then swept the road with fire. Every vehicle was destroyed or damaged

 DISK 1, TRACKS 8-9: Route 9 and the Rough Riders.

FEBRUARY 5-8, 1968	FEBRUARY 23, 1968	FEBRUARY 29, 1968	APRIL 14, 1968	JUNE 19-JULY 5, 1968
NVA attack Hill 861 Alpha, Lang Vei, and Hill 64.	Enemy gunners bombard base with more than 1,300 rounds in heaviest attack.	NVA launch regimental size attack against base.	Marines break out of siege and attack and seize Hill 881N.	Khe Sanh Combat Base is destroyed and abandoned by American forces.

and every man was a casualty—twenty-four of the force were killed. A single, wounded Marine escaped and struggled to run back the entire distance to Ca Lu to alert Capt John Ripley of the attack. Ripley dispatched a reaction force to counter the ambush, rescue the casualties, and evacuate the dead.

But despite this devastating ambush, the engineers continued their work and sufficiently improved the road during the next several weeks to allow armed convoys to make the run from Ca Lu to Khe Sanh, thus bringing supplies by land instead of the expensive airlifts. These convoys were nicknamed "Rough Riders." For the first time since 1964, Route 9 was open.

"I was the commanding officer of Lima Company, 3rd Battalion, 3rd Marines at Ca Lu," said Capt Ripley. "My company was given the mission to provide security for the Rough Riders attempting to move supplies along the road to Khe Sanh. Once the convoy arrived at Ca Lu we would board it, secure it, and move out to Khe Sanh, unload, and return."

It sounded routine, but there was nothing simple about the run.

"The condition of Route 9 from Ca Lu to Khe Sanh was incredibly bad," said Ripley. "It was pitted, holes washed out, completely overgrown in places, and rock slides had covered part of it. It was an impassable route."

Despite all the negatives, it was the only road, and the Marines intended to use it. If the road was bad, though, the bridges were worse.

"The road was cut into a cliff side on the north side and there were no guard rails anywhere along the road," said Ripley. "It was a tactical nightmare. There was no way you could secure your position unless you had a company of infantry moving ahead of you at every step."[1]

The bridges along the road defied description. One look at them would have been enough for any rational engineer to throw up his hands, condemn them as impassable, and walk away. But the Marines did not have the luxury to shrug and walk away. They looked past the obvious and examined these dilapidated, skeletal structures, and concluded that somehow they would make these "bridges" work. Somehow they would push a 60-ton tank across them.

"I would never in my life have thought that vehicles could have crossed such a bridge," said Ripley. "The surfaces had completely worn away so that as you crossed, you were looking down through it into the river. You crossed on the stringers, that run longitudinally across the bridge."

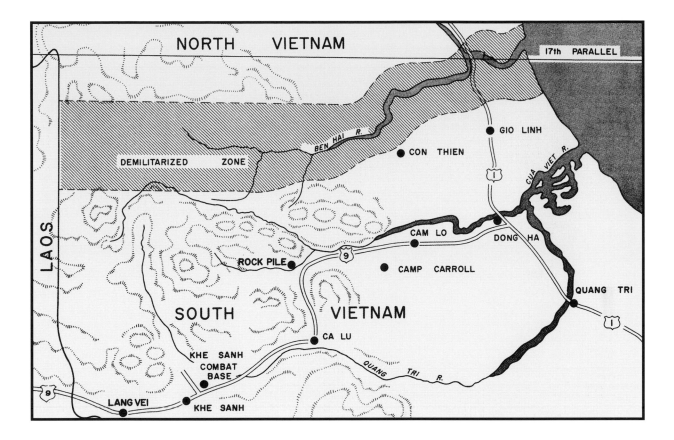

Driving was a nerve-shattering experience. A driver had to creep across making sure the tires remained on the stringers and did not slip off, thereby wedging between the beams and forever trapping the vehicle. Once across, he had to negotiate a road overgrown with jungle, completely hiding culverts. A vehicle proceeding along what looked like solid roadway could suddenly plunge off the edge of an invisible culvert and into the river below.

It was along this impossible path that the Rough Rider sought to supply Khe Sanh. The security force included a rifle company of Marines, reinforced by armored vehicles including tanks, Dusters, Ontos, and quad-.50s mounted on trucks.

The Ontos sported six 106mm recoilless rifles. The Dusters and quad-.50s were popular weapons from World War II capable of enormous firepower. The Dusters had twin 40mm guns mounted on a tank chassis, firing 2-pound projectiles in four-round clips at two hundred forty rounds per minute. The round was high-explosive with a tremendous blast and fragmentation effect, but its highly sensitive, point-detonating

A map of northern Quang Tri Province. **OPPOSITE:** A security force patrols ahead of a convoy on Route 9.

fuse was less effective in the jungle. In dense vegetation, the round exploded before penetrating.

Its sister weapon, the quad-.50, easily overcame that shortcoming. Old-timers called it, "Whispering Death." Each .50-caliber gun fired eight hundred rounds per minute, translating to thirty-two hundred rounds per minute when all four fired simultaneously. Gunnery instructors described the quad-.50 as "the best way to move 20 meters of jungle back 30 meters."

"We would leave Ca Lu early in the morning, and this was a two-day operation," said Capt Ripley. "We would proceed out to the Hairpin Bridge. The Hairpin Bridge was a former French bridge built many years ago, and was not passable. We built a new, heavy, Class 60 bridge to take the heaviest stuff, and remained overnight, securing it in one of the most remote places you've ever seen in your life."

The next day, the main convoy pushed out to the newly erected bridge site with the quad-.50s in front, along with a vehicle carrying a spare bridge. Then the convoy pushed across the bridge and began up the long gradient toward Khe Sanh.

"We would always keep the vehicles moving," said Ripley. "We would prep fire with both artillery and our own weapons. We'd fire at likely ambush points. The quad-.50s would defoliate the jungle in front of them."

After the four-hour trip, there was no dilly-dallying around. The convoy unloaded its cargo as fast as possible and readied for the dangerous return trip. When they reached the Hairpin Bridge, the Marines dismantled the Class 60 bridge, loaded it up, and the whole convoy returned to Ca Lu.

The Marines who made this nerve-wracking trip over several months never made it without feeling that unseen eyes watched them and that they were walking into the killing zone of an ambush every step of

Members of Company C, 1st Battalion, 26th Marines man an outpost near a bridge on Route 9 just east of the combat base, August 1967. **OPPOSITE:** Engineers repair a bridge on Route 9.

the way. But the supplies and matériel kept the remote outpost alive, even though some of the runs seemed less than vital.

"I'll never forget on one trip out there," said Capt Ripley. "There were three pallets of dehydrated cabbage, and I couldn't help thinking: Here I am risking my life to protect dried cabbage which nobody is going to want to eat, and everybody probably despises; and somebody is getting rid of it in a cushy spot like Da Nang, while they're having proper food and we're protecting this crap to take it to Khe Sanh."[2]

The apprehensions of Capt Ripley and his Marines as they traversed the twisting road were not unfounded. The unseen eyes that they suspected were, in fact, watching, and the NVA were very concerned about the Rough Rider convoys. Resupplying Khe Sanh ran counter to NVA plans to isolate the base. Somehow they had to stop it. They devised an ambush they hoped would be as effective as the "perfect ambush" they had sprung at the Elbow.

Using night and inclement weather as cover, the North Vietnamese pushed through the jungle and began to prepare the ambush site along Route 9 between Ca Lu and the Hairpin Bridge. They actually set up living quarters in the dense jungle that surrounded the road, and in some cases made living space in the overgrown culverts along the road over which the Rough Riders passed.

The ambush killing-zone was massive, almost 5 miles long, with continuous trenches and mines above the road, and mines and booby traps below the road. Mortar fire could completely blanket the road.

There would be no escape. If successful, the ambush would bring the column to a halt, unable to proceed forward or backward. Then the ambushing NVA would pour devastating fire on the column from the steep slopes and trenches above and parallel to the road. The deploying Marines would detonate the mines and booby traps as they maneuvered to counterattack, and the only escape for the convoy would be to plunge down the steep cliffs into the raging river.

By the middle of July the site was ready and the NVA moved into position. On July 21, the largest convoy to attempt the Route 9 run formed in Dong Ha. It included almost ninety vehicles and several of the Army's 175mm self-propelled artillery pieces. It would proceed to Ca Lu where it would be joined by its security, and then advance to the Hairpin Bridge to cross for the final run to Khe Sanh. The big 175mm guns would give the Marines at the combat base a much greater range to cover targets to the north and west.

At Ca Lu, Capt John Ripley's Lima Company waited for the convoy. As Dong Ha signaled that the convoy had departed, a platoon from Company M set off from Ca Lu to patrol the road to the west.

The 2nd Platoon of Company M set off in the morning heat and humidity, and proceeded west, carefully

Ambush survivors carry a wounded soldier to safety. **OPPOSITE:** An Ontos, with its six 106mm recoilless rifles.

observing the dense terrain that surrounded the road. They proceeded for 2 kilometers and then 3. The forty-man unit walked in two columns, spread out in formation, and the point man moved slightly ahead. Four kilometers came and went. At the 5-kilometer mark, the road bent out of sight.

Just around the bend was the beginning of the massive, 5-mile ambush. It ran all the way to the Hairpin Bridge, and the North Vietnamese would trigger it only after all the vehicles of the convoy had entered the killing zone.

The point man of 2nd Platoon slowly inched around the bend and paused as more and more of the continuing road came into view. Half way through the turn, he was shocked to see an NVA soldier urinating on the side of the road. Unaware that the Marine patrol was anywhere nearby, this soldier had obviously decided to abandon his covered position to relieve himself in anticipation of the big action to come.[3]

The Marine opened fire, and instantly the NVA soldiers on the slope of the steep hill returned fire. The rest of the platoon deployed forward to engage the enemy force. The platoon commander radioed back to Ca Lu that he was in contact with an enemy platoon, but the fire became so intense that he quickly changed his estimate to an enemy battalion.

LtCol Robert C. Needham, commanding 3rd Battalion, 3rd Marines, ordered his platoon to disengage and return to base, but 2nd Platoon could not free themselves from the fire of the numerically superior enemy. Frantically, air support and artillery were brought to bear on the enemy to assist the engaged Marines. As the firefight raged, the convoy from Dong Ha arrived at Ca Lu.

The remaining platoons of Company M moved to the firefight accompanied by two Army vehicles carrying twin 40mm guns and quad-.50s. The NVA greeted this reinforcing column with more than two hundred rounds of mortars and a fusillade of small-arms fire.

Arriving aircraft saturated the steep slopes with heavy fire, and the Army guns shredded the foliage, pinning the enemy down. The column reached the Marines of the 2nd Platoon just as two tanks arrived to further punish the enemy force, and the Americans were able to disengage and return to Ca Lu.

On July 25, the convoy completed its journey to Khe Sanh. The 175mm guns stayed behind. Several more convoys negotiated the run, but in early August, vehicular traffic stopped. The massive ambush had failed, but its ambitious attempt was not in vain.

Its very size and the thought of the destruction it could have inflicted on precious rolling stock was enough to slam the door on Route 9. Khe Sanh would again be resupplied only by air.

The NVA continued to strike vehicles on Route 9. On August 21 and again on September 7, NVA units ambushed small convoys, with mixed results. During the August attack the enemy knocked out four vehicles, but the attackers had to break contact when Marines reacting with lightning quickness almost trapped the ambushers.

Emboldened by their August attack, the NVA tried a second ambush at almost the same point between the Rockpile and Ca Lu. This time the Marine reaction was even swifter, and they pinned the enemy to the ground in an eight-hour firefight that killed almost one hundred NVA soldiers.[4]

But the enemy forces were not finished. In a year that had seen the North Vietnamese attempt to overrun Khe Sanh and then close Route 9 with an attempted ambush, they now targeted Con Thien for a September offensive meant to disrupt the South Vietnamese elections and bring about a major defeat

Marines and Navy corpsmen load casualties onto an H-34 helicopter at Con Thien.

of a significant American force. Con Thien was a strategic Marine outpost just 2 kilometers south of the DMZ. The Marines dug in on this small hill, only 158 meters (less than 520 feet) tall, that had a commanding view of the surrounding terrain. It was also the western anchor of the barrier, nicknamed "McNamara's Line," now under construction. The land had been bulldozed and cleared to form a 600-meter (approximately 655-yard-wide) track stretching east for 8 miles.

The September attack began with a particularly destructive bombardment on the air facility at Dong Ha. Forty-one artillery rounds smashed into the helicopter base there, igniting and destroying the ammunition- and fuel-storage facilities. The resulting explosions and fires sent a 12,000-foot column of smoke into the sky. Seventeen helicopters were damaged, but more important, the helicopter squadron was forced to relocate its base to the south toward Da Nang.

But it was on Con Thien that the enemy gunners focused. During September they pounded the hilltop with two hundred rounds per day. On the 25th, the outpost was hammered with more than twelve hundred rounds. Following the artillery came a series of ground attacks as the NVA went all out to overrun Con Thien. But each attempt was hurled back. While the hilltop could accommodate only one battalion within its perimeter, two additional battalions were positioned to the south as reaction forces. The enemy observed the locations of all Marine forces and launched a seven-day bombardment. Marine patrols met heavy resistance. After several sharp encounters, the enemy's 90th NVA Regiment withdrew into the sanctuary of the DMZ.

But the artillery, mortars, and rockets did not retreat, and continued with the greatest bombardment of the war to that time. From September 19 to 27, they struck Con Thien with more than 3,000 rounds. To counter the heavy bombardment, the Americans unleashed a devastating counter-battery attack of its own. More than 12,000 artillery rounds, supplemented by 6,148 naval gunfire rounds blasted enemy positions, and B-52s and other aircraft flew more than five thousand sorties in a maximum effort against the NVA attackers. At the end of this massive counterfire, the NVA attacks on Con Thien greatly diminished. The enemy had failed to pull off a great victory before the onset of the northeast monsoon.

What the enemy didn't know was that they had been the victims of Operation Neutralize, an air offensive utilizing a newly conceived tactic called SLAM. "By the first week of October 1967 the siege of Con Thien was over," said Gen Westmoreland. "It was broken by tenacious, aggressive Marines, and by a new concept of marshaling firepower known as SLAM."[5]

The acronym stood for "seeking, locating, annihilating, and monitoring," but in plain language it meant marshaling "the entire spectrum of heavy fire support—B-52s, tactical air, and naval gunfire—in close coordination with artillery and other ground fire," Westmoreland explained. "For forty-nine days SLAM strikes pummeled the enemy around Con Thien and demonstrated that massed firepower was in itself sufficient to force a besieging enemy to desist."[6]

At the same time as the NVA were attacking, American forces of the 101st Airborne Division captured a vital enemy document and forwarded it to U. S. Military Assistance Command Vietnam (USMACV) headquarters in Saigon. It was entitled, "The Thirteenth Resolution of North Vietnam Lao Dong Party."

The Thirteenth Resolution* was a rambling, boring, single-spaced, thirty-one-page directive filled with the high-minded propaganda common in Party documents. But besides extolling the virtues of the Communist Party with familiar words like "struggle," "dedication," and "sacrifice," and castigating "America and its puppet," there were several key sentences suggesting a shift in the wartime posture of North Vietnam.

"Our forces grow stronger and are now capable of defeating the enemy," the resolution proclaimed. It called for increased military struggle and to "counter the enemy's pacification program by disrupting his sweep operations." The population was exhorted to "double the production efforts to support the front line."

There was also a grim warning predicting heavy casualties. The resolution called for the destruction of entire battalions of American and ARVN troops. "Attrition warfare is normally waged, and creates no problem. The criterion set out for this dry season was to kill 10,000 Americans . . . and 100,000 puppet soldiers."

The resolution ended with typical stilted propaganda. "We must currently rise up to Chairman Ho's appeal and sacrifice our lives and offer our power to gain a complete victory. The everlasting glory always pertains to our heroic Party, heroic people, and heroic troops."

In Washington on November 21, President Lyndon Johnson sat down to breakfast with eight men. They were all high-ranking political and military advisors, including Gen Westmoreland and Gen Wheeler (JCS). The president was concerned over intelligence reports that the Communists were preparing a big offensive to achieve a significant victory on the battlefield. He asked for a status report on a speedup of U.S. troop movements to Vietnam. "We need to get all the additional troops moved as fast as we can," he said.[7]

The meeting adjourned, and Gen Westmoreland went to address the National Press Club. There he gave an optimistic report on the progress of the war.

"I am absolutely certain that whereas in 1965 the enemy was winning, today he is certainly losing,"[8] the general said.

During this speech and later as a guest on television's *Meet the Press*, Westmoreland predicted that in "two years or less," South Vietnamese armed forces would assume more of the burden of the war and American forces would begin withdrawing.

This was a welcome statement to a nation whose patience had been stretched. President Johnson and South Vietnamese president Thieu both expressed approval of the address to the Press Club. Both were optimistic, but couched in that optimism were the nagging concerns about increased enemy activity, especially in the north around the DMZ, and of more references to the French battle at Dien Bien Phu.

As the tension mounted, the weak began to wilt. Robert McNamara changed his military philosophy again. On November 1, he told President Johnson he had doubts that they could accomplish their objectives in South Vietnam.

Then he made an unbelievable proposal. In the face of a known massive enemy buildup against American forces, he recommended stopping all bombing in the North before the end of the year. McNamara explained,

*Ho Chi Minh had promulgated Resolution I in 1918.

"We would hope for a response from Hanoi . . . the lack of any response . . . would demonstrate that it is North Vietnam . . . blocking a peaceful settlement."[9]

Friends, advisors, generals, ambassadors, and cabinet members told the president they were against this proposal. Clark Clifford said, "I am at a loss to understand this logic."[10]

This latest assertion was too much, even for Lyndon Johnson, who had consistently backed McNamara, and the president rejected it. Since 1965 ten bombing halts and pauses had produced nothing. Almost seventy peace feelers had been ignored or rejected by Hanoi. In frustration, Johnson gave the enemy grudging admiration. Calling up an Alamo comparison, the president said, "They can't be accused of being hypocrites. They've given the same answer from the start. It is just like the answer that Travis gave at the Alamo when they asked if he would surrender. A cannon shot!"[11]

One month later, Gen Wheeler delivered an address to the Detroit Economic Club. He was not optimistic. The pressure in northern I Corps had been accompanied by regimental-size attacks to the south at Loc Ninh and Dak To in November.

Wheeler told club members, "There may be a Communist thrust similar to the desperate effort of the Germans in the Battle of the Bulge in World War II."[12]

Three days later, on December 21, President Johnson gave a gloomy forecast. He had been briefed that captured enemy documents indicated an all-out attack was coming to bring about a turning point, and that two more NVA divisions were noted moving to the south toward Khe Sanh. He told members of the Australian Cabinet in Canberra, "We face dark days ahead." He told them he thought that Hanoi would try for a military victory of some kind and might resort to using "kamikaze" tactics and human-wave assaults.[13]

At Khe Sanh, Marines patroling the area around their base found signs of increased enemy activity. NVA trucks frantically moved supplies along the Ho Chi Minh Trail into the DMZ and Laos. The Year of the Goat was coming to an end. The Year of the Monkey was at hand.

....

Gen Earle Wheeler, Chairman Joint Chiefs of Staff.

CHAPTER 4

THE INTRUDERS AND THE LISTENING POST

Naval Construction Battalion soldiers and their fifteen-ton rock crushers. **OPPOSITE:** Col David E. Lownds, commander 26th Marine Regiment.

Col David E. Lownds was forty-six when he took command of the 26th Marine Regiment on August 14, 1967. Lownds had been a young lieutenant during some of the fiercest action in the Pacific during World War II. He had been a platoon commander during the battles of Kwajalein, Saipan, and Iwo Jima, and had twice been wounded. More recently he had won the Bronze Star during the Marine action in the Dominican Republic in 1965.

But Lownds commanded the 26th Marines in name only, since the shuffling of battalions in and out of Khe Sanh usually left him overseeing only one battalion commander. The 26th Marines had been formed during World War II as part of the 5th Marine Division that fought at Iwo Jima, but it was subsequently disbanded. Vietnam had required an increased Marine force, and 5th Division was reformed in 1966. Two of its regiments, the 26th and 27th, were eventually committed to Vietnam.[1]

The day after Lownds took command of the 26th Marines, he closed the Khe Sanh airstrip so that a Naval Construction Battalion ("Seabees") unit could install a layer of crushed rock under the aluminum plates of the runway to protect them from buckling. Torrential monsoon rains had caused erosion and washouts that were undermining the vital airstrip. The twenty-eight Seabees of Unit 301 soon earned the moniker "Rock Crushers," as their three 15-ton machines pulverized rock from a hill 1,500 meters (about 1,600 yards) southwest of the Khe Sanh perimeter. By December 2, they completed the enormous task,[2] and the 3,900-foot airstrip was again operational.

On November 14 the commanding general of the 3rd Marine Division, Gen Bruno Hochmuth, was killed in a helicopter crash, and Gen Rathevon McCall Tompkins hurried from his stateside post to

DISK 1, TRACKS 10-12: Searching for the enemy.

FEBRUARY 5-8, 1968	FEBRUARY 23, 1968	FEBRUARY 29, 1968	APRIL 14, 1968	JUNE 19-JULY 5, 1968
NVA attack Hill 861 Alpha, Lang Vei, and Hill 64.	Enemy gunners bombard base with more than 1,300 rounds in heaviest attack.	NVA launch regimental size attack against base.	Marines break out of siege and attack and seize Hill 881N.	Khe Sanh Combat Base is destroyed and abandoned by American forces.

replace him. Tompkins arrived as intelligence reports bristled with information of new enemy activity in the DMZ area.

On December 13 Tompkins received a call on the secure scrambler phone from Gen Robert E. Cushman Jr., overall Marine commander, revealing details of the new threat: There were four NVA regiments within 12 miles of Khe Sanh. Tompkins dispatched the 3rd Battalion, 26th Marines (3/26) to Khe Sanh to join the 1st Battalion (1/26). The new battalion was airlifted into the combat base on December 14.

Chaplain Ray Stubbe attended a 1st Battalion briefing the following night and heard excited rumors fueled by the arrival of 3/26. What was next?

"First, 2/26 is also coming," the chaplain said. "Second, 3/26 is going into Laos, and third, the base is going to be attacked tonight. People sniffers had been out recently. These were devices able to sense people by ammonia. A plastic overlay on the map had several hundred dots all over the northern part of our area of operations. This jolted everyone into the realization that the enemy was out there in numbers, and out there close to us!"[3]

On December 19, the Combined Action Company (CAC) Headquarters in Khe Sanh village, several kilometers from the base, took small-arms fire and some mortars. It was a small attack, but it marked the first time the enemy had fired on Khe Sanh since June. 3/26 set off on a long patrol to the north and west, but after four days had made no contact with the enemy even though the unit had seen signs of activity. Fresh foxholes and well-used trails proved the NVA was moving in the area between the base and the Laotian border.

Christmas Day, 1967, was as peaceful as any back home in the United States. After the 1100 services, Chaplain Stubbe walked outside and was treated to the strains of "Joy to the World" broadcast from an overhead aircraft. In the evening, Col Lownds went into Khe Sanh village where he watched a Marine PFC dressed up as Santa Claus distribute candy to the Bru Montagnard children. Lownds was moved. "It makes me sick when I see all the protestors and here is a young man risking his life for bringing life to others."[4]

The last week of the year produced another battalion sweep. This time 1/26 swept toward the Rao Quan River to the east of the 881/861 Hill complex. The Rao Quan provided a natural thoroughfare from the DMZ into Quang Tri Province and to

Route 9. But although 1st Battalion found newly constructed bunkers, small weapons caches, and freshly used trails, its patrolling triggered no major contact. Lownds could sense the enemy presence but could not find them.

He now readjusted his forces to protect Khe Sanh Combat Base. 1st Battalion reinforced with L/3/26, provided base defense. I/3/26, with two platoons of M/3/26, manned Hill 881S. K/3/26 perched atop Hill 861, and the final platoon of M/3/26 provided the base reaction force. They would be the firemen to seal off any enemy penetrations. The Marines occupied the base in force and manned the hills which stood like sentinels barring the northern approaches.

On New Year's Day, 1968, 492,000 Americans in South Vietnam enjoyed the last hours of a cease-fire that the South Vietnamese government had announced for Allied forces from December 31 to January 2. Pope Paul VI had made an appeal for a day of peace on January 1.

But the "day of peace" was a frantic one for the North Vietnamese Army. During the thirty-six-hour cease-fire, American aircraft sighted and photographed eighteen hundred trucks in the panhandle area of North Vietnam north of the DMZ. This massive traffic, nine times the normal amount, was headed south.[5]

Members of 26th Marines patrol near Khe Sanh, November 1967. **OPPOSITE ABOVE:** Gen Rathevon McCall Tompkins, commanding general 3rd Marine division. **OPPOSITE BELOW:** Chaplain Ray W. Stubbe.

Gen Westmoreland had not been idle during this period of increased enemy activity. He seized the opportunity to prepare for the major battle he had sought with the main enemy force. He planned operations that would sweep the four northern provinces to Laos and planned for a possible amphibious invasion north of the DMZ to hook down and trap NVA forces in their sanctuary.[6] If the previously elusive enemy army was going to come out for a showdown, Westmoreland was ready to take them on.

The two battalions of the 26th Marines stationed at the two-mile long, half-mile wide Khe Sanh Combat Base and its surrounding hills cautiously enjoyed the last hours of the day of peace. Lownds knew they were not alone in those thickly covered piedmont hills. The next day the colonel received additional intelligence reports indicating two NVA Divisions and possibly part of a third had moved into the Khe Sanh area.

The 325C Division, veteran of the Hill Fights, was thought to be in an area to the north of Hill 881S. The 304th Division, veteran of Dien Bien Phu, was to the southwest of the base, and a regiment of the 324th Division was in the central DMZ 10 to 15 miles northeast. A fourth division was confirmed north of the Rockpile.

As dusk approached on January 2, the companies defending the base deployed their listening posts outside the perimeter. Each company usually had three or four LPs outside the wire. Company L, defending the west or "Red Sector," was no exception.

"A listening post [LP] was a fire team—four riflemen—which was sent out by each platoon to monitor a likely avenue of approach of our lines,"[7] said Capt Richard Camp, commanding Company L.

While a listening post was a must to provide early warning and security, it was also vulnerable to being overrun or encircled. The first rule for an attacking force was to drive in the outposts, thereby blinding the defenders to the details of the attack.

When the enemy approached, those manning a listening post created a dilemma for the company commander. The first tendency was to pull them in out of harm's way, but pulling a listening post in too soon robbed the commander of his eyes to the front; ordering them in too late could spell their doom. The CO's toughest decision was to order them to hold their ground and remain unseen while in the midst of the enemy.

....

PFC Daniel Allen, machine gunner for 3rd battalion, 26th Marines. **OPPOSITE:** On Hill 881S, members of India Company look for enemy artillery positions.

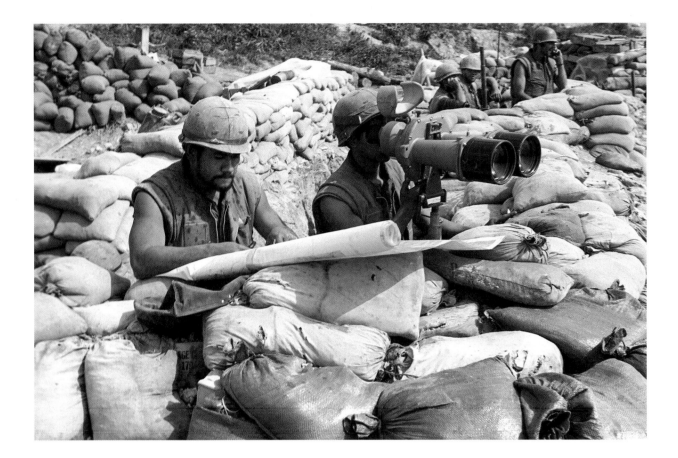

Marines assigned to listening-post duty could not be squeamish and had to possess great patience, nerves of steel, and the discipline to hold their fire and not reveal their positions even with the enemy breathing down their necks. If the post could remain undetected in the enemy midst, the advantage was enormous.

Listening Post Lima 1/1 (1st Squad, 1st Platoon) was positioned 400 meters (almost 440 yards) off the western edge of the airstrip, 80 meters (about 88 yards) in front of the company lines screening its right flank. There, a small draw rose from a valley to the end of the runway suggesting a good enemy approach to the perimeter. The LP located itself close to a distinctive landmark called "the Hanging Tree" because of its unusual shape. This landmark could make it easy for a reaction force to find the outpost, should an emergency arise in the ink-black night.

At 2030, dead silence gripped the western sector of the base and eyes strained to see in the darkness. Reports of the enemy's presence had caused the Marines to see battalions of NVA crouching to attack in each irregular shape to the front. More than one man stared for long periods at suspicious spots, trying to detect movement.

The silence of the evening was at last broken not with a bang but with the tiniest change in the quiet hiss of the radio, just audible above the squelch setting. The company's radio pit was a large fighting hole covered over with a tarp to keep light from making it a target in the night. Suddenly that little hiss, heard only by the radio operator, stopped and a voice quieter than the hiss transmitted. It was the listening post. In a low whisper, the voice reported movement to the front.

The company radio operator notified Capt Camp, who was at the radio in a flash, attempting to contact the LP, but there was no answer. A second, third, and fourth attempt still did not raise the LP, and the radio hissed quietly. Camp finally transmitted that if they could hear him, they should click the handset twice. Almost immediately the hiss was interrupted by the double click.

"And then we waited," said Capt Camp. "The adrenaline went straight through me. I had four Marines out there who thought they saw or heard something. It was darker than pitch. I had no idea what was coming in on them, and maybe they didn't either."

Camp pressed the handset hard to his ear as if that force could raise the listening post where his transmissions had not. "I was listening so hard, I almost missed the faint whisper coming in over my handset," Camp said. The whispered message was short and to the point. "We see something. Out!"

That was it—no details. Just a monotone voice Camp could only assume was whispering within close proximity to the enemy. He went into action and ordered his reaction force to stand by. The reaction force consisted of the ammunition humpers from the company's mortar section.

"The eight men in the reaction force were all mortarmen . . . " said Capt Camp. "Moreover, they were all very junior, all privates first class and lance corporals, if that. They were faced with the prospect of having to advance beyond our prepared defenses in the dead of night. Once they were in the open, they would have to locate a well-camouflaged friendly position they had never seen."[8]

Marines look out from their bunker at the base. **OPPOSITE:** Marine snipers on Hill 881S look for NVA troops.

But the 1st Platoon Commander, 2Lt Nile Buffington, knew exactly where the listening post was. He had personally placed them out at the Hanging Tree. Capt Camp sent his eight-man force to 2Lt Buffington with orders to be ready to reinforce the LP.

"The reaction unit was alerted to saddle up," said PFC Charles Thornton Jr. "Movement had been detected in front of the perimeter, and the company commander was sending us out to investigate."[9]

Suddenly Camp's radio came alive again. The feeble transmission was so low that he strained to hear. He didn't hear it all, but he heard enough. The team leader at the LP said, "We see something. Six of them just walked by us." Seconds later the Marine at the LP continued, "You want me to tell you what they are armed with?"[10]

Capt Camp told the LP, "Hold your position," and ordered Lt Buffington to take the men out.

"These people were very unorganized," said Buffington of the reaction force. "They really didn't know what they were doing. They had been set in behind our lines for backup, and they came with me. The only way we could do this was for me to walk point, because I was the only one who knew where to go."

So the reaction force of mortarmen and 2Lt Buffington formed up. In the time-honored tradition of the Marine Corps, "Every Marine is a rifleman." From the commandant to the cooks and bakers, every Marine is first and foremost a rifleman and expected to perform as such when called on. Buffington's force was no exception. So in battle formation, 2Lt Buffington and his "riflemen" moved toward the Hanging Tree.

"We moved up to and through our concertina wire," said PFC Thornton. "It was so dark you literally could not see your hand in front of your face. Our mortars from behind the lines began popping flares overhead.

The night was illuminated in a very strange manner as the flares slowly drifted through the cloud cover, swinging back and forth suspended on the parachute. There were intervals of darkness and light between the rounds fired.

"The lieutenant had us get on line, spread out, and begin moving into the darkness ahead. We walked on line, hunched over and listening only to the sounds of the night and our hearts pounding in our chests with anticipation. I heard the lieutenant, just off to my right, shouting to someone to identify himself."

2Lt Buffington had seen someone in front of him. At first he was worried a patrol from 1/26 had been sent out and had gotten lost and moved in front of his lines, and he did not want to open up on friendlies.

"You could make out their silhouettes," said Buffington. "I spoke to them in Marine language. 'You sons-of-bitches, you better identify yourselves!'"

But the intruders said nothing and in the murk and gloom seemed to just stare in the direction of Buffington's voice.

....

NVA officers lay dead near the Hanging Tree. **OPPOSITE:** PFC Charles Thornton.

"I said it twice. 'You goddam sons-of-bitches—you better identify yourselves.'"[11]

PFC Thornton heard Buffington. "He said, 'Identify yourselves or we will fire.' Just at that moment, all hell broke loose. There were weapons firing from all around, and tracer rounds cutting through the darkness. We returned fire in the direction from which the first shots began. It seemed like an eternity."

The volume of fire was enormous. The reaction force plus the four-man listening post delivered a sustained sheet of fire to the front. Small trees fell like wheat before the scythe. And then it was silent. The Marines listened for sounds of movement, but there were none.

"We again got on line and swept through the area where we thought the fire had originated, and found nothing and encountered no additional resistance, and returned to base," said PFC Thornton.[12]

"We were all shaking, knock-kneed, and went back through the lines and made our report to battalion," said 2Lt Buffington. "The first thing they wanted to know was 'Where's the bodies?' We went back out and we were scared to death. We didn't find anybody. Our listening post was still there."[13]

At the battalion briefing the following morning, LtCol James Wilkinson told his staff that the incident the previous night indicated poor fire discipline. There had been no apparent visible targets, he said, and a lot of ammo had been uselessly expended. He reiterated division policy that stated there would be no firing unless there was a definite target.[14]

While the colonel's briefing on fire discipline was taking place, 2Lt Buffington and his men were again approaching the Hanging Tree for a daytime look around. The broken limbs and mown grass and bushes pinpointed the location of the firefight. The Marines had little trouble locating their former adversaries. Five riddled NVA soldiers, stiffened by rigor mortis, lay where they had fallen. It seemed the Marine fire discipline had been just right.

"They were pretty well laid out in a row," said Buffington. "There were five of them, dressed in green. They all had ChiCom grenades. They had been reaching for them when we opened up, but they never got them out. We felt one of them got away. The belts had been cut off their bodies and the map pouches had been taken. There were blood drippings. The person who got away was wounded

and was leaving a blood trail."[15] The blood trail led off to the southwest. Intelligence had pinpointed the NVA's 304th Division to the southwest.

It seemed that in a daring effort at reconnaissance, ranking NVA officers had approached the Marine lines. They had gathered close to the Hanging Tree to look over the defenses and consider approaches for a possible attack. They had paced off distances and reconnoitered their avenue of approach, but the eyes of the alert Marines of Lima LP 1/1 had spotted them and cut their mission short.

The encounter at the Hanging Tree confirmed intelligence reports of enemy soldiers massing for an offensive. Gen Robert Cushman sent Col Lownds the last battalion of the 26th Marines to beef up the defense. When 2/26 arrived on January 17, Lownds sent them to Hill 558 to block the approach along the Rao Quan. The three battalions were now operating together for the first time since the Battle of Iwo Jima.[16]

....

President Lyndon B. Johnson (center) examines a terrain model of the Khe Sanh area in the White House situation room, February 1968.

Gen Westmoreland, at MACV Headquarters in Saigon, moved swiftly to design another SLAM operation like Operation Neutralize that had successfully crushed the enemy at Con Thien. He ordered Air Force general William M. Momeyer to prepare a two-part SLAM operation code named Operation Niagara.

"I gave it the code name, Niagara, to invoke the image of cascading shells and bombs," said Westmoreland. "The first part was to be a comprehensive intelligence-collection effort using every available means to pinpoint the enemy . . . " The second part would be the killing punch, including "carefully coordinated round-the-clock shelling and bombing by all available artillery and aircraft . . . "[17] Westmoreland would unleash the great arsenal of American supporting arms on the North Vietnamese Army, which had chosen to mass at Khe Sanh.

At the White House, President Lyndon Johnson kept well briefed on intelligence reports of enemy activity. Aerial photo interpreters had discovered two new roads originating across the Laotian border. One terminated 17 miles northwest of Khe Sanh; the second crossed the border only 8.5 miles from the base.[18]

The war had sapped Johnson's strength. Seventeen thousand Americans had been killed, and Hanoi continually rejected all peace feelers. It frustrated Johnson how "a raggedy-ass little fourth-rate country" could stand up to the United States.[19] Now the NVA threatened Khe Sanh. Ironically, this enemy was able to mass in the very sanctuaries that the president had allowed to go untouched. North Vietnamese soldiers marched toward the battlefield, spared from destruction by American bombers because of his target restrictions.

THE WAR HAD SAPPED JOHNSON'S STRENGTH. SEVENTEEN THOUSAND AMERICANS HAD BEEN KILLED, AND HANOI CONTINUALLY REJECTED ALL PEACE FEELERS.

The newspapers and press succumbed to the temptation to compare the Marine position with the 1954 French position at Dien Bien Phu. Johnson had heard the comparison so often that he had a terrain model of the Khe Sanh base placed in the White House situation room, surrounded by large aerial photographs. The names of Colonel Travis, Davy Crockett, and Jim Bowie were never far from his mind. One night, as he flew aboard Air Force One, he remarked, "It's another Alamo."[20]

Despite these seemingly gloomy reports, some of Johnson's staff had reasons to be encouraged. The Dien Bien Phu reporting drowned out the results of a significant Harris poll showing that the American people were, in fact, taking a tougher stance on the war. Forty-nine percent to 29 percent favored invading North Vietnam; 47 percent to 21 percent favored invading the DMZ, 42 percent to 33 percent favored mining Haiphong harbor, and a hard-core 25 percent did not oppose bombing China or using atomic weapons.

Some of the surprised staff urged the president to incorporate those results into his upcoming January 17

State of the Union address. They felt that this was a clear indication that a portion of his low 48 percent approval rating was because many Americans wanted him to get tougher in Vietnam, not vice versa. It seemed there were lots of Texas Rangers in America.[21] Johnson rejected his staff's advice.

What made Khe Sanh so important now when it had been so unimportant at other times? Indeed, since 1962 both the Americans and the NVA had had mixed emotions about Khe Sanh. The only time the Americans wanted to hold it was when the NVA wanted it. If the NVA left, then so did the Americans.

Its real value was that it was situated to monitor access routes to the northern provinces of South Vietnam from Laos and the western reaches of the DMZ. This was very important to the NVA in their trek from North Vietnam into South Vietnam. Their road networks included the Ho Chi Minh Trail through Laos and the Santa Fe Trail that skirted the western edge of South Vietnam. It was also important to Gen Westmoreland for any future plans he might employ for a possible thrust into Laos.

There was simply no easy passage into and out of South Vietnam for several hundred miles. The Annam Cordillera served as a barrier between Laos and Vietnam. This great mountain system stretched along the western edge of the Vietnams from 200 miles above the DMZ to approximately 200 miles below. But there was a significant break in the mountain range where Route 9 ran across Laos and through the mountains into South Vietnam at Khe Sanh.

The Mu Gia Pass and Keo Neua Pass 100 miles above the DMZ allowed the NVA to slip out of North Vietnam, enter Laos, and make this end run around the DMZ and enter South Vietnam. In January 1968, both sides wanted Khe Sanh.

On January 14, an eight-man Marine recon unit, Dockleaf, returning from a four-day patrol, moved down the south face of Hill 881N toward Capt Dabney's forces on 881S. But before they reached the base of the

Lt Thomas Brindley on Hill 881S. **OPPOSITE:** Capt William Dabney, commander India Company, 3rd Battalion, 26th Marines.

hill, an NVA force caught them in an ambush, killing or wounding six and pinning down the survivors in a hail of fire. Gunships flew support missions to pin the NVA. The wounded survivors of the team managed to break away from the battlefield but left their two killed comrades behind. A platoon from Company I was later able to recover the bodies.

Four days later, a second recon team made contact with an NVA force, again on the southern slopes of Hill 881N. The team was pinned down and unable to move because of superior NVA fire but were able to call in mortars and artillery and to signal their plight to Khe Sanh. Company I provided the 3rd Platoon as a rescue force.

"Lt Brindley volunteered to take his platoon to assist," said Capt Dabney. "Time was critical because the recon team could not carry its own

casualties and Brindley's platoon had 4 kilometers [2.5 miles] to cover. The platoon had to be back on 881S by dark; we couldn't leave large units out overnight.

"Brindley's 3rd Platoon shucked its packs, flak jackets, and all except weapons, ammo, and water, and literally double-timed to 881N in three squad columns . . . . In less than two hours, at 1600, the platoon found the recon team, set up a landing zone to evac the wounded, and returned to 881S with the six uninjured team members in tow. There was no contact, but we discovered that the team had abandoned a radio and some shackle sheets."[22]

The sheets were classified, used to encrypt messages for secure transmission. In enemy hands they would compromise security. The following day, January 19, Dabney dispatched his 1st Platoon under the command of 2LT Harry Fromme to patrol from 881S to the ambush site and try to recover the missing radio and the encryption sheets.

The patrol departed at dawn, slowly working its way down the northern slope of 881S and then up the facing, southern slope of 881N. Following a finger of land veering toward the northeast, each man moved with deliberate caution, keenly aware of the enemy presence.

At noon, Fromme and his men noticed there was a discernable change in the trail patterns. Most of the patrolling Marines knew the trail patterns like the backs of their hands, and the slightest changes were immediately obvious.

As Fromme's reinforced platoon moved slowly northward up the finger of land leading to the crest, an NVA force of equal strength unknowingly approached along the same track to the south. The contact was inevitable, and it occurred 500 meters (less than 550 yards) below the crest of 881N. The Marines' point got the first shot off and killed the NVA point, and the firefight began. Fromme's force engaged the NVA, who moved into bunkers. Three Marines were instantly wounded, and the lieutenant ordered his men to fall back so he could get mortars and artillery on the target. As the Marines moved down the slope, PFC Leonard Newton covered their maneuver with machine-gun fire.

Newton fired his M-60 in deadly bursts into the NVA positions. The ammunition belt whipped in the air as the gun ejected the spent brass cases in a steady stream. The roar of his gun dominated the battlefield. He briefly ducked down to clear a jam, but was standing again in an instant, blazing away long after the last of his fellow Marines had made good their withdrawal. Again his weapon jammed, and the young machine

Lt Harry Fromme, Sgt Michael Jones, and SSgt Taylor on Hill 881S.

gunner knelt to clear it and then returned to his standing position, firing with complete abandon. As he poured fire into the enemy soldiers, a return bullet struck Newton and killed him.*

The platoon was able to withdraw to 881S, but had not recovered the missing radio or shackle sheets. Capt Dabney decided that he would conduct a company-size patrol in force the following day.

As the enemy encircled the Marines at Khe Sanh, there was one casualty that was not unwelcomed to the Marines. The "McNamara fence" had been a millstone around their necks. It had been slow progress and high cost, and promised increases in men and matériel to implement the system had suddenly been forgotten. The Leathernecks accused MACV of reneging. MACV charged that the Marines were not serious about the job. Westmoreland let the Marines know that he was being pressed from "higher headquarters to meet a fixed time schedule." The general referred to schedule failures as "slippages." And these slippages "must be supported by factors recognized as being beyond our control." He told the Marines that "Project Dyemarker was operational necessity."[23]

The Marines felt that "the screws are being tightened." A senior Marine general opined that a commander should be tactically handling his troops, "rather than build the damn line that nobody believed in, in the first place." His complaints fell on deaf ears, and as the enemy encircled, he asked, "How in the hell were you going to build this thing when you had to fight people off while you were building it?"

The bickering, finger-pointing, and ridicule continued while the Marines worked to make significant progress. It was backbreaking and done in the face of enemy observation and within the range of their guns, and still Gen Westmoreland was not satisfied. "I have had no end of problems," he stated. "[It] seems that the Marines have had little experience in construction of fortifications and therefore lack the know-how to establish them."[24]

The Marines took great exception to his left-handed barb and countered that they saw the whole concept as an obstacle to fighting the war. Westmoreland seemed to micromanage even the construction of bunkers, suggesting sloping fronts as opposed to solid fronts. To the Marines, this was absurd. They were amazed that the commanding general should be concerned with "such trifles." Many described the observations of MACV as "nitpicking." Westmoreland was not to be outdone. He referred the Marine commanders to military field manuals for guidance in preparing defensive positions.

Arguments raged over bunkers, fortifications, size, and numbers; over who manned what; and how trench lines and barbed wire would be laid. Gen Tompkins said that "Dyemarker influenced almost everything we did and they wouldn't let us off the hook."

Westmoreland was in command, and despite their glib remarks, the Marines were fighting a losing battle. They needed an ally and, just in the nick of time, got the help they needed from the least likely of sources. It came from the NVA, which encircled Khe Sanh and the Marine positions across the DMZ. With the enemy at their doorstep, the generals, Marine and Army, agreed to stop Dyemarker until the enemy could be sorted out. The Marines quit building the fence, consigning Robert McNamara's barrier to the scrap heap. To the Marines, that was just where the project had always belonged.

*PFC Leonard Newton was posthumously awarded the Silver Star.

CHAPTER 5

HILL 881N: THE OPENING ATTACK

Capt Dabney and his men on the radio.

TIMELINE	APRIL 24, 1967	MAY 13, 1967	DECEMBER 1967	JANUARY 21, 1968	JANUARY 31, 1968
	Hill Fights begin at Khe Sanh	Hill Fights end. Marines fought off elements of the 325C NVA Division in a two-week battle that cost the enemy 824 KIA. 168 Marines were killed and 443 wounded in the struggle.	General Westmoreland decides to reinforce Khe Sanh in the face of enemy buildup.	NVA attack hill 861 and bombard combat base exploding ammo dump, and attack Khe Sanh village. Siege begins.	NVA launch countrywide Tet Offensive.

While the Marines occupied Hills 881S and 861 to the north of the base, the NVA occupied some high ground of their own. Dong Tri Mountain (Hill 1015), looking like an inverted teacup, was to the east of the Rao Quan River and slightly to the east of the Marine radio station on Hill 950. Unable to drive the Marines from that lofty perch six months earlier, the NVA now invested Hill 1015 with their antiaircraft artillery and positioned their guns to threaten the airstrip and aircraft that attempted resupply.

Throughout the land to the west and south of the combat base, the NVA placed numerous other antiaircraft artillery positions on high ground and hilltops. Near their base camps, supply trails, and trench complexes, they employed single-gun units, but in their vital storage areas and distribution points, they placed multiple guns, usually in a triangular formation, to throw up a wall of steel at any intruding aircraft.

Each position was selected for its commanding view of the surrounding terrain. Communications trenches connected each of the guns. Well-constructed bunkers protected the ammunition-storage areas and fighting holes, and often included overhead cover.

Their big defensive position atop Hill 663, 5 kilometers (3.1 miles) south of Route 9 and 8 kilometers (5 miles) southwest of the base, included fifty fighting bunkers that doubled for living quarters. The NVA troops constructed the bunkers in a mutually supporting, circular arrangement and, for concealment, placed the entire position just below the crest of the hill. Trees and high elephant grass made the position virtually invisible, while the hill afforded them excellent visibility. Logs were strapped to 12-inch support beams, arranged teepee-style overhead, and then embedded into the bunker's floor.[1]

This strong position dominated the southern and western approaches to Khe Sanh, and protected the NVA supply lines entering through Laos and North Vietnam. With these approaches firmly in their hands, the NVA simply had to kick the Marines off the outpost hills 881S and 861 to complete their encirclement of the combat base. Thus they would dominate all the high ground and would bring about a second Dien Bien Phu.

 DISK 1, TRACKS 13-14: The battle on 881N.

FEBRUARY 5-8, 1968	FEBRUARY 23, 1968	FEBRUARY 29, 1968	APRIL 14, 1968	JUNE 19–JULY 5, 1968
NVA attack Hill 861 Alpha, Lang Vei, and Hill 64.	Enemy gunners bombard base with more than 1,300 rounds in heaviest attack.	NVA launch regimental size attack against base.	Marines break out of siege and attack and seize Hill 881N.	Khe Sanh Combat Base is destroyed and abandoned by American forces.

PFC John Corbett, a twenty-year-old mortarman, arrived at Khe Sanh during the NVA encirclement.

"As soon as I got off the airplane, I looked around. It wasn't that big a base. I was by a makeshift air tower. It was a structure of sandbags and ammo boxes painted red, and it had lettering on it, and in gold-stenciled letters it said, 'Welcome to Khe Sanh.'

"I got mustered to an office where they sifted through my paperwork and sent me down to the mortar squad. I was assigned to a hootch, semi belowground. It was dug in the ground, and timbers coming out and a structure on top. The roof was sandbagged and had small steel matting across the top. For the interior effect, they had a parachute hanging on the inside of the ceiling.

"The next day I went to familiarize myself with the base. What struck me about the base was the beauty surrounding it, the mountains and the valleys. It was a beautiful sight."

Khe Sanh's makeshift air tower and welcome sign. **OPPOSITE:** PFC John Corbett having coffee near his bunker.

But the beauty of the country around Khe Sanh was quickly forgotten when Corbett went to his orientation lecture. He was surprised that there was only one other Marine present. After a short while, a lieutenant with a big cigar in his mouth came into the room and walked straight to a large map hanging prominently on the wall. He snapped his pointer on the map and turned to face his two-man audience.

"He pointed to Khe Sanh on the map," said Corbett, "and said, 'Here is Khe Sanh.' And there were red Magic Marker boxes all around that point on the map. The lieutenant said, 'These are Red divisions, Communist, North Vietnamese divisions. You are surrounded. It's only a matter of time before they try to overrun this base. When you leave this tent, take your entrenching tool and start digging a foxhole.'"[2]

The lieutenant took his pointer and left the room. Corbett's orientation was over and he immediately returned to his area to start digging and filling sandbags, piling them in layers on some discarded pallets on the top of his bunker. When his overhead cover was two layers thick, Corbett looked around and saw that many other bunkers had five or six layers of sandbags. But he concluded that two layers were enough for him.

"I was kind of lazy," he said, rationalizing that more sandbags would not keep fate from playing the decisive card. "If anything was going to hit it, it's going to hit it."

As a finishing touch, Corbett found an old street sign in a pile of junk. What a street sign was doing there he could not imagine, but he retrieved it and placed it in the left corner of his trench. His trench became known as "West Dickens Ave."

On January 18, two late-coming Marines arrived at Khe Sanh and immediately moved to the command center. Maj Robert Coolidge and Capt Mizra M. Biag were part of a three-man Intelligence Augmentation Team. The third member of the team, Maj Jerry Hudson, was already there, serving as the 26th Marines intelligence officer.

Capt "Harry" Biag had the title of "Target Information Officer," and although his title did not seem daunting, his mission was. Like a hired assassin, his job was to stalk his targets, fix them in his crosshairs, and liquidate them. But his marks were not individuals; they were the NVA's encircling 304th and 325C Divisions. Biag made it his business to study everything about them: their movements, their posture, their tendencies, and the tactical significance of their general order contained in the language of the 13th Resolution. Biag placed himself in his enemy's mind to better understand him and to anticipate just what he was up to.

When Harry Biag arrived at Khe Sanh he had already formulated several assumptions about his adversaries. First, he presumed that the NVA attack plan was the brainchild of a supreme headquarters, not the plan of some field force commander. If that was true, he saw the fact as an advantage he could exploit.

"Because of this," Biag explained, "the commander in the field could not, and would not, alter the plan . . . "[3]

The captain further reasoned that since the NVA field commander could not change the plan, he might be forced to follow it rigidly even if the tactical situation screamed for change. If retreat was not an option,

Jack Corbett's bunker, "West Dickens Ave."

he might continue to feed his troops into a meat grinder, or to hurl and batter them against a stone wall. Marines knew well the tactics of the Japanese in World War II, who continued to attack, inviting their annihilation, even when there was no hope of success.

Might this commander do the same? Harry Biag thought it was a possibility.

He then concluded that the enemy's tactics at Khe Sanh would be predictable. It would be a siege in the classic sense of the word: encirclement followed by a slow but deadly strangulation. The overall NVA commander, Gen Vo Nguyen Giap would employ the very strategy that had delivered his dramatic victory at Dien Bien Phu, modified by his more recent, unpleasant experience at Con Thien.

On the very day that Capt Biag and the Intelligence Augmentation Team arrived at Khe Sanh, a special meeting of generals took place to the east at the Dong Ha headquarters of 3rd Marine Division. Gen Tompkins welcomed Air Force Gen William McBride, the commander of "Task Force Alpha." This innocuous-sounding name was a fitting mask for the top-secret Infiltration Surveillance Center at Nakhon Phanom, Thailand, 130 miles northwest of Khe Sanh. McBride privately briefed Gen Tompkins on the possibility of installing a unique electronic battlefield, an idea that bristled with intrigue and high-tech innovation.

Air Force aircraft would crisscross the entire Khe Sanh countryside, seeding enemy avenues of approach and suspected marshaling areas with something called ADSIDs (Air-delivered seismic intrusion device). These devices were spike buoys and acou-buoys, high-tech electronic hardware that had been earmarked for use in the now defunct "McNamara Line."[4]

BIAG MADE IT HIS BUSINESS TO STUDY EVERYTHING ABOUT THEM: THEIR MOVEMENTS, THEIR POSTURE, THEIR TENDENCIES, AND THE TACTICAL SIGNIFICANCE OF THEIR GENERAL ORDER CONTAINED IN THE LANGUAGE OF THE 13TH RESOLUTION.

McBride explained that two hundred fifty sensors could cover the trails and approaches. Once installed, these sensors would detect enemy movement and sound, and relay those signals to a station on a high peak or to an orbiting manned aircraft or drone. Signals would be transmitted to the giant computers at "Naked Fanny," the American nickname for the Royal Thai airbase at Nakhom Phanom.[5] Within five minutes the computers could digest and analyze the information and spit back readouts and fire data to the CP at Khe Sanh. Tompkins liked what he heard and approved the plan.

In addition to this high-tech support, Col Lownds sported a formidable assortment of conventional supporting arms. Five 90mm-gun tanks from the 3rd Tank Battalion were dug in at the base, and 1st Battalion,

13th Marines provided artillery support with three batteries of 105mm howitzers, one battery of 155mm artillery, and a 4.2-inch mortar battery. Far to the east, at Camp Carrol and the Rockpile, along Route 9, the Army's 2nd Battalion, 94th Artillery could train its long-range guns to cover Khe Sanh. These 175mm weapons could fire 20 miles and hurl devastating, 147-pound projectiles into the heart of enemy positions.[6]

But despite the buzz of activity and the maps filled with red dots, Col Lownds' men could not make contact with the suspected massive enemy force. His Marines had fought with some small units on two consecutive days on the slopes of 881N, but those brief firefights were the only encounters. Active patrolling had revealed nothing more. So, on January 20, Capt Dabney mounted up his company to return to the previous contact area to see what was up.

"It was obvious to me something was about to happen," said Dabney, "so I requested to make a reconnaissance in force to 881N."

At 0500 on January 20, Dabney's men jumped off and began their descent down the northern slope of Hill 881S in zero-visibility fog.

"We moved silently down the hill," said Hospitalman 3rd Class Mike Ray. "We slipped down through the waist-high elephant grass. We came down through the fog cover. As we went deeper, the bright sun turned into a faint glow. The fog must have been several hundred feet thick."[7]

Dabney's men worked down to the low ground between the two hills and began their slow ascent up the foreboding slopes of Hill 881N. The company advanced up two parallel ridges leading to the crest, Capt Dabney moving with his 1st and 2nd Platoons on the western ridge, and Lt Thomas Brindley moving with his 3rd Platoon and a seven-man recon team on the eastern ridge. The movement was slow due to the steepness of the slope and the caution of the Marine columns. Their caution was not unwarranted.

Unseen by the Marines, ahead was a battalion-size NVA force on a defensive line anchored on four small mounds that connected the two ridgelines.[8] The enemy force had moved into those positions after the previous day's contact. Capt Dabney paused as he approached the area. To his front was one of the small mounds. He reasoned that an enemy contact would most likely develop here, and he prepared to attack with the two platoons moving with him. But then Dabney noticed a possible advantage.

The fog had lifted and he could see Lt Brindley's reinforced platoon on the eastern ridge exactly opposite him, four hundred meters (about 440 yards) away. Brindley's force was poised to seize a small hill to his front, and if they could take that hill, they would be in a perfect position to pour devastating fire into the mound ahead of Dabney.

Dabney ordered Brindley to attack, and the 3rd Platoon moved forward. Immediately they came under automatic-weapons fire and a hail of rocket propelled grenades. Three Marines were seriously wounded in that initial exchange, and Lt Brindley could not get a fix on the enemy through the thick elephant grass. Dabney ordered Brindley to break off and evacuate his wounded. The young lieutenant called in effective artillery and 106mm recoilless rifle fire to cover his withdrawal, and moved back 200 meters (about 220 yards) to set up a landing zone.[9] At the zone was Lt Richard M. Foley, the executive officer of Company I.

"Lt Brindley reported to Lt Foley what happened," said PFC Kenneth D. Brewer, "and was limbering up his pitching arm! He went around and talked to every man, asking how he was and giving reassurance."[10]

The two lieutenants discussed how to take the hill should they again be ordered to do so, and decided that Foley would provide a base of fire with his machine guns while Brindley attacked with his reinforced platoon.

But on the western ridge, Capt Dabney had decided on role-reversal. He would now advance with his 1st and 2nd Platoons, seize his mound, and then provide covering fire for a second attack by Brindley's force. 1st Platoon moved to deploy, but before it could even begin to attack, the force was taken under fire from the mound to its front as well as from the mound on the opposite ridgeline ahead of Brindley's 3rd Platoon. The flanking fire from that eastern ridge was the most devastating, just as Capt Dabney had envisioned it would be. His 1st Platoon was unable to advance.

....

Two Marines look for signs of NVA activity from bunkered positions on Hill 881S.

Now a second LZ had to be set up two hundred meters down the western ridge. A CH-46 helicopter attempted to land, but the NVA seemed to be everywhere. Antiaircraft weapons slammed .50-caliber rounds into the approaching aircraft, stitching its fuselage and setting it on fire. The chopper crash-landed to the west of the LZ, and Lt Michael Thomas, commanding the 2nd Platoon, with quick thinking, led a rescue force to extract the crew before the aircraft was engulfed in flames.

The dug-in enemy force had met Capt Dabney's attacks on both ridges and stopped them cold, but Dabney was not finished. He ordered Brindley to again attack the mound to his front, and Brindley was ready. He moved his platoon into an attack position under cover from devastating mortar and artillery fire delivered from 881S, and from Lt Foley's machine-guns. The fire completely covered the enemy's position, and machine guns from the 1st Platoon on the western ridge added support, firing across the 400-meter span into the flank of Brindley's objective.

The attacking force formed an assault line, and Lt Brindley placed himself front and center. He rose and signaled the attack. The Marines on the line stood with their lieutenant, then surged up the 30-degree slope, hurling grenades and firing their weapons. The crest was 75 meters (slightly more than 80 yards) away, and the NVA brought all of their weapons to bear on the advancing line of Marines. From his position on the western ridge, Capt Dabney had a ringside seat for the attack. He could see the line moving and some men falling.

"Brindley was in the lead despite the fire, and led the Marines up and over the crest by the sheer force of example," said Capt Dabney.[11]

"He kept the men on line by moving the left flank and then waiting for the right, all the while giving commands, 'Keep on line; keep firing!'" said PFC Brewer.

The sheer force of Brindley's attack swept up and over the crest, but just at the moment of triumph, a sniper's round felled the courageous lieutenant.

"He screamed and grabbed for his shoulder," said Brewer, "and rolled to the right on the ground." The dying Brindley shouted his last words: "Keep low, keep going, stay on line."[12]

On the western ridge, Capt Dabney's radio crackled with the terrible news. The attacking force was almost out of ammunition, and all the squad leaders and sergeants were hit. "No one's left in charge up here," the radio operator yelled. "What should I do?"[13]

Dabney led his 2nd Platoon with Lt Michael Thomas across the gully separating the two ridgelines to reinforce his shattered, leaderless 3rd Platoon. Thomas moved up to the front line to consolidate the position, and began evacuating the wounded, even though he was subjected to continuous heavy enemy fire. He directed the Marines' fire against suspected enemy positions and was able to suppress some of it. When his men reported that eight Marines were missing, Lt Thomas located five, and, hoisting them individually on his back, carried them to safety. He was almost exhausted when he found the sixth man, and was carrying him to safety when he was wounded in the face by enemy fire. Thomas refused medical attention and continued his mission. Finally he could go no more and collapsed.

When informed that there were still two wounded men on the reverse slope of the hill, he waved everyone off and inched forward to try to reach them. Within 20 yards of the wounded Marines, Thomas was fatally shot.[14]

Dabney's company now occupied both ridgelines. The NVA had been thrown back on the eastern ridge, and air strikes napalmed and bombed their retreating forces. The battlefield was strewn with 103 of their dead. But the cost had also been heavy to Dabney's company. His battalion commander, having moved to 881S to monitor the attack, now asked Col Lownds for reinforcements to continue the assault. Lownds denied the request and ordered Dabney to break off the contact and return to 881S.

"We lost forty-two from India [Company]," said Capt Dabney. "Seven killed including Lieutenants Brindley and Thomas,* plus all the recon team were casualties. A CH-46 was shot down and all the crew wounded. Contact began about noon, and at 1500 it was obvious

that whatever we found was more than we could handle. The rest of the afternoon we spent evacuating the wounded and the dead, recovering the helicopter crew, and breaking contact.

"The mission was to still hold 881S, so withdrawal was essential—not that there was much of a choice since the prospects of success were dim. There were a bunch of those guys up there, and they'd come prepared to fight. We hosed down 881N and all the ground between it and 881S till dark, with air, 81s, 60s, and all the artillery we could get during the night. For once we knew where they were."[15]

As India Company limped back to their positions on 881S, they were unaware of the extraordinary event that had caused Col Lownds to recall them.

*Lts Brindley and Thomas were posthumously awarded Navy Crosses.

Lt Thomas Brindley.

CHAPTER 6
THE ENEMY STRIKES

A South Vietnamese soldier and several Marines take cover during a volley of incoming.

	APRIL 24, 1967	MAY 13, 1967	DECEMBER 1967	JANUARY 21, 1968	JANUARY 31, 1968
TIMELINE	Hill Fights begin at Khe Sanh	Hill Fights end. Marines fought off elements of the 325C NVA Division in a two-week battle that cost the enemy 824 KIA. 168 Marines were killed and 443 wounded in the struggle.	General Westmoreland decides to reinforce Khe Sanh in the face of enemy buildup.	NVA attack hill 861 and bombard combat base exploding ammo dump, and attack Khe Sanh village. Siege begins.	NVA launch countrywide Tet Offensive.

While Capt Dabney's men slugged it out with the NVA on the slopes of Hill 881N, 5 miles to the southeast, Khe Sanh Combat Base buzzed with activity. At 1400, just beyond the perimeter wire on the eastern end of the runway, a solitary figure approached the Marine lines carrying an AK-47 rifle and a white flag. He captured the attention of all who saw him, and his slight figure filled the gun-sights of astonished Marines.

"Early in the afternoon, Bravo Company's 2nd Platoon reported the presence of a possible NVA waving a white flag on the northeastern side of the runway," said Capt Kenneth W. Pipes. "I moved some 500 meters [almost 550 yards] outside the wire. The NVA soldier initially disappeared, so I shouted, 'Marine *dai uy*' [captain] several times as we proceeded. The NVA soldier reappeared and surrendered. He was a lieutenant."[1]

The fire team accompanying Capt Pipes quickly apprehended the enemy soldier and turned him over to Gunnery Sergeant Max Friedlander of the 17th Interrogator-Translator Team.

"When we got to my bunker, the first thing I did was offer him a cigarette and ask him if he was hungry," said Friedlander. "I got him something to eat and he devoured it quickly.

"He identified himself as Lt La Thanh Tonc. He was married and had several children, and was very disillusioned, especially with politics. He didn't like the way many officers had treated him, and he was disgruntled because he had been passed over for promotion."[2]

Friedlander learned that Tonc had not even gotten a letter from home in over two years. The Marine sergeant tuned his radio to music from the north. Tonc's face brightened, and he said that he had not heard music since he left home. When the NVA lieutenant seemed comfortable, Friedlander began his interrogation and Tonc was very willing to talk.

The NVA lieutenant told Friedlander that 881N was presently surrounded and a company of sappers was poised to attack Hill 861. Once they had seized 861, the NVA would begin the general attack against the combat base with two regiments. Heavy artillery and rocket fire from the northwest would prep the base prior to the ground attack.

DISK 1, TRACKS 15-17: The siege begins.

FEBRUARY 5-8, 1968	FEBRUARY 23, 1968	FEBRUARY 29, 1968	APRIL 14, 1968	JUNE 19-JULY 5, 1968
NVA attack Hill 861 Alpha, Lang Vei, and Hill 64.	Enemy gunners bombard base with more than 1,300 rounds in heaviest attack.	NVA launch regimental size attack against base.	Marines break out of siege and attack and seize Hill 881N.	Khe Sanh Combat Base is destroyed and abandoned by American forces.

Tonc continued as Friedlander wrote furiously. In addition to the general bombardment, the enemy would mortar the Marine positions on Hill 950 and would pound the parked helicopters with a massive barrage while antiaircraft guns protected the mortars from any attacking aircraft.

Tonc had more to say, but Friedlander could wait no longer. He left Tonc to an assistant and raced off to Col Lownds. The colonel read Friedlander's notes and immediately sent the information up the chain of command. Friedlander went to Lang Vei to notify the Army Special Forces camp. When he returned to continue his interrogation, Tonc told him more.

"The information I got was just endless," said Friedlander.[3]

The prisoner had identified himself as the commanding officer of the 14th Antiaircraft Artillery Company, 95C Regiment, 325C NVA Division. He revealed the disposition of the assault regiments, the 95th and the 101st, and said that in a little over ten hours, at 0030 on January 21, elements of the 325C would attack 881S, 861, and the base itself. As spectacular as this information was, there was more. Tonc said there would be a second attack, by the 304th Division, smashing in from the west, paralleling the runway, to collapse the entire Marine defense.[4]

....

Building bunkers at the combat base. **OPPOSITE:** GnySgt Max Friedlander.

While Capt Dabney fought on 881N and Lt Tonc surrendered at Khe Sanh, Task Force Alpha was busy at work. Helicopters crisscrossed the Khe Sanh valley while the gunners stood in the doors and dropped the small anti-intrusion devices of the defunct McNamara Line. The detectors plummeted to earth and stuck like darts into the ground, lodged in the dense undergrowth, or hung in trees. These aircraft continued their patterns until they had sown the seeds of the first electronic battlefield. Seventy-two sorties deployed three hundred sixteen sensors in forty-four strings of nine modules each.[5]

The North Vietnamese Army boldly moved for a decisive victory. It was the eve of the battle they imagined would put an end to American interference. Fourteen years after Dien Bien Phu, their conquest of the South seemed close at hand.

The NVA had worked hard for this day. It had consistently and effectively exploited a program of international deception with willing believers. It had secured sanctuaries in neighboring countries by denying its soldiers were there, shifted to an offensive strategy, developed an attack plan, and now had troops massed at Khe Sanh. The NVA's movement into the battle area and encirclement of the Marine base had been shrouded by the monsoon and the impenetrable fog of Khe Sanh. The enemy force now stood poised and cocked like a giant catapult ready to hurl its massive force against the Marine bastion in a bold attempt to "kill 10,000 Americans," and bring about a military victory as ordered by Ho Chi Minh's 13th Resolution.

But despite their bold maneuver and their optimism, the commanders and soldiers of this massive North Vietnamese force could not imagine the terrain they were stepping onto was a battlefield unheard of in military history. They had no idea that although the Marines had not seen them mass and still could not see them, they could hear them and detect their movements.

On Hill 861, Kilo Company, 26th Marines, was also busy on January 20. They were well aware of the fight by India Company on 881N. They could hear the sounds of battle and see the aircraft dive in. Cpl Dennis Mannion, the artillery forward observer, was listening to the artillery requests coming from India Company.

"Sometime around noon . . . someone on the western side of the hill spotted five or six North Vietnamese soldiers on top of the ridge, 500 yards away from us. They weren't visible for more than a couple of seconds,

but Capt Norman Jasper, the Kilo Company commander, asked me if I could fire some artillery at that spot. We fired thirty or forty rounds from the base . . . most of them impacted pretty well right up on that hill."

Capt Jasper ordered a patrol out for a ground assessment of the mission. Mannion volunteered to join the patrol.

"We went out the north gate," Mannion said, "and crossed over a deep, wooded ravine, and on up to the ridgeline west of Hill 861. Just as we got up into the area where we could see the impact of the rounds and smell the cordite, we got a call on the radio to come back in. The patrol leader replied that we were right at the spot where the shells had landed, and asked permission to drop down over the western side of the ridge, just to see if there were any blood trails or bodies. Capt Jasper personally came up on the radio and told us to come back—immediately, without even taking another look around."[6]

Noticeably disappointed, the patrol retraced its steps to 861, and was back in the lines by 1700.

"As soon as the patrol was back, I was called with all the platoon commanders and platoon sergeants to a command meeting at Capt Jasper's command-post bunker," said Mannion. "The captain told us that we were supposedly going to get attacked that night by a fair-size number of North Vietnamese soldiers."[7]

Jasper placed his company on 100 percent alert for the evening and registered concentrations (firing coordinates) for the big 175mm guns at Camp Carrol 19 miles away and for the artillery at the base. There was a "dead space" however, that could not be covered by fire from those supporting arms. On the northwest corner of Hill 861, a steep side descended into a ravine. Fire from both the base and Camp Carrol was masked by the hill itself and could not impact into this ravine.

Hill 861 defenses consisted of barbed concertina wire sandwiched between two belts of barbed-wire tanglefoot, and inside that was the trench line, bristling with bunkers. Behind the bunkers were the crew-served weapons: 106mm recoilless rifles, 60mm and 81mm mortars, and two .50-caliber machine guns on the summit by the company command post.

"We settled in to wait," said Mannion. "Everybody cleaned their weapons and we ate our C-rations for dinner. Eventually it got dark. It wasn't a real clear night, but it wasn't the worst fog we had seen up there. It was very dark."[8]

PFC Elwin Bacon stared into the night. "There was no visibility. I couldn't see outside my foxhole. I had to focus with my ears for the perimeter watch, not my eyes. Hopefully, if anyone was out there, he would set off a trip-flare."[9] Each Marine strained his senses to detect anything that might approach.

At 2030, Marines on the northwest corner of the hilltop heard noises down in the deep ravine. The 1st

Platoon manned that part of the line, and Cpl Dennis Mannion went to the platoon command post in hopes of getting fire on the enemy.

"From there I could hear the NVA outside the wire," he said. "They were talking and giving commands. I could hear the wire being cut . . . the tinny sound when the wire sprang back in both directions. We threw grenades and popped flares but never fired a shot. The North Vietnamese took it with laughter and an occasional scream. They kept right on cutting . . . as if they were out there on a high school field day."[10]

The unnerving sounds and the presence had the Marines poised, each man gripping a hand grenade, with other grenades at the ready. The night wore on. Shortly after midnight, the long-awaited attack started.

"At 1230 we began to take incoming rounds," said 2Lt Linn Oehling, commanding the 2nd Platoon, manning the southwestern perimeter. "The area that was hit the hardest was at the COC [combat operations center] on the top of 861. My platoon was situated down from the top, around the point. I was on the western side of the hill. My lines on the western side were supplemented by Sgt Stahl, who was acting as gunnery sergeant for the 4.2 [mortars]. We took incoming, kept our heads low, and wherever we heard movement, made sure that we never opened up with our small arms or automatic weapons, but threw grenades."[11]

....

Observing an air strike from atop Hill 861. **OPPOSITE:** Cpl Dennis Mannion on Hill 861.

"The enemy had put satchel charges on our wires out there, and they had it all prearranged," said PFC John Lewis, a machine gunner with the 1st Platoon. "They set them up, and then set them off. They had it very well planned. The rockets and mortars and then the satchel charges went off, and then they got through our lines, just like that."[12]

"We had incoming, but everyone was pretty well calm and relaxed," said PFC Michael James, a rocket squad leader in the 1st Platoon. "We had one incoming round hit behind us, up by the .50-caliber machine gun. It was directly behind us. I ran up the hill to see if anybody was hurt, and came right back down. We started getting a few more mortars; then rockets hit us, RPGs, and everything seemed to break loose. Our 106 [recoilless rifle] got blown up, and they tore the hell out of our CP. They were trying to cut the wire and were blowing it up. They had satchel charges, a lot of them, and bangalore torpedoes. It was very effective."[13]

"The firefight commenced at exactly 0310," said 1st Sergeant Bernard Goddard. "They hit us with RPGs . . . and then they let us have it with 82s. They walked those 82 mortars right up the line, up and down

....

The 106mm rifle position on Hill 861 that was destroyed on January 21, 1968. **OPPOSITE:** 1Lt Jerry Saulsbury and 2Lt Linn Oehling

the hill, and they were goddamn effective, very accurate. My CP group was in the bunker, and the rest of us were outside the bunker, just in case they did break through the wire. They started opening up with .50-caliber, and the .50s were buzzing right over our heads.

"I got zapped, and I patched up my one leg wound. It never hit the bone, I don't know how—real lucky. Then I got zapped in the ankle; that stunned me a little bit, but my leg swelled up fast. I made a pressure bandage on it, so I didn't lose too much blood. But then I got zapped in the neck. I thought that was it. I slammed my index finger up in my neck, and undoubtedly I stopped the bleeding."[14]

The NVA poured through the breached wire between the lines of 1st and 3rd Platoons. The Marines fought and fell back, and then sought to close the opening in their lines.

"Once the wire had been breached," said 1Lt Jerry N. Saulsbury, now in command of the company, "the bunkers that had been knocked out served as a very good bridge for the NVA to jump across our trench line. The flat roofs offered a good area for them to run across and gain enough momentum that they could jump the trench lines. It furnished a flat runway for them to leap across."[15]

"We lost three bunkers right off the bat," said Sgt Mykle Stahl. "The NVA were sticking bangalore torpedoes under the wire. LCpl Mutz and his people were knocking them off with grenades and rifle fire. My people supplemented the lines. We were being hit pretty strenuously. We owe a lot to holding the lines to our two machine gunners. One was PFC Curtis B. Bugger, and one was LCpl Billy Moffett."[16]

When the attack began, Bugger and Moffett were at their position on the .50-caliber machine gun, up high near the CP. Bugger was all business, constantly feeding cans of belted ammunition to the gun, first on one side, and then on the other, and Billy Moffett fired the big gun in a never-ending, guttural roar. The stream of tracers painted red streaks in the foggy night and just cleared the heads of Marines in the trenches.

"We were just about getting overrun on the lines down there," said Moffett, "so Sgt Stahl came up and said we needed some firepower down on the lines. So that's what we mainly did; fired down on our own lines, just above our own men's heads, to try and keep them back if we could."[17]

Eighteen-year-old PFC Gerald F. "Slick" O'Neal, who was in Moffett's gun section, lay in a shallow trench just outside the command bunker. The initial enemy onslaught had destroyed the bunker and seriously wounded Capt Jasper, putting him out of action. The company gunnery sergeant was dead, and the 1st sergeant severely wounded in the neck. The higher command structure of Kilo Company was shattered.

"As the battle intensified, someone shouted, 'NVA inside the wire,'" said O'Neal. "I moved into an old bomb crater at the base of the .50-cal."

Just above O'Neal's head, Billy Moffett blazed away.

"He fired the .50-cal continuously, never letting up to cool the barrel. The incoming fire he was drawing was tremendous. There were 82 mortars dropping all around us, and a steady stream of RPG fire. I could see green tracers from heavy machine guns coming into our little area from two different directions. The snap of AK-47 rounds going over my head and into the .50-cal position was steady. Throughout this, Moffett never stopped firing.

"I cursed myself for taking a position so close to the .50-cal. I cursed Moffett for firing the gun continuously. The NVA fire that he drew was so heavy it was impossible to move. I looked up and over my shoulder, and I saw the barrel of his .50 glowing bright red. I hoped it would melt, so he would have to stop firing."[18]

The NVA also saw Moffett's red, devastating gun. Some of their soldiers managed to slip around to the rear, to try to take him under fire. Their first shots killed PFC Bugger, but Moffett managed to drive the attackers off with grenades.

"A few minutes later," said O'Neal, "I heard him say in a shockingly calm voice, 'Slick, come up here and help me.' Stiff with fear, I managed to climb into the position with him. I'll never forget his calm face or his soothing voice. He was only two or three years older than me, but he talked to me like a father would to his child. There was no fear in his eyes, only dead calm. As I tried to take up the normal position of the A-gunner, he said, 'No. Stand over here. Bugger is laying there.'"[19]

Although supporting arms could not bombard the ravine where the NVA had massed to deliver their attack, they were not immune from fire. Quite unexpectedly, the "dead spot" that had offered them cover and concealment erupted with explosions. Bill Dabney's mortars on Hill 881S had a perfect line to the target.

Part of the 3rd Battalion command group was still on Hill 881S after controlling supporting arms for Capt Dabney's afternoon fight. Weather had isolated them on the hill, and they had a ringside seat for the NVA attack on 861.

Maj Matthew Caulfield, the battalion XO (executive officer), rationed some of the hill's 81mm mortar ammunition, and the gunners began to fire rounds into the flank of the attacking NVA force. Throughout the assault, mortarmen from 881S poured six hundred eighty rounds into the defilade and onto the northwestern slope of the hill.

On Hill 861, Sgt Stahl noticed that there was no fire coming from the 3rd Platoon position, and began to maneuver through the trench toward their first bunker. Two Marines followed him.

"There was a tremendous volume of fire from our front, from four or five North Vietnamese who were in the trench line, advancing toward us from the 3rd Platoon sector. The fog was very thick there, and they didn't see us until about the time we saw them. There was a furious firefight. I emptied one magazine, popped it, threw another magazine in, and went through that, too," said the sergeant.

Stahl killed the first NVA, but the second enemy soldier killed one of the Marines and wounded Stahl before falling to the fire from LCpl Dennis Mutz. Stahl continued to fire, and he and Mutz dispatched the last two. But the fight was far from over.

"The next thing I knew, I was face to face with a North Vietnamese. I had run through my second magazine. I had no bullets left in my M-16. He had me. He fired, but nothing happened. In that instant, I cringed and tightened up. Quicker than I could react, he bayoneted me in the right chest. Then Mutz shot him. The point of the bayonet punctured me and ripped downward . . . . It broke a rib and left a gash."

The bayonet also damaged Stahl's M-16, so the wounded sergeant grabbed the dead NVA's AK-47 and his magazine pouch. When the fire became intense, LCpl Mutz stopped but Stahl continued. He moved forward until he finally came upon the first 3rd Platoon bunker, looming ominously before

him in the artificially lit fog. Stahl's grenade narrowly missed the small aperture, and bounced off the side and again wounded the Marine sergeant. But the blast also drove the enemy from the openings, allowing him to roll forward to the base of the bunker. With a second grenade in hand, he rose up and dropped it inside, eliminating the two occupants.

"I was looking for 3rd Platoon Marines to link up with, but could not find any. In the next bunker were more North Vietnamese. I took it out with a hand grenade and then sprayed it through the aperture with my AK-47."

Stahl continued his one-man attack. At the third bunker, he fired into the opening from a distance, and suddenly heard "*Chieu Hoi.*"* He knew it was a word that signaled surrender, and ordered the occupants out. Three soldiers exited.

"Two had their hands up, but the third was an arrogant, defiant type of guy. When I motioned them back down the trench line with my AK-47, the last one tried to grab my weapon. I broke his jaw with the AK's butt."[20]

*Chieu hoi is translated as "open arms," and was the name given to an amnesty program begun in 1963 to encourage Viet Cong and NVA soldiers to defect.

Sgt Mykle Stahl with an NVA AK-47 captured in the January 21, 1968, fight for 861.

Stahl finally found Marines in the fifth bunker. The gap in the lines was 75 meters (about 80 yards), and the sergeant led Marines from other parts of the perimeter to fill in the dangerous gap. He then manned a silent machine gun position until first light.[*]

"The first sign of it letting up was daylight," said PFC Elwin Bacon. "We were able to make out silhouettes, but the fog was still so thick that we couldn't really see much. The NVA withdrew, but some of them got caught and were unable to get outside the wire.

"We found NVA bodies all the way up to the command post area. It was saturated with bodies. There were dead bodies everywhere I looked."[21]

Lt Tonc's information and timetable had been accurate. An estimated three hundred soldiers had attacked Hill 861, had briefly breached the Marines' position, had smashed the command post and the company command, and then had been hurled back with terrible loss by Marines fighting under new leadership, as Marines always do. Intelligence reported hearing the NVA commander call for reinforcements, but none came.

As the victors policed the battleground, they counted forty-seven dead NVA soldiers. Four Marines had been killed and eleven wounded. There were lots of drag marks and blood trails, and in the days and weeks to come, a horrible stench arose from the ravine. Those NVA soldiers killed and caught in the tangle of wire remained where they fell.

"We never went outside the trench line to do anything about the North Vietnamese who had been killed . . . within our three, concentric rows of wire," said Cpl Dennis Mannion.

"Using heavy binoculars . . . I was able to see clearly that the bodies turned to skeletons within three weeks. There was no flesh left on them—just skeletons wearing North Vietnamese uniforms, packs, and helmets."[22]

On Hill 881S, Capt Dabney had braced for the attack Lt Tonc had predicted. But it never came. Could the company's earlier battle on the slopes of 881N have stymied such an attack? No one could say, but when the NVA assault did not come, Dabney turned his guns to support the Marines on Hill 861, pouring withering fire into the NVA's flanks and pulverizing the area behind them where their reserves would be massed.

Tonc had also predicted a general attack against the combat base with two regiments, preceded by heavy artillery and rocket fire. Maybe that prediction would be wrong, too.

During the night, as the fight on Hill 861 raged, recon team Nurse was on Hill 689, far to the west, surrounded by a fifty-man NVA force that had detected the team's presence and was bent on their annihilation. The team had walked out from the base on January 20, the day before.

"We ended up on the backside of 689 that night: swift, silent, and surrounded by fifty NVA for most of the night," said LCpl Sandy Reid. "One-oh-fives out of the base provided covering fire, and fired approximately twenty-four hundred rounds in our support. We had a Spooky [C-47 gunship] flying for us until the fog came in and they couldn't see our strobe any longer."[23]

---

[*]For his heroic action, Sgt Stahl was awarded the Navy Cross. The heroic action of LCpl Billy Moffett was not recognized with a personal decoration and he joined a long list of unsung heroes.

"Thirteenth Marines fired 'box-me-in' fires all night long,"[24] said Maj Jerry Hudson, regimental intelligence officer.

"Sometime early in the morning, the base started taking incoming, and our 105 support was withdrawn. By the time morning came, the NVA seemed to have had enough of us, and things were pretty quiet. We had inflicted a fair number of casualties on them . . . and our team leader, Sgt Caldwell, decided that our best option was to make our way back to the base on foot."[25]

The incoming that Reid saw was, in fact, the fulfillment of Tonc's warning. At 0530 an enormous barrage of rockets, mortars, and artillery hit the base. Helicopters, trucks, tents, and even Col Lownds' quarters were destroyed. Marines ran for the trench lines, while artillerymen manned their guns for counter-battery fire.

"I was lying awake at four o'clock," said Jack Corbett, the 81mm mortarman, who had recently built his bunker, "West Dickens Ave." "I had the top bunk, so my face was closest to the top of the hootch ceiling, and what was keeping me awake was a big rat trying to eat through the timbers and into the canvas. And I'm figuring this rat is right next to my face here, and it won't be long before he breaks through this parachute silk, and I'm going to be eaten next. So I'm lying there, and lit a cigarette. All of a sudden I heard a noise that

THE DUMP EXPLODED IN A SERIES OF BLINDING DETONATIONS. BURNING FUEL IGNITED LIKE GIANT MOLOTOV COCKTAILS; TEAR GAS ROLLED ACROSS THE FIELD IN A GAS-CLOUD REMINISCENT OF WORLD WAR I, WHILE AMMUNITION "COOKED OFF" IN SYMPATHETIC VOLLEYS.

I wasn't very familiar with. One of the guys yells out, 'Incoming!' Everyone was flying out of the hootch to take shelter, and they knocked over the little candle and the ammo box with my glasses on it.

"After thumping around the floor looking for my glasses, I couldn't find them, so I figured that I had to get the hell out. My night vision isn't that good and I am almost blind as a bat without my glasses . . . so William Donner started yelling to me: 'Just follow my voice.'"[26]

Enemy rounds set off fires. The most dangerous one raged inside the main ammo dump. Efforts to extinguish it were as life-threatening as they were futile. The flames first licked at, then encircled, and finally engulfed the piles of shells and stacked boxes. The inevitable happened: The dump exploded in a series of blinding detonations. Burning fuel ignited like giant Molotov cocktails; tear gas rolled across the field in a gas-cloud reminiscent of World War I, while ammunition "cooked off" in sympathetic volleys. The dump became a roaring, exploding inferno.[27]

"Charlie Battery had three guns on 881 South and three guns on the base at the far eastern edge of the perimeter," said Capt William J. O'Connor Jr., the battery commander. "The perimeter was only 25 yards

from our most eastern gun. The airstrip was located 100 yards to our northeast, and the main ammunition dump was located between the airstrip and Charlie Battery's position.

"When the first volley came, we lost all electrical power, and the ammunition dump took its first direct hit. The cannoneers immediately manned their guns and started returning fire on their assigned counter-battery targets. We only had two guns in action at the time. Gun No. 5 was out of action due to a faulty recoil mechanism. However, when the incoming continued, we put him back in action, figuring we needed everything we had."[28]

"At 0500 I was in the exec pit," said 1Lt William L. Eberhardt, XO of Charlie Battery, "and we had three or four rockets that came in ahead of all the other volleys. They landed in our vicinity, and also in the ammo dump just to our left. Another officer took over the fire missions, and I went out to check the guns.

"One gun went down because of a dud that landed in the parapet. We weren't sure if the rounds that landed in the pits were being shot from enemy mortars or rockets, or whether they were ones that were blown from the dump; but the ones that came out of Gun No. 1 came from the enemy.

....

One of the many ammo dump explosions on January 21, 1968. **OPPOSITE:** Marines take cover in the combat base trenches.

"Other rounds were stuck in the parapets throughout the area. We just had three guns, and if you lose one, you lose a third of the battery. All we could think of was trying to get those rockets and mortars silenced. Until we could get them stopped, we didn't have time to worry about the duds or the ammo blowing right there."[29]

"I started outside the FDC [fire direction center]," said Sgt Ronnie Whitenight, "and an enemy mortar had stuck in the wall of Gun No. 1's parapet. Everybody hollered that there's a dud in the wall, so they all got off the gun and headed into their bunkers. I ran over and took it out, and threw it in a deep ditch behind the FDC.

"Gun No. 2 was out of action for a while. They were getting incoming rounds from our own ammo dump—illumination and high-explosive rounds were too much for them to stay on the gun. Mr. Eberhardt and I went over there and cleared them out. I removed duds for about three hours from the pits."[30]

The guns continued to fire despite all adversity, even when communications were lost.

"One of the cannoneers on Gun No. 1, LCpl Pelitier, ran down to the pit," said Capt O'Connor, "and we'd write the fire commands out on a piece of paper, and he'd deliver them to the guns. We were delivering fire on known rocket and mortar positions that were being spotted by FOs on 861 and 881S, and on the base perimeter. As we'd get each fire mission, we'd write it out, give it to Pelitier; he'd run out and give it to the guns, and come in again to pick up the next fire mission. All this time we were getting continuous incoming, and also getting rounds from our own ammunition dump."[31]

LtCol James Wilkinson, commander of 1st Battalion, 26th Marines, was in his bunk when the first enemy mortar impacted. He was fully clothed except for his boots. He quickly stepped into them, grabbed his helmet and gas mask, and raced for his command bunker.

"Suddenly it dawned on us that the enemy's objective was to hit our ammunition dump, which was just adjacent to my command post. The enemy gunners were very accurate, since most of their rounds were impacting right in the middle of the ammunition dump.

"This was not just an ammunition dump filled with small-arms ammunition," said Wilkinson. "This ammunition dump had 105 artillery rounds . . . ammunition for the 106 recoilless rifle, TNT and C-3 explosives, and even a large amount of tear gas.

"About 9:30 in the morning, the fires that had erupted in the ammunition dump created a tremendous explosion. Almost everything exploded simultaneously, followed by other explosions that rippled and rippled for several minutes. The initial explosion was so huge that it created a shock wave."[32]

GnySgt Bill Martin was at the command bunker next to the dump area when it exploded.

"When you take a direct hit, you don't hear an explosion like you would if the explosion was a little

Marines watch the fire in the ammo dump burn beneath a layer of fog.

bit away. You just hear a ringing sound in your ears—you don't actually hear an explosion.

"I was shaving, and the Major, who was on duty, yelled, 'Gunny Martin! Go out and run a crater analysis, and I don't believe you're going to have to look very far for the crater.'"[33]

Maj Ronald W. Campbell also raced from shell crater to shell crater, gathering fragments and carefully measuring the angles of the crater's core to determine the caliber and direction of fire of the enemy guns. Ammunition men crawled to and from their guns to avoid the flying projectiles and debris hurled from the dump by the ear-shattering explosions.[34]

"A steady stream of 105mm rounds were hurled through our command-post bunker's entrance by the continuous explosions in the adjacent dump," said Capt Ken Pipes. "Many of them were smoking when they landed. One of my Marines cradled each one in his arms and ran outside with it. Many of those rounds exploded after he left them in the open."[35]

"The noise from the impacting rounds got worse, between what was blowing up in our dump and the rockets and artillery rounds hitting around our sector of the base," said PFC Corbett. "We took cigarette filters and stuffed them in our ears, and held them there. I could hear Donner screaming that he needed ammunition. So being the new guy on the block, it was my job to run to the ammo bunker, get ammo, and return as fast as I could.

"I ran to get the ammo, and the noise of the explosions was unbearable, but the shrapnel was coming from all directions: shrapnel the size of long lawn mower blades, whizzing through the air. But there was not just one; there were thousands of them, and it was like walking through a maze of someone throwing knives at you.

"When I got to the gun pit, they had taken a hit with an 82 [mortar] that did not explode. Their sandbags were on fire from the heat from our dump and the hot shrapnel that had landed on them, igniting them. The men were in the gun pit singing the Marine Corps Hymn."[36]

Just when it seemed it could get no worse, it did. Marines from the Combined Action Company, in the village of Khe Sanh, several kilometers southwest of the base, reported the NVA were attacking from the west along Route 9. Lt Tonc had warned of a two-pronged ground attack, from Hill 861 and from the west, parallel to the airstrip. The attack from 861 never occurred, thanks to the efforts of Kilo Company to hold the hill, but elements of the 304th Division smashed into Khe Sanh village.

Col Lownds was distressed. "We had three things going at once, and my concern was, with all of these forces around me, that they might start closing the base. Intelligence, over a short period of time, had told us that there were three enemy divisions. It was at that time that we decided to fight a set-piece battle."[37]

With the enemy on their doorstep, the decision to fight was a welcomed relief to many Marines who had chased the NVA all over the countryside—sometimes finding them but more often seeing them melt into the jungle or skip over the border into their internationally ignored sanctuaries when the going got tough.

"It had been very frustrating for several months at Khe Sanh, seeking out the enemy, but rarely finding the enemy," said LtCol Wilkinson. "Now we knew the enemy was there. In fact, he was all around us."[38]

CHAPTER 7

THE ENCIRCLEMENT

Marines in the combat base trenches during the siege.

	APRIL 24, 1967	MAY 13, 1967	DECEMBER 1967	JANUARY 21, 1968	JANUARY 31, 1968
TIMELINE	Hill Fights begin at Khe Sanh	Hill Fights end. Marines fought off elements of the 325C NVA Division in a two-week battle that cost the enemy 824 KIA. 168 Marines were killed and 443 wounded in the struggle.	General Westmoreland decides to reinforce Khe Sanh in the face of enemy buildup.	NVA attack hill 861 and bombard combat base exploding ammo dump, and attack Khe Sanh village. Siege begins.	NVA launch countrywide Tet Offensive.

Elements of the 66th Regiment of the 304th NVA Division smashed into Khe Sanh Village at first light, surrounding the Huong Hoa District Headquarters manned by two platoons of the 915th Regional Force Company of the ARVN and a Marine Combined Action Platoon (CAP). The large enemy force expected to overwhelm the one hundred seventy-five Vietnamese and American defenders easily.

Army Capt Bruce B. G. Clark also had a four-man advisory team with the Regional Forces (RF), and the Marines had a second platoon, just down the street, both from Combined Action Company (CAC) Oscar under the command of 1Lt Thomas B. Stamper.

CAP O/1—with ten Marines, one corpsman, and an equal number of Bru Montagnard tribesmen—was ensconced in a separate defensive position inside the District Headquarters compound with the South Vietnamese and the Army advisory team. CAP O/2 was located in its own barbed-wire compound in a small hamlet 200 meters (about 220 yards) to the west along Route 9.

"The base started taking real heavy incoming," said Lt Stamper, "and right away we ordered everyone into the trenches; grab your rifles, flak jackets, and everything. Fifteen minutes later, I started to go out of the bunker, walked out the door, and saw a red pen flare. That's when all hell broke loose around the entire compound—360 degrees around the thing."[1]

CAP O/2 was under command of Sgt Roy Harper. As the NVA attack began, Corpsman John R. Roberts was on watch in the bunker manning the PRC-25 radio.

"Everybody got in their fighting holes," said Roberts. "It was just before daylight when they hit. That morning they threw a hand grenade inside my bunker, and I had a case of white phosphorus hand grenades right there next to me. Harper was barefooted, and no shirt on, and he ran up that plank, grabbed that grenade, and threw it away before it exploded.

"I had seven guys wounded in the first thirty to forty seconds, and I was running from one gun position to another, firing a few rounds, trying to treat the wounded. I was talking to Col Lownds, and

DISK 2, TRACKS 1-4: Flying missions over Khe Sanh.

telling him what we were up against, because they could all hear the firefight but didn't know what was going on."[2]

The main enemy fire came from the front and right flank of the compound, dominated by a French coffee planter's house and a Buddhist pagoda. These locations offered the enemy excellent firing positions and an unhindered view of the compound.

Sergeant Harper manned the observation bunker and moved to the top of the tower attempting to direct fire, but an NVA gunner fired an RPG that hit the bunker, and shrapnel hit Harper in the face. Roberts and another man pulled the sergeant to safety in the trench. The Marines and the Bru tribesmen fought furiously against the overwhelmingly superior enemy, who seemed to have endless ammunition.

"PFC Biddle was standing on top of the sandbags, with an M-60 machine gun, letting them have it," said Roberts, "no flak jacket, no helmet; just bare skin; and just standing up there, cursing them for everything and firing at the same time. They'd come at him, and he would keep cutting them down. And then they shot an RPG and blew the whole sandbag infrastructure out from under him, and he fell down. Boy, that really pissed him off, and he climbed back up there and let them have it again."

"Doc" Roberts fought as best he could alongside his Marines, who gave him a case of hand grenades to start lobbing on the enemy, who were belly-up to the wire.

....

Incoming rounds explode and burn at the base. **OPPOSITE:** 105mm howitzer crew working.

"I'd never thrown a hand grenade," said Corpsman Roberts, "and we were trying to throw them out as fast as we could. They gave me a case, and I started to throw my first one, and it rolled off the right side of my fingers, and went about 3 feet and blew up, and wounded three of our own guys.

"One of the guys jumped on me and said, 'God dang it, Doc, you just patch everybody up and leave the fighting to us!'"[3]

At the District Headquarters, the fighting was equally fierce. Capt Clark fired his own mortar rounds, with no propelling increments, so they blooped out of the tube as if in slow motion, to impact just outside the wire. The supporting artillery from Khe Sanh Combat Base ringed the compound with steel from their 105 howitzers, but still the NVA attacked.

"We took a lot of fire from the pagoda," said Capt Clark. "We knocked that out with artillery, on the third round. We fired at least five hundred rounds of 81s, all without increments."[4]

Sgt John J. Balanco, with CAP O/1 inside the District Headquarters compound, was everywhere on the tiny battlefield. He constantly moved from bunker to bunker, keeping up morale, distributing ammunition, and readjusting the line.

"I went from bunker to bunker, and never stopped," he said. "The officers called in .ir strikes and artillery, because the NVA were in the wire. When we got hit, they came from all points. Cpl Russell probably killed more NVA than any other Marine, with his machine gun. I walked up to his gun, and like . . . the tip of a cigarette glows orange; well the whole entire barrel of that gun was that color. He never let up. They kept coming, and just kept coming toward him. They were actually coming from within the village. Russell had someone feeding him the rounds; they were constantly feeding the gun.

"We were constantly calling in artillery and air strikes on ourselves. It was scary as hell when those jets are dropping their bombs that close to you."[5]

Naval and Marine air forces had reacted to the presence of the enemy like sharks to the scent of blood in the water. The enemy had exposed himself, and at bases to the south, the fighters and bombers lit their afterburners and roared off the strips, pummeling the countryside with their shock waves. Despite the overcast skies and cloud cover, they stacked over the battle area, waiting for the controllers to direct them in.

From Chu Lai, 120 miles to the southeast, Marine attack aircraft of VMA-311 rolled for take-off. Maj Darrell L. Guttormson was the operations officer, and his mission began at 0900.

....

Bombs from American air strikes detonate just outside the defensive barbed wire of the base. **OPPOSITE:** Marines watch as a fire burns on the base.

"VMA-311 had the hot-pad duty that day," said Guttormson, "and the next scramble team included myself, Lt John Hawkins, and Col Leonard from the wing. We were scrambled at 0900, and had three aircraft—two carrying ten 250-lb. snake-eye bombs, and the other aircraft carried 500 lb napalm bombs.

"We proceeded to Khe Sanh, met by FINGERPRINT 53 [FAC]. We were the first flight in that day, and 53 said he had gooks all over the place. We approached the target and were given the 'roll and heading,' the target elevation, the friendly situation, the terrain altitude, and a prestrike brief. The operation was very close to Khe Sanh and generally southwest of the airstrip. We were given the mark by the FAC, and rolled in and delivered our ordnance on the target. As soon as we had completed, there was another flight checking in. This was to be the story throughout the day, continuing on even after dark."[6]

The Chu Lai airstrip became a hotbed of activity. Aircraft took off while others landed. The Marine aviators flew fifty-four sorties in support of Khe Sanh, and each returning aircraft had to be refueled and rearmed. The clerks and office workers shed their normal duties to join the ground personnel in this frantic rearming and refueling activity. All hands pitched in to roll and load 250-pound bombs.

With each bombing run, the NVA attack staggered. Capt Clark, in Khe Sanh Village, ringed his compound with artillery fire, and the Marines at the combat base fired over 1,000 rounds of variable time (VT) ammunition, designed to burst over the heads of the enemy force and create an enormous killing field. The NVA was inexorably hammered into submission. Whatever impetus they maintained after their initial attack was stopped cold by a devastating bombing run by an A-6 Intruder from VMA (AW) 522, the Marine all-weather attack-bomber squadron based at Chu Lai.

The squadron had first earned its reputation during World War II, having the distinction of destroying more enemy aircraft than any other all-weather attack squadron, and all their kills were by radar.

The Marines of the current 522 Squadron were no less proud, and their unique aircraft was recognized as the finest bomber in the air fleet, capable of lifting off with an incredible 9 tons of bombs.

Their mission was to attack and destroy surface targets, day or night and in any weather, and the Intruder bristled with a complicated radar system. It sported numerous "black boxes," and a state-of-the-art computer, weapons-release system, and search radar.

Capt Ronald M. D'Amora's A-6 took off at 1730 from Chu Lai, armed with twenty-eight 500-lb. bombs, and headed north.

"We proceeded up to Dong Ha, and PLUTOCRAT ALPHA [air coordination station] told us we had a priority mission over at Khe Sanh. AMERICAN BEAUTY DELTA [FAC] was controlling the strikes, but we had trouble finding the area due to the overcast. When we got there, we couldn't find our targets since the airborne controller had run out of flares, but there were a bunch of A-4s, A-6s, and F-4s all running the target at the same time. There were five to eight aircraft hitting the target.

"One F-4 had run out of bombs, but had plenty of fuel, and he had a blue cross on his plane, so we joined up with him, and he led us into the target. I made a dummy run, came around, and dropped one bomb to verify with the FAC that we were on target, and made four succeeding runs."[7]

....

A collection of shell casings from artillery fired at the encircling NVA.

With each run, D'Amora unleashed seven bombs on the exposed NVA. The earth shuddered, and geysers of dirt and smoke shot skyward. The Marines watched the folding fin, snake-eye bombs from the A-6 arch downward and impact into the enemy lines. With each ear-shattering *crump*, the CAP Marines cheered and yelled, "Get some." If the shocked enemy survivors had time to recover from the first bombing run, they had only seconds to change positions before the Intruder was on them again, and again, and again.

Like a giant eagle with a 53-foot wingspan, the bomber roared in, its two 9,300-pound-thrust engines screaming as the bombardier called off final data from the glowing screen to his front and the pilot's thumb released the next deadly load.

When the smoke had cleared, AMERICAN BEAUTY DELTA flew in for a bomb-damage assessment. One hundred NVA bodies lay sprawled below, and three bunkers and 30 feet of trench line were split apart and destroyed.[8] Other observers later reported long lines of NVA porters carrying dead and wounded toward Laos.

"It was a wild melee up there with three F-4s, two A-6s and three A-4s in the pattern at the same time, with everybody running in," said D'Amora. "While we were running in we received automatic-weapons fire, and small-arms fire."[9]

The multiple NVA attack of January 21 was broken. Nowhere had the ground attack succeeded. However, the bombardment of the combat base in support of the ground attack had been a huge success. The Marines found themselves perilously low on artillery and mortar ammunition.

"1st Battalion, 13th Marines had fired 'box-me-in' fires all night long," said Maj Jerry Hudson, "which, combined with the draw-down of ammunition during the battle of Khe Sanh village and the attack on 861 . . . and the loss of the ammunition dump; the artillery ammunition situation was 'critical,' to say the least."[10]

The artillery commander relied on an ammunition reserve of twenty thousand rounds, but the events of January 21 had reduced his reserve to less than five thousand rounds, and the NVA forces now surrounded the combat base. Resupply would be a big problem.

The bombardment had reduced the 60-foot by 3,900-foot runway to only 1,800 usable feet, but in a cold-blooded display of courage, pilots and crews of C-123 aircraft braved the gauntlet the same night. They landed by the light of flares and delivered 26 tons of supplies and munitions. On the planes' run-ins and takeoffs, NVA machine guns and mortars tracked them up and down the runway as if they were moving targets in a shooting gallery. The following day, twenty sorties delivered another 88 tons.[11]

That very night, Gen Westmoreland's SLAM operation, titled Niagara, began. There were five hundred ninety-five sorties of attack aircraft, and forty-nine B-52s.[12] The big bombers pulverized avenues of approach and possible enemy marshaling areas.

The defenders at the District Headquarters in Khe Sanh Village and the isolated Marines of CAP 0/2 hunkered down for the night, expecting a renewed attack after dark, but the NVA had neither the numbers nor the stomach for it. Most of their attacking force lay dead in the street, strewn in the fields, and tangled in the defensive wires. NVA survivors had taken positions in nearby huts and buildings, and resorted to firing sporadic mortar and small arms to let the Allied defenders know they were still there.

At the combat base, the perimeter was alive with activity. In the vicinity of the Hanging Tree in the Red Sector, Marines in the line observed a platoon of enemy soldiers crawling toward the wire. Aided by flares and night-vision scopes, the Marines engaged the NVA in an hour-long firefight, killing fourteen. The Leathernecks observed survivors dragging the dead and wounded back from the wire.[13]

The fighting was over for the day. Despite numerous attacks, the NVA had not fared well. They had begun a classic offensive against a defended position, and tactics called for the attackers to drive in the defender's outposts. But the outposts at 881S, 861, and Khe Sanh village had not been driven in, and the forward observers at those posts had been able to call in murderous fire on the attackers. The NVA losses on 861 and at Khe Sanh Village had been horrific, and the Marines of India Company had frustrated the attack on 881S. As the battered NVA forces passed the night, they began to hear the ominous rumblings that would come to define their daily existence.

The rumblings were the bombs from the B-52s, as Operation Niagara eagerly began to engage the exposed, concentrated forces. The American bomber crews flew and attacked with renewed vigor. They were like wild animals suddenly released from the crippling bombing restrictions that had hobbled their efforts. In this battle there would be no sanctuaries.

A C-123 lands on the airstrip as an enemy round explodes. **OPPOSITE:** Ammunition boxes stacked outside the mess hall at the CAC-O District Headquarters in Khe Sanh Village.

Marine casualties for the day were surprisingly low: Nine Marines had been killed, and another thirty-seven wounded and evacuated. It was hardly the start that Gen Giap had anticipated.

At the District Headquarters in Khe Sanh Village, Capt Clark radioed Robert Brewer, the senior advisor and CIA officer in Northern I Corps, headquartered at Quang Tri. He reported to Brewer that he was short of ammunition and if the Marines evacuated back to the base, he would not be able to hold his position.

Brewer called a meeting of all the advisory team and ARVN senior commanders, and they concluded that they had to reinforce the compound the next day. But that was easier said than done, since the NVA controlled the buildings in the village and all access to the compound.

"The District HQ was really an indefensible position," said Brewer. "One side of the compound was abutted in the city; the houses were right up against it. On the other side there was an orchard of coffee trees. I made plans with Bruce Clark . . . we would come right to the District compound, on the coffee orchard

side, blast an opening in the orchard, and put troops in right next to the headquarters. We'd put them right into the compound.

"The province chief agreed that we should send RF companies out there. We airlifted . . . with ten or more Hueys. My deputy, LtCol Joe Seymoe, felt it important to lead these choppers in. I said, 'Go Ahead.'

"We sent our own FAC because we were going to blast those trees, and we had four sets of fighters aloft, but another FAC was in the vicinity and we couldn't get ahold of him, so he radioed to the oncoming choppers to hold up, because we couldn't get the fighter strike in yet. Col Seymoe understood that the strike wasn't to come off at all, and took it on his own to land at the Old French Fort."

But the NVA forces that occupied the Old French Fort immediately fired on the arriving Hueys, dropping them from the sky or riddling them on the ground. Thirteen pilots and fourteen crewmen were killed in the onslaught. The seventy-four assaulting ARVN soldiers were killed or missing. It was a disaster.

"Seymoe's chopper was blown up, and away, and down the hillside, about 100-feet away, and came to rest upside down. One side gunner was killed; the pilot and co-pilot climbed out through the broken Plexiglas nose, and the other gunner got out.

....

On the base, Marines struggle to extinguish a fire burning in a downed CH-53 helicopter. **OPPOSITE:** A Huey gunship circles over Khe Sanh.

"The NVA were pouring down the hill. Col Seymoe was pinned to the ground by the bar that holds the stretchers. The plane was on fire but had not yet exploded. The pilot, co-pilot, and the gunner were shooting at almost point-blank range at the NVA coming toward them, and trying to pull Seymoe out. The fire spread, got to the petrol tanks, and blew up. Then there was no hope. The three of them ran around the chopper, down the ravine, and made their way to the combat base."[14]

Maj Tom Stiner celebrated his thirtieth birthday in full flight away from his downed chopper. The NVA were everywhere.

"I picked up two grenades and clips for my carbine, and started downhill. I bumped into an enemy force, and surprised them as much as they surprised me. They were walking, and I ran through them. I kept running, and they were chasing me, and firing and yelling. It didn't sound too friendly. I would run until I just couldn't run anymore. So I would find a bushy area and hide, then run some more."[15]

It took him thirteen hours to traverse the 3 kilometers (1.9 miles) to the outer fringes of the base defensive wire, where he promptly set off an antipersonnel mine that wounded him with shrapnel. The detonation alerted a Marine sentinel who promptly shot him and triggered all the Marines along the line, to open fire. The wounded Stiner flattened himself to the earth and shouted from his position that he was an American and not the enemy, but it took some time to convince the wary Marines.

The encircled Marines at CAP O/2 pondered their fate. They could stay in their isolated position and hope for a rescue force, or attempt to join CAP O/1 and the larger force at District Headquarters. They chose the latter and radioed to CAP O/1 that they were coming and to cover them.

"We had seven of our nine Marines wounded," said Doc Roberts. The ones that had leg wounds and more serious, I wrapped them with ace bandages as tight as I could, and I gave them an injection of morphine, and then we broke out. The last thing that they expected from us was for us to attack. And we just shot them as we ran through them, and got over to CAP O/1. We were shooting to both sides as we ran through. Everybody was just so juiced up. Our emotions and our adrenaline were pumping so hard. A couple of the guys were grabbing other guys around the waist and helping them; and Taylor made it out with his bagpipes!"[16]

As soon as the Marines had consolidated at the District Headquarters, helicopters flew in to rescue them, leaving Capt Clark and his Vietnamese forces behind.

"The minute those Marines got on the helicopter and flew away, it was like somebody had deflated the RFs. So we walked out, and were turned away at the combat base, but the FOB-3 folks took us in. We went

through the town, and there was a little trail, a very steep little cut that went by Hill 471, and then got up on the ridgeline, and came down into the combat base. About 3:30 we told the Special Forces guys about all the weapons we captured. It was over a hundred of them, and we left them behind. They got their own helicopters, and we conducted a raid back into the District Headquarters that afternoon, and recovered all the weapons. I booby-trapped everything I could get my hands on, especially the beer and the food. We were picking up off the helo pad when the NVA were coming back in the front door."[17]

With the evacuation of the Marine CAPs and the Army advisors team with the 915th Regional Force Vietnamese from the District Headquarters, the NVA had finally driven in one of the outposts.

The airspace over Khe Sanh was crowded with planes on January 22, waiting to attack the many targets identified by the FACs. LtCol Harry T. Hagaman, the commanding officer of squadron VMFA-323, led a flight of attack aircraft into the battle area, which bristled with enemy antiaircraft fire.

....

A wounded Marine is carried toward a medevac helicopter.

"The FAC had a suspected AA [antiaircraft] site south-southwest of the field, and marked the target on the side of a small hill. He cleared the start of my run, and I rolled in, firing six Delta 1As and four Delta 9s. My speed was 450 knots, and I rolled out at 2,000 feet, 500 meters [about 550 yards] from the target. Just as I pulled the nose up off the target, I noticed a heavy stream of fire coming out of the target's position, and as the nose lifted up into the sky, I felt a tremendous impact in the center of the aircraft, and immediately the aircraft burst into flames and started to tumble, with the rear of the aircraft proceeding in an upward arc over the front of the nose. As the aircraft started to tumble, I lost all control of the flight system. I immediately tried to right the system by applying full right rudder. This was to no avail. As the aircraft spun around, my RIO [radar intercept officer] ejected. He ejected on the first turn. On the second flip, I realized the aircraft was mortally wounded and there was no way to recover. The cockpit was engulfed in flames and smoke. My ejection was smooth. I hit the ground and rolled over in 8 to 9 feet of elephant grass, and sat up and felt my arms and legs and shoulders to see if I was in good health. I was in a small valley on the side of a hill, and proceeded away from the touchdown point, making my way through the grass. There was heavy weapons fire from the south-southwest, and also the crack of a .50-caliber machine gun.

> ## I NOTICED A HEAVY STREAM OF FIRE COMING OUT OF THE TARGET'S POSITION, AND AS THE NOSE LIFTED UP INTO THE SKY, I FELT A TREMENDOUS IMPACT IN THE CENTER OF THE AIRCRAFT, AND IMMEDIATELY THE AIRCRAFT BURST INTO FLAMES AND STARTED TO TUMBLE . . .

"I looked up and spotted a helicopter, 200 feet above me, and I waited for three or four minutes, and realized the helicopter was coming in from the west, looking for me in the grass. I popped a smoke signal, and he proceeded directly to my position, hovering 10 feet in the air. Because of being on the side of the hill, he could get no closer than 6 feet above me. The bottom of his landing skid was at the limits of my reaching up. I stood there patiently with all my equipment, waiting from them to hoist me into the helicopter, but he had no hoist equipment aboard. There was a rope, no hook on the end, and the crew chief indicated for me to wrap it around my body. A crewman attempted to pull me up into the helicopter but couldn't lift me. The pilot lowered the helicopter down further, and they reached with both hands and got ahold of my wrists. They lost their grip, and I fell on the hill in the grass, and they threw out another rope with a sling on it, and I pulled myself up into a chinning position. They grabbed the back of my torso harness and pulled me into the helicopter."[18]

Before the NVA could exploit their success of driving in the outpost at Khe Sanh Village with another thrust toward the base, 1st Battalion, 9th Marines arrived the same day to reinforce the 26th Marine Regiment.

The area to the west, close to the rock quarry that had supplied the material for the runway repair, afforded the enemy an ideal approach to the base. With the loss of the village outposts, Col Lownds decided to place the newly arrived battalion 1,500 meters (about 1,600 yards) to the southwest of the airstrip. The following day, the approach from the southwest was again effectively outposted and blocked.

LtCol John Mitchell set up his battalion perimeter around the quarry and outposted a small hill knob 500 meters (about 550 yards) farther to the west with a platoon from Company A. It became known as Outpost Alpha, garrisoned by two officers and sixty-four enlisted men, and was often called "Hill 64." The reinforced platoon was positioned to give LtCol Mitchell "as much warning as possible, before the enemy reached 1/9's MLR [main line of resistance].[19]

The area around the rock quarry was not set up for immediate defense. Lt James R. Talone said, "We had no wire, and elephant grass was right up to the road; you had 10 to 15 meters (33 to 50 feet) of cleared

An Air Force jet lays a smoke screen to obscure the enemy's view of a supply plane landing on the airstrip.

area, and one corner of my sector was heavily wooded." It took the 1/9 Marines two weeks to carve out a proper defensive position.

Col Lownds made one other move in this gigantic test of strategy and counterstrategy. After the battle for Hill 861 on January 21, he discovered that Kilo Company had a blind spot, just to their east. A hilltop of equal size masked their view into the valley between their position and that of 2nd Battalion on Hill 558. He detached Company E, commanded by Capt Earle Breeding, and positioned them on the second hill, dubbed 861A.

"We had to walk up 861A that night," said Capt Breeding, "and that was single file up a marsh and a draw, and luckily we met no resistance, because we could have been swallowed up. We set in a circular defense. The troops were absolutely exhausted. At first light we set in our positions and started digging."[20]

On that same night, the NVA launched another attack to secure terrain necessary for their planned all-out attack on Khe Sanh. But this attack was not in South Vietnam; it was in Laos.

On the night of January 23/24, three battalions of infantry, supported by armor, attacked the Laotian BV-33 Battalion, better known by its call sign, "ELEPHANT." The battalion sat astride Route 9, just across the Laotian border, and guarded the airstrip at Ban Houei Sane. ELEPHANT served as early-warning eyes to Army Special Forces and blocked the most important approach from the west to Khe Sanh and the Special Forces camp at Lang Vei.

Capt Charles Rushforth III was a Forward Air Controller flying missions around Khe Sanh, and was scheduled to fly that night. He had previously been a FAC flying missions in North Vietnam, called TALLY HO, but had recently been pulled to fly Khe Sanh. He flew the small Cessna O-2 that he described as "meant for little old ladies to fly around the Hawaiian Islands, rather than fight a war in."[21]

But the Cessna's ability to fly "low and slow" was perfectly suited to find and observe enemy targets and mark those targets for attack by high-performance fighter-bombers.

"That little O-2 is just kind of hanging there," said Rushforth. "not moving too fast, and almost in suspended animation. It's a real mind-bender; tends to make something of a fatalist out of you."[22]

Just before takeoff at 0330 for his scheduled six-hour flight around Khe Sanh, he was informed that ELEPHANT was under attack. As he arrived on the scene, he found that ground fog and clouds were solid up to 2,500 feet. A flare ship was up, trying to light the area in spite of the fog.

Rushforth couldn't see the battle area, but saw the distinctive mortar and gun flashes, and his radio crackled with a panicked voice.

"HOUNDOG, this is ELEPHANT. Sah, continue flare! Sah, continue flare," said the Laotian soldier in his heavy accent.

"Their western perimeter was broken," said Rushforth. "The NVA came down Route 9 in trucks and tanks. I couldn't put air in visually and had to 'sky-spot,' and there is usually a fifteen-minute delay in radar bombing. We had fighters available, but they couldn't get in, so we flew them on coordinates, overhead, using our radar guidance."

The fifteen-minute delay seemed like hours to the Laotians under attack on the ground.

"'Sah, you air-strike coordinate—now, sah! Sah, you help us!'

"I felt sick and helpless," said Rushforth. "'Air strikes coming, soon, ELEPHANT.' 'Sah, we wait long time. VC come! Many, many trucks; many VC. You air-strike, sah!'

"I couldn't put in B-57s with funny bombs,* because of the fog and clouds. 'Sah, VC come; many more! Many more! We run! We run! They come to our command post!'

"I could see the flashes. If only the sun could hurry. 'Sah, we run east on highway. You bomb command post. Many, many VC.'

"The sun was just under the horizon, and we began to see the terrain. After much effort, we were finally

---

*A bomb with incendiary shards, capable of melting armor.

Old Lang Vei village. **OPPOSITE:** Capt Charles Rushforth III (right) with his commanding officer.

able to see the command post area down through the fog. The sky-spots had been pretty good—right on Route 9. I called for more fighters for visual bombing, and eight F-100s arrived. I dropped down through the clouds and told them to go after the flare. They rolled in and got good hits. There was a large fire in the command post.

"Things started to clear up, and they really hit the road. I could hear that little fellow as he ran down the road toward Lang Vei. 'Sah, we run. We go to Lang Vei.'"[23]

The remnants of BV-33 fled to the east and took up new positions in Old Lang Vei, just west of the "new" Lang Vei Special Forces Camp. For whatever reason, the use of armor in the attack at Ban Houei Sane, although reported,[24] was not highlighted and received little attention at any level of command. Perhaps the report was dismissed as panic in the ranks of BV-33. Because of the clouds, fog, and overcast, none of the air forces respond-ing to the attack on Ban Houei Sane had seen tanks.

But someone had confirmed them. Capt Rushforth said, "We debriefed at Da Nang, and got a FLASH [most urgent] message to 7th Air Force Headquarters, and then phone-called directly to Col Woody for report. Found out that they did have five tanks. I think we got one on our attack on Elephant command post."[26]

The Laotian troops and the Army Special Forces strongpoint at Lang Vei were now sandwiched between the forces of the NVA in Laos and those ensconced in Khe Sanh village.

"Route 9 was completely held by the enemy," said Gen Tompkins, "complete from Khe Sanh village to the Laotian bor-der. The hills to the north of Route 9 were completely held by the enemy."[26]

CHAPTER 8

EMBRACED BY THE ENEMY

Members of the 37th ARVN Ranger battalion

TIMELINE	APRIL 24, 1967	MAY 13, 1967	DECEMBER 1967	JANUARY 21, 1968	JANUARY 31, 1968
	Hill Fights begin at Khe Sanh	Hill Fights end. Marines fought off elements of the 325C NVA Division in a two-week battle that cost the enemy 824 KIA. 168 Marines were killed and 443 wounded in the struggle.	General Westmoreland decides to reinforce Khe Sanh in the face of enemy buildup.	NVA attack hill 861 and bombard combat base exploding ammo dump, and attack Khe Sanh village. Siege begins.	NVA launch countrywide Tet Offensive.

The days following the fall of Ban Houei Sane were ones of frenzied preparation for the anticipated NVA ground attack. First Battalion, 9th Marines dug furiously at the rock quarry, scrounging for defensive materials to build bunkers with overhead cover, and cleared fields of fire in the encircling trees and elephant grass.

Company E, on Hill 861A, also dug trenches, built bunkers, and strung tanglefoot and concertina wire. "You dig foxholes first," said Capt Earle Breeding, "and then convert to trench lines; we tried to get engineering supplies, barbed wire, tent stakes, sandbags, but we had very little. We cleared fields of fire as far as we could, but as the terrain falls off, you can't shoot around a curve, so in some places it was only 20 yards."[1] Both units registered artillery and mortar concentrations, and final protective fires.

On January 27, the last reinforcements to the combat base arrived. The ARVN 37th Ranger Battalion, under the command of Capt Hoang Pho, landed at the airstrip and were immediately assigned to partially prepared defensive positions on the east end of the runway.

The runway sat on the crown of the plateau, which was the geographic feature of the combat base, and while the western edge of the strip terminated on a gentle, descending slope, the eastern end came to an abrupt stop and plunged off a steep face into a deep, wooded ravine.

The Marines were unable to encircle their defensive lines around the eastern end, and were forced to cut their perimeter short, so that their line actually crossed the runway, hundreds of yards from the eastern end. The arrival of the ARVN Rangers allowed for a better arrangement. Lownds positioned them so that they tied in with the Marine lines parallel to the runway on either side, and extended the crossing 200 meters (about 220 yards) further down the strip, closer to the steep escarpment. The ARVN became a "blister" on the old Marine lines. Two Ontos, with their twelve recoilless rifles, covered the only "gap," caused where the runway bisected the Ranger perimeter.[2]

Air and artillery initiated unrelenting attacks against the NVA, which was no longer an elusive, hit-and-run force. They delivered thousands of bombs and shells in an effort to disrupt NVA formations and maneuvers. The Fire Support Coordination Center (FSCC) became the hub of activity.

DISK 2, TRACKS 5-9: Attack on 861 Alpha.

FEBRUARY 5-8, 1968	FEBRUARY 23, 1968	FEBRUARY 29, 1968	APRIL 14, 1968	JUNE 19-JULY 5, 1968
NVA attack Hill 861 Alpha, Lang Vei, and Hill 64.	Enemy gunners bombard base with more than 1,300 rounds in heaviest attack.	NVA launch regimental size attack against base.	Marines break out of siege and attack and seize Hill 881N.	Khe Sanh Combat Base is destroyed and abandoned by American forces.

"The daylight hours were passed in a vulgar free-for-all," observed Capt Harry Biag, the target information officer, "wherein air and artillery attacked anything and everything that looked peculiar. At night it was a different matter. Finding part of a target complex led to predicting the rest.

"Our entire defense philosophy was to allow the enemy to surround us closely, to man about us, to reveal his troops and logistic routes, to establish his dumps and assembly areas, his truck parks and artillery, and to prepare his siege works as energetically as he desired.

"Once the enemy had finally embraced us, we had him fixed. His battle plan, directed from higher headquarters, forced him to stay and continue."[3]

The new $2.6 million United States Embassy in Saigon was on Thung Naht Boulevard. It was a white, six-story, reinforced-concrete structure, resplendent with a teakwood door entrance; a 10-foot-high wall surrounded the complex. Completed in September 1967, it was dubbed "Bunker's Bunker" in honor of the American ambassador to South Vietnam, Elsworth Bunker.[4]

On January 24, three days after the first attack on Khe Sanh Combat Base, Ambassador Bunker sent an urgent cable to President Johnson. In view of the enemy's posture along the DMZ, Bunker expressed grave

An ARVN Ranger in a trench at the base. **OPPOSITE:** A Marine inspects an Ontos that lost one of its tracks.

doubts concerning a planned forty-eight-hour truce during the upcoming Tet holiday season. The Communists had announced they would cease hostilities for one week. Because of past truce violations, Bunker said, he saw "little reason to presume that North Vietnam forces intended to observe the ceasefire . . . when it is not to their advantage."[5]

This cable reinforced the message Gen Westmoreland had sent to Johnson right after the Khe Sanh attacks. The general had told the president he believed that "the enemy will attempt a countrywide show of strength just prior to Tet.'"[6] He also told Johnson he thought that the NVA saw a similarity between Khe Sanh and Dien Bien Phu.

There it was again—the specter of Dien Bien Phu. Talk of the old battle buzzed in and around the Pentagon, the National Security Council, Saigon, throughout the MACV network, and especially in the press briefing rooms.

A worried President Johnson called for data relating to Dien Bien Phu and Khe Sanh.[7] Westmoreland was determined to hold Khe Sanh and deny the enemy's grand design to seize the two northern provinces of South Vietnam. In the process, he planned to destroy the NVA forces with massive firepower. The president was determined to hold with him, and like Col Travis at the Alamo, he drew the line in the sand with his sword. On January 29 he called the Joint Chiefs of Staff to the White House and asked them to step over the line and defend Khe Sanh. "I don't want any damned Dien Bien Phu,"[8] the president demanded. In his Texas drawl, it came out "Din Bin Phoo." He called for each Chief to state that he was confident that Khe Sanh could be held. Gen Earle Wheeler then sent a memo to the president expressing Gen Westmoreland's confidence.

"General Westmoreland stated to me that . . . we can hold Khe Sanh, and we should hold Khe Sanh. He reports that everyone is confident. He believes that this is an opportunity to inflict a severe defeat upon the enemy."[9]

All the generals stepped over the line.

Shortly before 0300, January 31, 1968, as the Tet holiday began, initiating the Year of the Monkey, fifteen sappers detonated explosives that blew a huge hole in the wall of Bunker's Bunker. They scrambled through, firing their weapons in an attempt to seize the embassy. The Marines inside denied them entrance to the chancery, but the attackers prowled the grounds and building complex for six hours, exchanging fire with embassy guards and staff. In the end, a platoon of MPs attacked, and the fifteen

sappers were soon dead, their bodies strewn around the embassy grounds along with five dead Americans and several South Vietnamese.

The attack on the embassy was the most dramatic, to the television camera's eye, of the numerous actions all across South Vietnam that became known as the Tet Offensive. The embassy was a shambles; its now-shattered facade and teakwood door, along with the battered emblem of the Great Seal of the United States, filled the camera's lens and made a poignant backdrop for newscasters. But few reporters and newsmen emphasized the fact that all fifteen attackers lay dead in the compound, their mission to take over the embassy a total failure.

In three days, the Communists hit thirty-six of the forty-four provincial capitals, five of the six autonomous cities, sixty-four of two hundred forty-two district capitals, and fifty hamlets.[10] One of the few places not attacked was Khe Sanh. Perhaps Operation Niagara had something to do with that.

President Johnson focused on Khe Sanh. He was worried, and a report that new captured documents indicated the NVA intended to reenact Dien Bien Phu didn't help.

....

MPs crouch behind a wall near two dead U.S. soldiers during the VC attack on the American Embassy, January 31, 1968.

That intelligence was reinforced by the testimony from a prisoner from 95C Regiment, 325C Division, who said that the plan of attack called for withdrawal to Laos if the first attempt to capture the base was turned back. Another assault was to be made after Tet, when maneuver elements would be supported by artillery and tanks, and reinforced by "twice as many troops." This second attack would start on February 3.[11]

Westmoreland reassured the president that his firepower would hold the base, but Johnson would not be assuaged. He voiced his concerns to Gen Wheeler that if things got bad, he may be forced to use tactical nuclear weapons.[12]

On February 3, there was a long luncheon at the White House. The subject was Khe Sanh. If the Marines at the base had to withdraw, the enemy would score a great victory. The possibilities of diversionary attacks were discussed and rejected, and an air of gloom settled over the attendees.[13] But if there was an air of gloom among the president and politicians in Washington, there was none among the fighting forces attacking the exposed NVA forces.

From Anderson Air Force Base in Guam, from Kadena Air Base in Okinawa, and from the Royal Thai Air Base in U Tapao, Thailand, huge B-52 Stratofortresses rolled out on the runways, their 48-foot "shark" tails towering over the landscape. When each aircraft was positioned for takeoff, the pilot and co-pilot pushed the throttles forward. Eight J-57 engines gulped fuel and air, and, with a deafening roar and 80,000 pounds of thrust, inched the massive aircraft, with its 186-foot wingspan, forward. Starting as if in slow motion, the Stratofortress lumbered down the runway, gathered speed, and lifted off, headed for Khe Sanh, its belly filled with as many as 108 bombs. At night, only red and amber instrument lights illuminated the faces of the six-man crew.

This was an Arc Light—code name for a B-52 strike—which lent its full weight of firepower to Operation Niagara. The mission was to annihilate the suspected twenty thousand to forty thousand NVA closely surrounding the Marines at Khe Sanh.

"The 'D' model B-52 had what we called the 'big belly' modification," said Capt Robert Karwoski, an aircrew navigator. "That allowed us to put eighty-four Mark-82, 500-pound weapons in the bomb bay. We also carried twenty-four M-117, 750-pound bombs on the wings. We had a total of 108 weapons—500-pounders, and 750-pounders—for a maximum gross weight of 60,000 pounds."[14]

After as much as a six-hour flight, the aircraft approached the target at 650 mph, and the crew prepared for the bombing run at 35,000 feet. In less than a minute, the computer had dropped the bombs and the aircraft were headed home. The earth literally exploded.

"You could neither see nor hear the planes," said Gen Tompkins. "Then suddenly, a long strip of earth just erupts . . . . Then a few seconds later, another nearby strip erupts . . . . One day I saw eight or ten North Vietnamese stagger out of the dirt of the first eruption, struggling for their lives, only to be engulfed by the second eruption."[15]

"The targets were designed to take maximum advantage of the vast power of one cell [three planes] of B-52s," said Capt Karwoski. "You're talking about 180,000 pounds of ordnance. We rarely went in and

dropped on our own targets; we were vectored in by the Combat Skyspot, the radar, which would vector-in the lead aircraft, and those of us in the second and third positions would offset ourselves, left and right, so that our weapons would not fall on the same spot, but to the left and right."[16]

Such was the drama of one Arc Light strike. The Air Force would fly 2,548 Arc Lights and drop 59,542 tons of bombs at Khe Sanh.[17]

Within several days of its dramatic start, the impetus of the Tet Offensive petered out, except at Hue City, where the Marines battled an enemy entrenched in the ancient Citadel. But the NVA remained very much in strength at Khe Sanh. Artillery and air strikes delivered twenty-four-hour bombardment on enemy locations as the *crachin* of the northeast monsoon cloaked the base with impenetrable fog. The *crachin* did not offer the NVA any respite from this constant bombardment. The sensors installed by Task Force Alpha were immune to the *crachin*, as was the A-6 Intruder, and the Americans heard and tracked the NVA's movements, and by examining their traffic patterns were able to develop an ability to predict where they were going. It was high-tech stalking, just as a predator might anticipate his victim's path and lie in wait for his arrival. This high-tech warfare was top secret, known only to a select few.

....

An A-6 Intruder prepares for takeoff from an aircraft carrier, 1967. **OPPOSITE:** Fog hangs like a shroud over the base.

Meanwhile, the drama of the anticipated showdown at Khe Sanh led journalists to invoke the name of Dien Bien Phu continually, even though all studies of the decisive 1954 battle revealed little in common with the present encirclement at Khe Sanh. The only comparable element was Gen Giap, the NVA commander, who was attempting to employ the same tactics that had worked for him fourteen years earlier.

At Dien Bien Phu, Giap had encircled the French forces in a valley 100 miles from the closest supporting French base. He had occupied the high ground with his artillery, and early in the siege had bombarded the tiny French airstrip below and rendered it useless. The French had only 100 aircraft available to support their base and had absolutely no bomber support with which to attack Giap's Viet Minh force. French artillery in the valley was literally under the Viet Minh's guns, and suffered constant bombardment from the high ground. The only way the French could support and reinforce their position was by parachute, and once a soldier had parachuted in, there was no way out.

Khe Sanh, on the other hand, was not in a valley; it was a plateau only 12 miles from a supporting U.S. base, and it had a usable airstrip even after the bombardment. Giap's army had not occupied the surrounding high ground, although it had tried. The Marines, in fact, held the high ground, and it was they who looked

down on the NVA, and it was they who directed their own artillery and the big Army guns at Camp Carrol to support their positions.

Additionally, fifteen hundred aircraft from the U.S. air armada stood ready to support the base. The heavy bombers, unfettered by restrictive rules, stood ready to pounce on the enemy's every movement. Those heavy bombers were virtually immune to the effects of inclement weather and Gen Giap's weapons.

Marine replacements and reinforcements arrived at Khe Sanh by aircraft, and the wounded and those ending their tours departed the same way. Men going on R & R were able to exit the base; reporters could fly in, take pictures, deliver stand-up television reports, and fly out; and mail arrived from home continuously.

But none of these readily available facts had the slightest effect on news reporting or the content of continuing news stories. Khe Sanh and Dien Bien Phu were always mentioned in the same breath and with the same foreboding of doom.[18]

....

An artillery tube is delivered to Hill 881S. **OPPOSITE:** A corpsman looks after a wounded Marine in the base's medical facility, Charlie Med.

Dr. Harvey DeMaagd, the battalion surgeon to 26th Marines, described daily life at the base after the bombardment began. It wasn't pleasant, but it was not mind-numbing either.

"I would travel daily from my end of the runway down to H&S [headquarters and service] for the morning briefing. But it was not too frightening an experience. Most of the time you could hear incoming, and most of the time it came from one particular direction. So as you're walking down the road, you are pretty much, subliminally, aware of places where you're going to fall to hide—in ditches or behind bunkers. Surprisingly, we were not too much intimidated."[19]

The Marines learned to adjust. The fog was not always their enemy; it also blinded the NVA gunners. As long as it shrouded the base, the Marines were relatively free to work and move around. Like Dr. DeMaagd, each man mentally picked out spots into which he would dive when the "incoming" alarm sounded. As the *crachin* burned off, work ceased and Marines retreated to their bunkers, anticipating the enemy bombardment as the base became visible.

In the early morning hours of February 5, seemingly on schedule with the revealed "second stage" of the attack, the NVA again attempted to seize the high ground. Having failed to budge India Company on 881S or Kilo Company on 861, it now attempted to kick Capt Breeding's Echo Company off its newly occupied

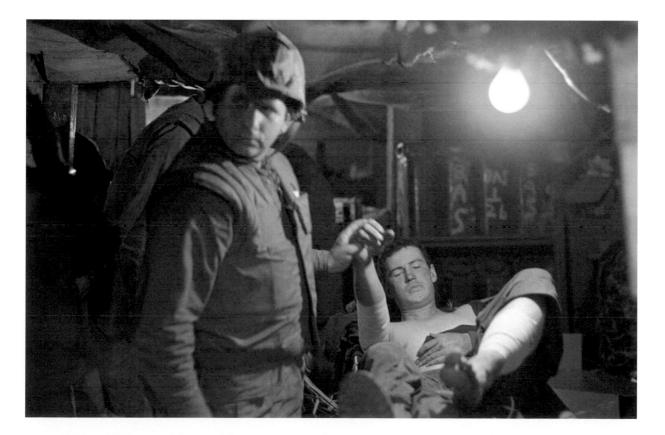

position on Hill 861A. Breeding's Marines had hardly had time to prepare the hill for defense, but they had strung some wire and were dug-in.

Having knotted the long grass to mark their route of approach to the slopes of Hill 861A, a battalion of NVA inched upward to their attack positions just outside the wire. Individual sappers crawled forward, slipped the long bangalore torpedoes under the barbed-wire strands while the main force crouched, awaiting the signal.

"It was the middle of the night, and we started hearing tin cans," said 2Lt Jeff Bodenweiser, commanding the 2nd Platoon. "We had these C-ration cans hanging on the barbed wire, and when those cans went, we knew there was something out there. Then the crap hit the fan."[20]

"They had a sapper unit with bangalore torpedoes, and they set them off," said Breeding. "It just cut the wire. We didn't have much wire, and they started pouring through. They had RPGs preceding them, and they pinned us down initially. That initial barrage landed right in the trenches. It was very heavy, but short-lived because their troops were going to advance. The troops came in, and that's where it became quite a melee. They advanced almost to the aid station."[21]

"When it all started, all I heard was one shot," said Cpl Eugene J. Franklin with the 60mm mortar section. "I thought it was just somebody who thought he saw something in the wire, and just fired. All of a sudden mortar rounds were dropping all around the gun pit, and around my hootch, and I had one man trapped inside his hootch when they busted the lines.

"I tried to get out to the gun pit, but concussion from one of the rounds knocked me back. I tried to get out again, and that's when I saw a couple of enemy troops coming up on the side of the hill. One of my men was trapped inside his hootch, and he tried to get out, but couldn't, and the enemy shot an RPG into the side."

Franklin managed to struggle out to the gun pit just in time to see NVA soldiers sneak up to the side of PFC Stevenson's bunker and drop a grenade inside.

"It blew him away," Franklin said. "I tried to fire the tube inside the gun pit so I could get the guys some illumination. I dropped one round down the tube, and it didn't go off. The tube was broken and had shrapnel holes through it."[22]

Lt Nick Elardo and and 2Lt Jeff Bodenweiser.

PFC Newton D. Lyle had the other 60mm mortar on the hill.

"Someone came over to our gun and said that Cpl Franklin's gun had been wiped out, and Red and Stevenson were dead. When we heard this, we pulled our gun from our position and went over there, and you could actually see the NVA running around on the lines, laughing and throwing ChiComs in bunkers, and you could hear the screams of our buddies, and we were running around firing mortar rounds out in front of the wire.

"After awhile we were told that all the men had been wiped out in the trenches in front of us, and we were to fire directly into those trenches. We lowered our tube and started firing mortar rounds all along the trenches. We were firing so close it was actually throwing shrapnel back in our own faces."[23]

Lyle's team started working their tube, oblivious to the enemy running wildly inside their lines. They fired their rounds as fast as they could and ran to the other destroyed gun to retrieve ammunition. They fired from 0330 until 0600, praying for daylight to come.

> "I TRIED TO GET OUT TO THE GUN PIT, BUT CONCUSSION FROM ONE OF THE ROUNDS KNOCKED ME BACK. I TRIED TO GET OUT AGAIN, AND THAT'S WHEN I SAW A COUPLE OF ENEMY TROOPS COMING UP ON THE SIDE OF THE HILL. ONE OF MY MEN WAS TRAPPED INSIDE HIS HOOTCH, AND HE TRIED TO GET OUT, BUT COULDN'T, AND THE ENEMY SHOT AN RPG INTO THE SIDE."

"We knew by daylight they would either have to pull back, or really get their asses kicked, because we could call in air strikes and artillery," said Lyle.[24]

Tom Eichler, platoon sergeant of the weapons platoon, had his six machine guns attached to the three platoons forming the perimeter.

"I was with the first platoon. We were protecting the finger that led up the approach to 861A. It was pitch dark, and I started hearing rounds. As soon as I heard the first four or five rounds, I started yelling and made my way through the trench line to first platoon, and checked my machine guns. When I walked up to my two machine gun positions, they were all wounded. I still had it in my mind that these were mortar rounds, and didn't realize that we were being attacked. It was pitch black and foggy, and all kinds of shooting going on."

Eichler took off his cartridge belt and his other gear, and picked up one of his wounded gunners in a fireman's carry. He started carrying the man back to the rear, but the NVA blocked his way.

"As I was running through the trench line, an NVA soldier jumped into the trench. There was nowhere for me to go; I didn't have a weapon, so I turned and started running the opposite way. He opened up with his AK-47, and was hitting the wounded Marine I had on my back. I could feel the

bullets hitting him. The Marine on my back was absorbing the bullets. I ran down the trench line and set him down, and another NVA jumped in, but he had his back toward me. He was shooting down the line with a B-40 rocket; just firing down the trench line. I hit him from behind and strangled him with the straps from his pack."[25]

Eichler returned to the shattered front line and rescued two more of his wounded Marines. He saw NVA soldiers in the holes, with Marine helmets on, just as the order came to pull back to the secondary defensive lines. Eichler got one of his men and set up a mortar with no base plate. They fired the tube with the base just resting on the ground. But in his excitement, Eichler had not pulled the propelling increments off, and the first rounds blasted out of the mortar to their 1,600-yard maximum range. He realized his error, ripped the propellants off, and began firing at zero elevation, and the mortars made a short flight and smashed into the trenches just yards in front of him and into the intruding NVA.

The attack had breached the lines of the 1st Platoon commanded by 2Lt Donald Shanley on the northwest perimeter.

Marines run between the combat base trenches.

"I was trying to figure out what the hell was going on," said Shanley. "There was an enormous amount of incoming, and SSgt Allen was in a hole right next to me. I went down there and was aware that PFC Mitchell's position had been taken out. The fog was very dense; visibility went in and out as fog does. There were times when the visibility was 3 to 5 feet, and then there were times when the visibility was 50 feet. I was surprised how quickly illumination occurred. But it was like high beams on an automobile in the fog. You can't really see any better; it's just brighter. I was aware that a North Vietnamese soldier was going across the lines 20 yards from me. I fired once, but my M-16 jammed. The attack came pretty much right up the middle. There was this finger, and my CP was centered over that finger, and that's the only way they could come with any kind of strength because it was enormously steep elsewhere. I was crouched on my back in this hole, and in the flare's light I could see a steady stream of automatic-weapons fire impacting in the ground right above my head.

"Suddenly Sgt Allen screamed that he had got this guy, and then I stood up. The firing had stopped, Allen looked over and gave me a sign that he gotten two of them, and there were two 20 feet from my hole. At a certain point, I was aware that there were men in my platoon area that weren't in my platoon. One of them was Sgt Eichler, who was truly a hero that night. I saw him and Cpl Johnson, and they seemed to be working as a team. I saw Cpl Johnson on the edge of a bomb crater to my left, standing up and firing, aiming and firing, and moving his rifle and firing. Allen got up, I got up, Johnson got up, and Eichler had been dragging cases of grenades down from the CP. All of a sudden the four of us were standing, where none had been standing up before. Everybody got up on line, and we walked across this big bomb crater that was 30 to 40 feet across. There were a lot of bodies of North Vietnamese soldiers on the ground."[26]

"We held that perimeter until the captain got some more men, and we just kept throwing grenades," said Sgt Eichler. "I know we threw two hundred that night. The next morning the front of the position had a lot of dead NVA in the trench lines, and a lot lying outside the perimeter. I took a patrol out and found a lot more bodies buried in shallow graves."[27]

During this attack, just as in the previous attack on Hill 861, Capt Dabney's Marines on Hill 881S poured mortar fire into the enemy's flank as it surged up the slopes of 861A, this time hitting them with eleven hundred rounds.

"Hill 558 also delivered 106 [recoilless rifle] fire across my eastern flank," said Capt Breeding. "They were shooting 20 to 30 meters down from the top. That was pretty good fire because they couldn't see their bursts. They had to compute their angle of fire.

"We had a seven-point illumination program. There were seven flares burning over us all the time. It was eerie; the fog was such that you couldn't see anything unless you had a flare very close to you."[28]

As the enemy attacked, Breeding radioed for supporting arms fire. The artillerymen of 1/13 went into action, unleashing protective fires on the slopes of 861A with three batteries. Four other batteries fired in the area where the enemy movement was the thickest, and the wall of steel rolled down the slope like a giant scythe. The Marine loaders slammed the rounds into the breeches, and the blocks closed behind the

rounds. An instant later, responding to the yank of the gunner's lanyard, the howitzers recoiled mightily, surrounded by a deafening blast. Only the spades of the trails held the weapon in check from its recoil and forced it to return to its original lay, bouncing on its tires. A pull of a lever opened the breechblock, extracting the hot, smoking, brass casing with a distinctive "pling," and in seconds a new round filled the empty space, to repeat the firing sequence. The only pauses in the fire missions were for slight adjustments to the elevation and traverse.

The second phase of the repetitive fire included four batteries of the 175mm artillery from Camp Carrol. The guns fired their 147-pound projectiles, propelled by separately loaded bag powder, into a broad "V" on the lower northeast slope of 861A. The steel rain crept up the slope, finally plunging into and pulverizing the earth a mere 200 meters (less than 220 yards) from the wire. The batteries from Khe Sanh filled in the gap. They joined this awesome barrage to sweep that small, dead space with their own fire, leaving no place for the enemy to hide.

....

An artillery team fires 105mm howitzer rounds from Hill 881S.

American aircraft flew TPQ-10 (radar) missions and struck several hundred meters outboard of, and parallel to, the massive artillery bombardment; the aircraft rippled their bombs in continuous flights to provide multiple bands of defensive fires around Capt Breeding and his defending Marines.

On that very night, Capt Biag had suggested that the enemy was massing for an attack, but he had not identified Hill 861A as the final objective. During the previous night he had tracked NVA movement from the northwest of Captain Dabney's positions on 881S. The sensors had first gone active, then silent, and then active again, tattle-tailing the enemy's movement and direction. After 4 kilometers (2.5 miles), the column turned south, and when the sensors southeast of 881S did not activate, Biag knew the column had stopped south of Capt Dabney's Marines. He estimated the force to be something less than two thousand, and engaged them with artillery fire and bombing runs.

But on this night, Biag thought the approach movement was over and an attack was imminent. He predicted the enemy would assault in the thick mist, with their regiments in a column and their battalions on line. The sensors had identified the NVA assembly area to the south of Hill 881S. Biag designed a killing field, 1,000 meters wide by 300 meters deep (about 1,100 yards wide by 330 yards deep). In the concealed confines of the FSCC, the target information officer penciled a gently curving line on his map, spanning 1,000 meters from the northeast to the northwest, around the sloping base of the hill. He then connected that line with two short, vertical lines representing the 300-meter sides. A second 1,000-meter line formed the base of Biag's eccentric rectangle, and completed the box that would become his anvil; the hammer would be thirty minutes of sustained artillery fire.

Beginning at 0300, five batteries of 1/13 artillery and the four batteries of 175mm guns from Camp Carrol lit the skies with their lightning flashes and saturated the box, relentlessly sweeping every square foot. At Nakhon Phanom, the technicians listened as the acoustic sensors broadcast the sounds of hundreds of enemy soldiers screaming and running in panic.

After the bombardment, the silence was ominous, but the NVA were not finished. Since there had been no sensors seeded near Hill 861 and 861A, the ground attack on Hill 861A by a force that had obviously escaped Biag's detection came as a complete surprise. Biag was crestfallen, and cursed himself for missing the force, but stoically noted that his oversight had been rendered harmless by the heroic work of the Marines of Echo Company. Although the NVA had managed to achieve some initial success, they had only gained temporary control of a portion of the hill, "from which," Biag said, "Capt Breeding was energetically heaving them!"[29]

"When the sun finally did come up," observed PFC Newton Lyle, "we thanked God for the ones of us that had lived. I had to go around and help pull two of my best buddies out of Cpl Franklin's positions. Stevenson had been killed instantly, and we went to the next hole to get Red out, but he was still alive; he had claw marks on the wall where he had tried to get out."[30]

Echo Company lost seven Marines killed and thirty-five medevaced, but the NVA had not seized the high ground, and they left 109 of their comrades on yet another hill the Marines would not surrender.

CHAPTER 9

THE ATTACK FROM THE WEST: LANG VEI AND OUTPOST ALPHA

A Marine and an ARVN Ranger in the trenches at Khe Sanh Combat Base.

TIMELINE	APRIL 24, 1967	MAY 13, 1967	DECEMBER 1967	JANUARY 21, 1968	JANUARY 31, 1968
	Hill Fights begin at Khe Sanh	Hill Fights end. Marines fought off elements of the 325C NVA Division in a two-week battle that cost the enemy 824 KIA. 168 Marines were killed and 443 wounded in the struggle.	General Westmoreland decides to reinforce Khe Sanh in the face of enemy buildup.	NVA attack hill 861 and bombard combat base exploding ammo dump, and attack Khe Sanh village. Siege begins.	NVA launch countrywide Tet Offensive.

After two weeks of attack, NVA successes were small indeed. They had forced the two tiny Marine CAPs in Khe Sanh Village to abandon their positions, and simultaneously had driven back the one hundred seventy-five-man Regional Force from the same location. Those Khe Sanh village forces took up new defensive positions at the combat base itself. But the NVA had not been able to exploit these successes in their attempt to attack Khe Sanh Combat Base from the south.

1st Battalion, 9th Marines had moved swiftly and strategically placed its one thousand–man force astride that very avenue of approach immediately after the NVA occupied Khe Sanh Village. The enemy was faced with the task of driving in yet another outpost as a prelude to a general ground attack. One of the new outposts was 500 meters (about 550 yards) in front of 1/9's main lines, on a tiny hill called "Outpost Alpha," manned by a reinforced platoon of sixty-six men from Company A.

But before they could even think about tackling Outpost Alpha, the NVA had to face another obstacle, an old one, the Army Special Forces Camp at Lang Vei, nine kilometers to the west. At the time, the Special Forces strongpoint actually consisted of two positions: Old Lang Vei, defended by the five hundred twenty-man, 33rd Royal Laotian Battalion that had been driven from its position at Ban Houei Sane; and New Lang Vei, one-half mile to the east, manned by U.S. Army Special Forces advisors along with four hundred fifty Civilian Irregular Defense Group (CIDG) personnel. The new camp was well wired, had four mutually supporting company positions, and featured a new steel-reinforced concrete Tactical Operations Center (TOC).

No enemy force could drive to the east from Laos to Khe Sanh along Route 9 without confronting the two Lang Vei positions that sat astride the road, blocking any advance. But on January 30, the day before the Tet Offensive began, an NVA rallier turned himself in to the new camp, called A-101, and revealed that the NVA planned to attack the strongpoint.

....

DISK 2, TRACKS 10-12: Heavy casualties at Lang Vei and Outpost Alpha.

FEBRUARY 5-8, 1968	FEBRUARY 23, 1968	FEBRUARY 29, 1968	APRIL 14, 1968	JUNE 19-JULY 5, 1968
NVA attack Hill 861 Alpha, Lang Vei, and Hill 64.	Enemy gunners bombard base with more than 1,300 rounds in heaviest attack.	NVA launch regimental size attack against base.	Marines break out of siege and attack and seize Hill 881N.	Khe Sanh Combat Base is destroyed and abandoned by American forces.

Long Dinh Du from the 8th Battalion, 66th Regiment of the 304th NVA Division, had important information. Unlike the earlier rallier, La Thanh Tonc, who had revealed the attack plan on Khe Sanh because he had not been promoted, Du had been fighting around Khe Sanh since January 21 and was despondent over huge losses.

He had participated in the attacks on the District Headquarters and the CAP compounds, and his battalion was at half strength. Continued air strikes and artillery bombardment were further thinning his unit, and sensing a grim future with the NVA, he opted to run away.

Two nights previous, his battalion executive officer, accompanied by a squad of sappers, had conducted reconnaissance of the camp. Two scheduled attacks had been postponed, but Du warned of one in the near future. Armed with this information and knowledge of the recent armored attack at Ban Houei Sane, Capt Frank C. Willoughby, commanding A-101, ordered one hundred of the new M-72 LAAWs (Light Anti-Tank Assault Weapon). He used fifteen of the weapons for familiarization firing and placed the rest in readiness.

In addition to the M-72 weapons, the camp also had two 106mm and four 57mm recoilless rifles, two 4.2-inch mortars, and twenty-one combined 81mm and 60mm mortars. Nor was the position lacking in machine guns: Two .50-caliber guns supported by forty-nine .30-caliber guns and thirty-nine of the older

Chaplain Ray W. Stubbe conducts worship for Seabees constructing the Tactical Operations Center at Lang Vei, October 31, 1967. **OPPOSITE:** Lt Paul Longgrear (front) with his Army Special Forces team prior to their deployment to Vietnam.

Browning automatic rifles (BARs) made A-101 a formidable defensive position.[1]

But Willoughby had some political obstacles. The commander of the Laotian forces at Old Lang Vei did not want to communicate with, much less take orders from a mere captain. Col Soulang wanted someone of nearly equal rank to speak with, so LtCol Daniel F. Schungel, the Special Forces commander from Da Nang, assigned his field-grade officers to be present at Lang Vei on a rotating basis.

"Since we acquired the Lao Battalion, plus some twenty-two hundred dependents, it was my policy to keep one of the company's three field-grade officers at Lang Vei . . . " said Schungel. "I relieved LtCol Headley . . . the afternoon of 6 February."[2] A few hours earlier, three enemy mortar rounds had impacted in the defensive area. At 1800 enemy gunners zeroed in on the A-101 positions not with mortars, but with big artillery.

"We received forty to fifty rounds of 152mm artillery," said Capt Willoughby. "All the rounds landed in the southern-perimeter wire, mostly in the area of 104 Company."[3] Company 104 was in the southeastern corner of the camp.

"I was in the TOC at the time the rounds started to come in," said SSgt Peter Tiroch. "The initial rounds hit in 104 Company; Sgt Fragos went there to help the wounded, and I linked up with him, and we made an attempt to find the direction from which the rounds came by analyzing shell holes and using the lensatic compass."

Tiroch informed the command center of the direction of enemy fire, but when no counter-battery fire was forthcoming, he decided to do something on his own.

"I got frustrated . . . and went to the 4.2 position, 30 meters [33 yards] to the west . . . . LtCol Shungel and 1Lt Longgrear were already in this position. We put the 4.2 in as near a firing position as possible to the enemy guns, then, using maximum charge, Lt Longgrear passed the high-explosive rounds to LtCol Shungel, who passed them on to me, and I dropped them in the tube."[4]

The rounds may have landed close to the enemy gunners; after firing several rounds, the three Americans received new enemy bursts short and long of their gun, and heard a number of rounds whistle over their heads headed for Khe Sanh. By 1930 all enemy fire had stopped.

But a more ominous sound replaced that of NVA artillery. The ARVN forces at Company 104 reported noises to the south.

"They said it sounded like engines running," said Capt Willoughby. "At the same time, the Mobile Strike Force OP west of the camp reported hearing noises. Around 2100, three trip flares went off in that area; illumination was fired with negative results. The OP opened up with their small arms and automatic weapons, and pretty soon the entire camp had joined in."[5]

Another trip flare ignited an hour later, but in both instances, no enemy appeared on the other side of the wire or massed for an attack. Another hour went by.

"The first indication of an actual attack came at approximately 2330 hours," said Willoughby. "At that time, 104 Company reported that there were enemy troops in the wire, and opened up with small-arms and automatic-weapons fire. Next the Mobile Strike Force OP started receiving incoming mortar rounds. My observer in the tower of the TOC reported seeing lights on the road leading to [the south to] Lang Troai."[6]

Lang Troai sat close to the Laotian border where the boundary line suddenly gouged deeply into South Vietnam, away from the normal east-west line separating the two countries. Willoughby reported the unfolding events to the artillery Fire Support Coordination Center at Khe Sanh and also to his parent

ARVN Rangers at Khe Sanh. **OPPOSITE:** The Old Lang Vei Special Forces camp along Route 9 (in background).

unit, C Company, at Da Nang. The ARVN soldiers at 104 strained their eyes to the south. Then came a truly shocking report.

"About fifteen minutes later, my observer informed me that there were two tanks sitting in our outer perimeter," said Capt Willoughby. "I went up out of the TOC, and verified that there were indeed two tanks sitting there with their searchlights sweeping the hillside, looking for our camp positions. I was informed that 104 Company was fighting with enemy troops in their wire."[7]

Sgt Nicholas Fragos was on guard. "I saw two men cutting the wire in front of a vehicle," he said. "The vehicle later was identified as a tank. Both men were cut down by small-arms fire from the perimeter, and the tank turned on its spotlight for about thirty seconds . . . before running over the wire."[8]

Fragos ran down to the TOC and reported what he had seen. The tank was destroying the bunkers in the 104 Company area with its main gun and spraying the adjacent defensive positions with its machine gun. Fragos retrieved some LAAWs from his position and began to arm them.

"I managed to load them one by one, handing them over to LtCol Schungel, and he fired at the two visible tanks. At this time we heard the 106 recoilless rifle fire at the tanks, and one . . . caught fire."[9]

Sgt Richard H. Allen was at the Old Lang Vei camp when the battle began.

"I was awakened at 0015 by SP4 Johnson telling me that the other camp was being hit. From our position, there was nothing we could really do."[10]

"I don't know who awakened me," said Sgt Tiroch at the battle site, "but the sentence that stuck in my mind was 'There are tanks in the wire.' I ran to the 4.2 mortar . . . and started to fire illumination toward the southeast, where tanks had been reported. Intermittently we dropped a few rounds of HE [high-explosive], thinking that there was possibly a ground attack behind the tanks."[11]

Capt Willoughby had given precise coordinates to the artillery of the tanks sitting in the wire scanning with their searchlights, but from the time of his artillery request to actual firing, fifteen minutes had elapsed, and the tanks had moved into the 104 compound.

"If we had received it in time, we could have knocked out the tanks in the wire. We were manning our LAAWs and our 106s. 104 Company lasted about forty-five minutes, until a tank got into

their area and started destroying their position with its main battle gun."[12]

But the battle in Company 104 area had not been one-sided. Sergeant First Class James W. Holt manned the 106 recoilless rifle in the center of the camp. Holt, the senior medic of the A-101 detachment, now found himself behind the one weapon made precisely to counter this armored thrust.

Holt peered through his lensatic sight and fired a .50-caliber marking round that streaked in a red line and impacted on the lead tank. The weapon's elevation and deflection were perfect, and he pushed the firing handle in, unleashing an enormous, blinding back-blast. The antitank round screamed from the barrel and smashed into the first tank, stopping it dead in its tracks. Holt swiftly reloaded, and his second round found tank number two.

"It must have been around 0300 that I saw SFC Holt," said SSgt Tiroch. "There were plenty of people in the 4.2 pit at this time and Holt seemed to be alone. I ran to his position to assist him by loading the projectiles.

Capt Frank Willoughby talks to his troops at Lang Vei Special Forces camp, August 1, 1967.

This was actually the first time that I had seen the tanks, and noticed by the illumination that two of them were sitting still and burning right at the outer perimeter. Another tank was moving around the two wrecks. The illumination went out at this time and Holt was unable to see his target through the sight."

But Holt's blindness was only temporary.

"Seconds later another illumination was popped," said Tiroch, "and SFC Holt apparently got on target, because he fired the 106, and the [tank], which was now some distance inside the perimeter, took a hit and went up in flames. At this time I noticed that there was only one round of ammunition left . . . . I loaded it into the chamber and Holt hit the last tank one more time to finish the kill."[13]

Four rounds—three tank kills, but now the weapon was out of ammo. There was no report of fire from the second 106, and both men left the gun, Holt to search the ammo bunker, and Tiroch back to the mortar pit. As SFC Holt disappeared into the darkness, he walked into obscurity. No one ever saw him again.

Sgt Emanuel Phillips, the radio operator of the A-101 team, was located in the TOC.

"Under Capt Willoughby's direction, all efforts were directed toward stopping the tanks and coordinating air support," said Phillips. "Five or six artillery missions had been delivered by the Marines on the southern approaches to the camp, and had been adjusted up to the outer wire. Tanks had been reported to be controlling the 104 Company area, and NVA were . . . in the bunkers. A large enemy concentration was reported on the northern perimeter, and VT [variable time ammunition] was called."[14]

The rounds from Khe Sanh detonated in the air over the Lang Vei camp, sending their deadly steel shards to the ground. The defenders hunkered down and the attackers scrambled for cover. 1Lt Thomas Todd was in supply bunker No. 1.

"I observed an enemy tank drive in front of my position, heading in the direction of the TOC. My position took a direct hit from an enemy artillery round . . . . I vacated the now destroyed bunker, and proceeded to the emergency medical bunker. An enemy tank stopped in front of the entrance . . . and fired one round, point-blank, into the stairway . . . . Another tank had positioned itself in front of the rear exit, and fired into the rear door. The two tanks then departed. Another tank drove past the front entrance, heading toward the TOC; this tank was followed by fifty enemy troops."[15]

At the 4.2 mortar pit, Sgt Tiroch joined in the attempt to knock out the marauding tanks. The 106s were out of ammo, and the Special Forces soldiers organized into tank-killer teams. But the M-72 LAAW abandoned them.

"I pulled the safety forward and attempted to fire the LAAW but it failed to fire," said Tiroch. "1Lt Wilkins fired a LAAW, hitting in front [of the tank], with unknown results. The tank stopped again, apparently to find out where he was being attacked from. Wilkins attempted to fire the second LAAW, and it failed to fire."[16]

The tank moved on, unharmed by the fire from the Special Forces team. Tiroch threw three grenades, aiming at the tracks and the vulnerable rear end, but the explosions failed to stop the lumbering vehicle. Other men threw grenades with no effect, and finally Sgt Burke advanced laden with a new supply of

LAAWs. Lt Wilkins grabbed three of them, and fired as the tank moved toward the dispensary. Two of the weapons misfired impotently. The third hit on the turret, normally a killing shot, but the tank moved on like an elephant bitten by a fly.

Undaunted, Lt Wilkins grabbed two more LAAWs and raced after his target, now on a path toward Company 102's defensive positions. His first shot hit the left tread—no results. His second shot missed the tank completely as it rolled on in its attack. Wilkins returned to the ammo dump for more LAAWs, intent on continued pursuit. But it was Sgt Tiroch who took the next shot.

"At this time an artillery round landed in the POL [petroleum, oil, lubricant] dump and set it on fire. The tank's outline could be seen directly behind it. SSgt Brooks and myself ran to the top of the team house and got the .50-caliber machine gun, with an enormous belt of armor-piercing ammo, and set it up, and began firing at the tank, and saw some sort of secondary explosion."[17]

A tank that had closed on the fortified TOC bunker began firing on the hunkered-down Special Forces soldiers in the 4.2 mortar pit. It had fired point-blank into the stairwell of the bunker, and now turned its machine gun to the mortar pit. Tiroch and a half dozen other men crawled toward the teamhouse.

"We came to a decision to E & E [escape and evade] through the northern perimeter, since this seemed to be the only place where there was no visible activity," said Tiroch. "We had made our way through the inner wire barrier and were in the process of going over the triple concertina when we started receiving heavy machine-gun fire."

The men moved through the bamboo and found a dry creek bed, and stayed there for the rest of the night. "We could still hear tank engines in the camp to our rear," said Tiroch, "and constant explosions and machine-gun fire." [18]

The NVA tanks now closed in on the TOC. Despite their gallant defense, the infantry was not equal to the firepower of the tanks, and the LAAWs proved totally ineffective. One tank parked on top of the roof, hoping to crush the TOC.[19]

Col Schungel fought valiantly against two tanks that had bypassed the two destroyed in the wire. Finally one was on top of him.

"I am not sure how many times he [the tank] was struck by LAAWs, but at least five were required to immobilize him. On each impact, there would be a great shower of orange sparks. When the crew survivors crawled out, 1Lt Quy and I killed them with grenades and small-arms fire."

The second tank bore down on Schungel and his team. The tank was buttoned up and poured a steady stream of fire into the Americans. Then it unleashed the devastating fire of its main gun.

"We were taking cover by some 55-gallon drums filled with rocks," said Schungel. "The main armament hit our barrels and caved in the entrance to the TOC. Lt Wilkins was knocked unconscious and crushed between the barrels, and Specialist 5 McMurray was gravely wounded. I was knocked head over heels by the concussion."[20]

The NVA attack pressed on relentlessly. Forty-five minutes after the fall of the Company 104 defenses, they had rolled up Company 101, and had pushed the defenders into the center of the compound. The eastern end of the camp fell first, and shortly afterward, NVA tanks smashed into the Company 102 and 103 defenses and occupied the western positions.

Col Schungel and Lt Wilkins crept toward the teamhouse. Inside, Schungel pushed Wilkins behind the bar and took up a position in the center of the floor observing both entrances.

"I cut the inner tubes on the doors so they would stand open," said Schungel. "There were still intermittent flares going off and I had a pretty good view. I saw a party of five NVA—three with AK-47s and two with satchel charges—approaching the north door of the team house. They approached, all bunched up, and when they were 5 meters [16 feet] away, I shot them all with one magazine."[21]

Schungel and Wilkins sought cover under the dispensary and remained there until daylight, listening to marauding enemy soldiers, just a board's width above their heads, knocking over bottles and rummaging through the building. Meanwhile, the largest group of Special Forces and ARVN soldiers was hunkered down belowground in the TOC.

> ## "THE MAIN ARMAMENT HIT OUR BARRELS AND CAVED IN THE ENTRANCE TO THE TOC. LIEUTENANT WILKINS WAS KNOCKED UNCONSCIOUS AND CRUSHED BETWEEN THE BARRELS, AND SPECIALIST 5 MCMURRAY WAS GRAVELY WOUNDED. I WAS KNOCKED HEAD OVER HEELS BY THE CONCUSSION."

"I saw one tank moving toward the TOC," said Sgt Fragos, "so I went downstairs, as I had expended all my ammo. The whole front door had been blown away by a round from the tank. There were twenty-five Vietnamese packed into the TOC, and amidst all the confusion, we heard a large explosion from the tower. We imagined it was blown away. Hand grenades started dropping down the tower and a burst of flame exploded. The place caught on fire from all the paper lying around. The smoke was so thick that it made visibility impossible. The smoke also made breathing impossible unless you lay flat on the floor.

"I saw the Vietnamese Special Forces camp commander, coughing and speaking some Vietnamese to his people, and the next thing I saw was all the Vietnamese make it to the outside of the TOC. I waited five minutes and went toward the door, and I heard someone calling us in English, and I shoved my head slowly by the door and looked up outside. The stairs and the cover of the stairwell were blown off. Outside was real light from Spooky [C-47 gunship] dropping flares."[22]

Fragos could see several Vietnamese lined up around the exit on top. One asked him to come out, but in the next instant, Fragos saw a helmeted NVA soldier with his weapon pointed at the prisoners. More hand grenades cascaded down, and then the enemy dropped a huge charge down the air vent, which detonated with an enormous concussion, knocking everyone senseless. Fragos awoke after 0330 and assumed everyone

else was dead. As daylight came, he watched as aircraft strafed and bombed the compound. Then a relief force from old Lang Vei approached the battered compound. It was a company of Laotians, led by SFC Eugene Ashley, attempting to reach the survivors buried in the TOC.

But the Laotians were squeamish and had no stomach for battle, and when they encountered the slightest resistance, they turned and fled.

"We got to the hill at the end of the 101 Company," said Sgt Richard Allen of the relief force. "There we picked up enemy machine-gun fire. I was on the right flank, Johnson on the left, and Ashley in the middle. Before we could advance, the indigenous retreated."

"We spread the men out and went up the hill," said Specialist 4 Joel Johnson. "There were dead NVA with weapons and equipment all along the hill. The Laotians left me pinned down up there by two machine guns. We pulled back to the gate and called in air. Then from out of the bush came Sgt Tiroch and SFC Craig."[23]

Lt Paul Longgrear looks at a map while his team moves along Route 9.

Allen raced to halt the fleeing Laotians, and brought several back at the point of his gun. The force reformed and attacked again, this time through some sporadic mortar fire, but it was too much for the Laotians, and when the NVA threw grenades, they again withdrew. The Americans gathered parts of the scattered force and made two more assaults, but could advance no closer to the TOC.

On the fifth and final assault they almost made it.

"We assaulted once more," said Johnson. "Tiroch, Allen, and Ashley were on one side. I was on the other. This time we made it past the bunker, and I tied in with Tiroch's element. We started receiving fire from our front and our troops ran. I finally got some men to stop running and we tried to flank the other side. Then someone told me an American was hit, and I saw Allen dragging Sgt Ashley. I immediately started mouth-to-mouth respiration, and was still doing it when a 105mm round knocked me out."[24]

Despite all efforts to revive him, Sgt Ashley had been mortally wounded.[*]

The eight men in the TOC could only peek out and watch the air strikes.

"A-1 Skyraiders made pass after pass, dropping their loads of napalm and bombs," said Sgt Fragos. "About 1400, I saw the captain digging himself out of the rubble. I had thought him dead since the big explosion."

The Skyraiders strafing and bombing the compound, CANASTA flight, were directed in by COVEY-688.

"All the A-1 guys were wonderful," said Capt Charles Rushforth, circling overhead in support of 688. "They were crazy—all balls—zipping through those treetops, firing away.

"The 500-foot overcast . . . began to open up right over the compound. We dropped 500- and 250-pound bombs and napalm. The enemy was hurt but still effective. SPUNKY HANSON [Lang Vei call sign] said, 'They're all over us out there. If you don't come down and get them, we've had it. Give them everything you've got!'"[25]

The A-1s responded with just that: Cluster Bomb Units, napalm, and machine guns. Inside the TOC it was decision time.

"We decided that it was getting late, and it would be suicide to stay here another night," said Sgt Fragos. "We had been without water or food for over twenty-four hours. Everyone was physically exhausted and close to the point of shock. I had thrown up seven times from the smoke and the gas, causing me to be dehydrated and weak.

"We decided to make a break for it since no more rescue operations would be attempted, and at 1530 Capt Willoughby called in all the napalm and bombs that the Skyraiders had to cover our withdrawal. With 1Lt Longgrear in the lead, each one of us climbed the stairs and dashed towards the supply bunker . . . . The stairs were blown away; all that was left was a hole to climb out of. We made our way to Highway 9 as the planes made dummy passes over the camp in support of us."[26]

A jeep carrying Ashley's body picked up the survivors and took them to the old camp where helicopters ferried them to Khe Sanh. Most of the Special Forces team then flew to Da Nang. The enemy, with twelve tanks and four hundred infantry, had successfully overrun Lang Vei, but at a fearful price. They left seven

---

[*]For his heroism above and beyond the call of duty, SFC Eugene Ashley was awarded the Medal of Honor, posthumously.

tanks smashed on the battlefield and two more heavily damaged. The Lang Vei defenders had not broken and run, but had stood and killed more than two hundred enemy soldiers.

The U.S./South Vietnamese forces had suffered heavily. There were more than two hundred killed or missing, including ten of the twenty-four Americans. But despite being overrun, the camp had stopped the attack, and the NVA was unable to advance closer to Khe Sanh. Still, the NVA had rolled back their first outpost.

News of the enemy attack spread like wildfire through the press. Headlines reported the enemy's "first use of armor." Of course, it was not. The attack at Ban Houei Sane two weeks earlier had been the first use.

Now the NVA attempted to drive in the second outpost, at Hill 64,* called Outpost Alpha, located 500 meters (about 550 yards) south of 1/9's defensive position at the rock quarry. Two officers and sixty-four enlisted men from 1st Platoon and the Weapons Platoon of Company A had occupied the outpost since January 23. The small, football-shaped knob was 40 meters long (about 130 feet) and half that wide, and steep sides

*Hill 64 did not refer to altitude and was most likely named because of the sixty-four men defending it.

A CH-54 "Sky Crane" carries a Jeep above Khe Sanh Combat Base. **OPPOSITE:** Jose Ruiz, a rifleman with 1/9 at Outpost Alpha, was killed in action in 1968.

protected the perimeter. Only on the northwestern end was the slope less than 45 degrees.

A trench encircled the perimeter, with bunkers connected to the trench line, and artillery and mortar concentrations ringed the entire outpost. Outpost Alpha's mission was to be the eyes and early warning for the entire battalion for any enemy attack coming from the south, the most likely avenue of approach.

"We had been getting probed constantly," said PFC George A. Einhorn. "Lang Vei got overrun the day before, and the main base camp was getting hit all the time. We were like on the gravy train out on Outpost Alpha."[27]

"When we arrived on Outpost Alpha, they said, 'This is where we're going to be. Start digging,'" said LCpl David Ford. "And we dug, and dug, and dug, it seemed like twelve hours a day. We were all exhausted but were under pressure to hurry up and dig deep, and build these bunkers, and get the wire up. We had not heard about Lang Vei being overrun. They just had us on alert. The NVA were probing our lines. At night you'd hear them moving about, around the wire, and that was a constant thing, so I didn't have any idea that we would be overrun; nobody did. It just came out of the blue."[28]

Under the cover of darkness and the overcast, a battalion of the 325C Division had moved into position to attack the outpost, not from the south, toward NVA lines, but from a position to the northwest, between the outpost and the friendly lines of 1/9. It was there that the slope was not as steep.

"They probably had been watching us for days, and we had a bad habit," said eighteen-year-old machine gunner LCpl Arnold Alderette. "I never cleaned my weapon on top of the bunker, but I know that the other squad always did so they could get the bright sunlight; so they knew exactly where our main weapons were. Our bunkers were about 8 feet in length and 6 feet wide. They were designed especially for the machine guns. We used a deeper hole so that we could stand and fire out of the parapet.

"When the battle began, I was on watch. It was pretty clear, pitch black, but a clear evening. It started out with a bugle. As soon as the bugle went off, my thought was that just a couple of days before someone had said that there were elephants carrying enemy supplies. So when I heard this bugle, my first thought was: 'My God, they're using elephants on us.' I was afraid that elephants could crumple up anything, and then there were several explosions right off the bat, and then small-arms fire. Then all hell broke loose from behind us."[29]

The attacking battalion first saturated the Marines at the rock quarry with three hundred fifty rounds of various fire to prevent any support to Hill 64, and then, at 0400, assaulted the outpost. Bangalore torpedoes blew holes in the wire and the NVA poured through. At other positions, they rolled over the wire on canvas covers.

"I was in my bunker," said 2Lt Francis B. Lovely Jr., commanding the Marines from the Weapons Platoon. "I heard a loud explosion, and ran out into the trench line and discovered we were being hit by a large enemy force. As I ran down the trench line, I ran into three NVA who had already penetrated the perimeter. Lt Roach, the platoon commander, had run across the top of the hill to try and bring in our on-call defensive fires. He was shot almost immediately by an NVA soldier who leaped up on a bunker and took him under fire. He was killed instantly. At that time, I took over the first platoon in defense of the hill. The NVA had penetrated our perimeter approximately two-thirds of the way through our hill, and controlled a great many of our grenades and our ammunition."[30]

LCpl James Rizzo transmitted frantically to battalion. "We got hit. Come and get us. We need help."[31] But there was no help, and moments later Rizzo fell in a hail of gunfire, mortally wounded in the chest.

"I HAD THE M-79 AND WAS THE GRENADIER," SAID PFC GEORGE EINHORN. "I KEPT FIRING IT STRAIGHT UP INTO THE AIR BECAUSE THAT'S HOW CLOSE THEY WERE TO US."

By 0500 the Marine position was reduced to one fifth of the hill. Still, the NVA could not push them off this last bit of terrain. The surviving Marines fought as individuals, and in twos and threes.

Pvt Lawrence Seavy-Cioffi moved about the position, exposing himself to fire, throwing grenades and collecting weapons from the destroyed bunkers and trenches.[33] As the artillery forward observer, he had been unable to get concentrations fired due to the proximity of friendlies, confusion, and lack of approval from Lt Roach. The young Marine collected twenty rifles that Cpl Edward O'Connor was able to put back into service.

"They came in from the rear," said Alderette. "You could see they came swarming just from the other side of the hill, which is where Cpl Burkhead had his machine gun. On top of the hill, the trenches were being held on the right-hand side. We had handed one of the machine guns over to PFC Raymond Rosales. He was keeping that right side pretty well, plus the forward observer [Seavey-Cioffi] was on that side, too. Lt Lovely was in the bunker, calling for reinforcements and artillery.

"We ran short of grenades . . . . Just to keep them on their toes and not to be tempted to charging, we would throw rocks. And when they wouldn't go off, then the enemy would come in and rush us again, and that's when we would throw the real grenades."[34]

"Everybody was busy fighting back and forth," said Cpl David Ford. "Alderette and I were on the top of the hill, and in the center of it, and were charging back and forth, and left to right and over toward the other far side where the enemy was. We were overrun and the NVA had two-thirds of the hill.

"There was a lull, and he had the gun [resting] on my shoulder, and we raised up and there were three of them, and they just fired point-blank at us. We didn't have many grenades, and were really getting desperate. Throwing the grenades had pretty much wiped out any chance they had of attacking. They really quieted down after a while, but we didn't know how many were left or how many were still coming up the hill, so we started throwing rocks, or a C-ration can, to keep them off guard."[35]

"I had the M-79 and was the grenadier," said PFC George Einhorn. "I kept firing it straight up into the air because that's how close they were to us. We kept moving constantly because every time I fired a round, I was getting grenaded. The M-79 made a big flash. It was a dead giveaway.

"Everybody was helping everybody. We pretty well expended the grenades, and we were under illumination, and Alderette started throwing rocks at them. He came running down to me and said, 'Get that grenade launcher, get that 79 moving all around the hill.' I asked, 'Where the hell am I going to fire it? I'm going to fire it on top of us.' And he said, 'Well, fire it straight up.' I didn't know where it was going to land. It was like a mortar."[*36]

At 0730 LtCol Mitchell had a relief column headed for Hill 64, still grudgingly held by the Marine defenders. By 0900 Company A commander, Capt Henry J. M. Radcliffe had reestablished contact with his beleaguered force, and after direct tank fire and air strikes, led a frontal assault over the crest and routed the remnants of the NVA force.

The attempt to take Outpost Alpha had cost the NVA force one hundred fifty dead, and their attacking force was shattered and in full retreat, hounded by the ever-present fighters, bombers, and gunships that pounced on their straggling formations. Marine casualties were terrible. Of the sixty-six defenders, twenty-one had been killed and twenty-six wounded. LtCol Mitchell pulled his battered force off the hill and incorporated them back into his lines. They had given him an early warning, stopped the attack, and held on until help arrived. His battalion stood intact in its defensive position, and the 325C Division was no closer to attacking the main defenses of the base than they had been two weeks earlier.

Thousands of miles away, President Johnson was a very worried man. His gloom was as heavy as the fog at Khe Sanh. He often wandered the hallways of the White House in the wee hours of the morning, making frequent stops in the Situation Room.[37] There he could chat with the duty officer, see reports from pilots returning from bombing missions, and study the features of the terrain map of Khe Sanh. Certainly as his eyes identified the outpost hills, the base, the runway, and then swept up the imposing slopes of the enemy-held terrain, his thoughts must have turned to the Alamo. Had Travis, Bowie, and Crockett been reincarnated into the persons of Lownds, Dabney, and Breeding?

*Thirty years later, PFC Einhorn, Cpls Ford and Feasel, and LCpl Rizzo (posthumously) each received the Bronze Star for heroism. In 2002, PFC Seavey-Cioffi was awarded the Silver Star, and Cpl O'Connor received the Bronze star.

On February 17, the president went to the Marine air station at El Toro, California, to see off the Marines of the 27th Regiment. He told them, " . . . the eyes of history itself are on that little brave band of defenders who hold the pass at Khe Sanh . . . . "[38]

The press found Khe Sanh irresistible. They goaded Col Lownds for comments, frequently bringing up the Dien Bien Phu comparison. Lownds delighted in tweaking them, and even feigned ignorance of the 1954 battle.

"My mission is to stay here, damn it, and we're going to stay here. It's only a question of how much Giap is willing to lose. I would hope it would cost him forty thousand to fifty thousand men, maybe more. What's there to panic about? We're here to stay. That's our job; that's what we get paid for."[39]

The reporter Michael Herr best presented the press's fixation with Khe Sanh and its perception of impending doom when he formulated a question for Lownds that he never asked. He wrote of a situation

....

President Lyndon B. Johnson at the White House in early 1968. **OPPOSITE:** Capt Bill Dabney (center) and his men in a bunker on Hill 881S.

where hordes of the enemy attacked, in human waves, absorbing all the death and destruction the Americans could dish out, and still advanced, undaunted.

"And what if they pass over every barricade we put in their way . . . and kill everything, defending or retreating . . . and take Khe Sanh?" he silently wondered.[40]

For the Marines, this all seemed a bit concocted. There was no gloom and doom. Capt Dabney said, "I never detected any fatalism or negative attitude. We had B-52s, and they were awesome when you turned them loose. We figured we could handle anything that came in close if they could break up the attack; and they could damn sure break up an attack. It never crossed my mind that the NVA had the capability to overrun an outpost of six thousand Marines."[41]

Capt Harry Biag was more succinct. "Newspaper correspondents never knew of the total weight and effectiveness of our artillery. Inexperienced as they were, they magnified the volume of enemy incoming and disregarded the relative ineffectiveness of the enemy artillery. The siege clearly established not only the bankruptcy of the NVA master plan, but also the ineptitude of their vaunted artillery. The press never saw this clearly."[42]

CHAPTER 10

THE VULGAR FREE-FOR-ALL

The combat base perimeter and Hill 861 during the siege.

TIMELINE	**APRIL 24, 1967**	**MAY 13, 1967**	**DECEMBER 1967**	**JANUARY 21, 1968**	**JANUARY 31, 1968**
	Hill Fights begin at Khe Sanh	Hill Fights end. Marines fought off elements of the 325C NVA Division in a two-week battle that cost the enemy 824 KIA. 168 Marines were killed and 443 wounded in the struggle.	General Westmoreland decides to reinforce Khe Sanh in the face of enemy buildup.	NVA attack hill 861 and bombard combat base exploding ammo dump, and attack Khe Sanh village. Siege begins.	NVA launch countrywide Tet Offensive.

If the press did not clearly understand Capt Biag's "vulgar free-for-all," and the sheer weight of American air and artillery on the encircling enemy, the NVA soldiers on the receiving end did. As the siege progressed, the landscape around Khe Sanh turned from green and lush and primitively beautiful to scarred, bombed-out, and cratered. Except for those areas occupied by friendly forces, hardly a square foot of the terrain had escaped the devastation of Operation Niagara.

Every avenue of approach to the battle area had been pummeled by continuous hammer strokes of bombs and shells. The entire 304th NVA Division occupied the area west and south of the combat base. Hoai Phong, a soldier of the 9th Regiment, described the constant bombardment.

"Here the war is fiercer than in all other places. It is even fiercer than in Co Roong or Dien Bien Phu. All of us stay in underground trenches, except the units that engage in combat. B-52s continue to pour bombs onto the area.

"If someone came to visit this place, he might say that this is a storm of bombs and ammunition which eradicated all living creatures and vegetation . . . even those located in caves . . . ."[1]

Another NVA soldier wrote: "U.S. forces are stronger than we were told in North Vietnam. When the 5th Battalion began infiltrating into South Vietnam, its strength was over five hundred men . . . . Malaria and bombs cut strength to two hundred men."

Soldiers in the 324th Division experienced continuing hardship. A captured diary revealed an element of despair.

"Rice is almost depleted and so is our salt. Dissension rose between the unit's soldiers and the political cadre. The situation is becoming worse due to lack of food, sleep, and worries. I feel too weak."[2] And again, "The heavy bombing of the jets and B-52 explosions are so strong that our lungs hurt."[3]

But despite heavy casualties, the enemy was still there, poised for a final attack to drive the Marines

DISK 2, TRACKS 13-18: Daily life under siege.

FEBRUARY 5-8, 1968	FEBRUARY 23, 1968	FEBRUARY 29, 1968	APRIL 14, 1968	JUNE 19-JULY 5, 1968
NVA attack Hill 861 Alpha, Lang Vei, and Hill 64.	Enemy gunners bombard base with more than 1,300 rounds in heaviest attack.	NVA launch regimental size attack against base.	Marines break out of siege and attack and seize Hill 881N.	Khe Sanh Combat Base is destroyed and abandoned by American forces.

from Khe Sanh. For the Marines to remain in position and continue to confront the enemy meant they had to be resupplied. Col Lownd's five battalions required 185 tons of supplies a day, every day, rain or shine—all delivered by air.

Under perfect conditions, it was a daunting task, but the conditions at Khe Sanh Combat Base were far from perfect. Visibility was poor most of the time, and the NVA gunners had zeroed in on the runway, converting it into a gauntlet-run. An aircraft had to approach from the east, over the steep ravine, since the only turnout was on the far western end of the strip.

After a steep approach, the pilot "planted" the aircraft and rolled out while standing on the brakes to ensure making the turn onto the nearest taxiway to the unloading apron. Making that turn was critical. A miss sent the plane to the far taxiway, and the far taxiway meant a stop in the unloading area, a turn-around, and a retrace of the aircraft's path to ensure enough runway for takeoff.

By making the first taxiway, the aircraft never had to stop moving. The ramp went down; arriving men jumped out and ran for cover as incoming rounds impacted. The crew pushed the pallets out, and departing

Parachutes carry supplies into Khe Sanh. **OPPOSITE:** A small parachute pulls a palette out of the back of a C-130 aircraft—one of many delivery systems used to resupply the combat base.

men jumped on. Wounded men were hustled out and placed on the floor on stretchers, and the aircraft made a right turn at the far taxiway, and a second right turn back onto the runway for takeoff, back to the east.

"The Marines on the ground did not want us in there," said Capt Doug Spitler, pilot of a C-130 of the 35th Tactical Airlift Squadron. "Our nickname was 'mortar magnets.'"[4]

But there were other ways to deliver supplies without landing. The air forces developed several systems for parachute drops. PLADS was the acronym for Parachute Low Altitude Delivery System whereby the aircraft flew 200 feet off the ground. The loadmaster lowered the ramp, released the locks on the pallets, and deployed a small parachute that dragged a larger one out the back of the plane. The larger chute then dragged the pallet out, which made one large, 90-degree swing, and hit the ground.

"Our crew was PLADS-qualified," said Spitler, "and they told us that the DZ [drop zone] was not secure. In other words, half a mile out was bad-guy territory."

Spitler's C-130 was carrying a planeload of ammunition, with all the pallets rigged in chutes for the drop.

"The problem was they had three very badly wounded Marines that they had field dressed and needed to get to Da Nang . . . because these guys were going to die if they didn't. 'What can you guys do? Can you land?'

"I talked it over with my crew. 'Captain, whatever you want to do is OK with us,' and I said, 'Well let's go get those guys.'"

The C-130 circled and the crew dismantled everything for the airdrop. Fighter aircraft came in to suppress enemy ground fire, and when all was ready, Spitler and his crew went in.

"It was very important we make the first turnoff," said Spitler. "We were very heavily loaded with five pallets of ammunition. But we just planted the aircraft in there in the first two or three hundred feet of runway. It's what they call an 'assault landing.' We just stood on the brakes to make the turnoff, and we did.

"We turned left, and the loadmaster opened the doors and got the ramp down. We turned right and went up the load ramp, and he said he was ready. I said, 'Dump it out. Go.'

"They had the three wounded ready. They just ran them on the plane, and just laid these guys on the floor. There wasn't time to set up the stanchions, or strap them in properly. We started taxiing and the loadmaster got the ramp up, and the first mortars came in—four or five of them. The tower said, 'Take off at your discretion.' They really didn't have a tower at Khe Sanh, just some controller in his bunker. It wasn't like we had a big traffic jam."

Spitler taxied and made his two right turns onto the runway, just as a mortar round hit one of the ammunition pallets he had just delivered and blew it up. Other mortars tracked the taxiing C-130.

....

A mortar explodes near the combat base airstrip.

"Then the mortars really started coming in," said Spitler. "One hit two or three hundred yards in front of us, right in the middle of the runway. We were already up to 60 knots, and now we were very light, and we just, kind of, raised the nose gear up over this little hole, and just flew through the smoke. Our total time on the ground was four minutes."[5]

The C-130 roared off the runway, flew to the east, and delivered the wounded men to Da Nang. For his action at Khe Sanh, Capt Douglas Spitler was awarded the Distinguished Flying Cross.

On February 10 all C-130 traffic was stopped from landing at Khe Sanh indefinitely after an aircraft carrying fuel bladders came in from the east and attempted to land.

"When Air Force aircraft were inbound, we would position ourselves over the eastern end of the runway," said 1Lt Tom O'Toole, an AO (air observer) flying in a tiny Cessna 01 Bird Dog. O'Toole was no stranger to the Khe Sanh battlefield. During the Hill Fights of 1967, he was awarded the Distinguished Flying Cross as a helicopter pilot for a heroic medical evacuation mission on Hill 881.

"When he came in and landed, we could pinpoint where the enemy .50 calibers were, and after the airplane left, we could go around and take care of them.

"When the C-130 came in, he came down, and shots were fired, so he pulled back up again. He came in from the east, as normally they do, went to touch down, took some .50-caliber fire and immediately pulled off to the right, and he took some hits that apparently started a fire inside. He hiked it around to the left, and tried to land back on the runway again, but when he did, he came in so hard and so fast, that when he touched down, you literally could see the entire PSP [matting] shift. And then he bounced back up into the air, and tried to come back down again, but when he did, his right landing gear was off the runway. Right next to the runway there were trenches and sandbags. At that point he was skidding down the runway. His right landing gear off the runway, his left on the runway, and the runway was scraping the entire bottom of the aircraft, which is causing more fire and friction, and at that point, everything blew."[6]

Two explosions rocked the plane as fire crews rushed out to spread foam. Several crewmembers were rescued, but six men perished in the resulting inferno.

With the base closed to C-130 traffic, they now had to rely on helicopters and parachute drops for resupply. Also complicating matters, 20 percent of Col Lownds' Marines were not at the base; they were on the hilltop outposts, and the hilltops were hardly suited to receive parachute drops. The supplies first had to arrive at the combat base to be repackaged and reloaded for helicopter delivery. The hills were also under constant enemy surveillance, and slow-flying helicopters approaching the hilltops were lucrative targets for NVA gunners.

"The problem was the enemy's capability to invest the hill with antiaircraft capability," said Capt Bill Dabney, who was on Hill 881S. "Normal helicopter operations were simply not possible. After you've lost four or five helicopters in the first couple of weeks, you say to yourself, 'We've got to have another way to do this,' because every time you lost a helicopter, it took two more to come in and pick the casualties up from that mess.

"One or two helicopters would fly up unescorted to the hill. With an internal load, you had to have a working party to unload the damn thing, and secondly, the helicopter was on the ground for two, three, or

four minutes. You couldn't hear the mortars pop, because it was sitting there gyrating. Inevitably in that sort of situation, the enemy would bracket, and then hit it; and if they had preregistered on that zone, they would hit the bird often with their first 120mm mortar round. It just wasn't working."[7]

Five choppers were shot down trying to resupply Hill 881S. The standard joke among helicopter pilots was that it was easy to find the Company I position. "Just look for the downed choppers. India always marks their zone that way."[8]

Finally the Marines came up with the solution for resupply. They called it the Supergaggle, and on February 24, they flew their first mission. The resupply would no longer be flown from Khe Sanh; the supplies would be staged and rigged in external cargo nets at Dong Ha, 30 miles to the east.

Simultaneously, 100 miles to the south, twelve A-4 aircraft would launch from Chu Lai as the sixteen CH-46 helicopters lifted off from Dong Ha with their cargo nets swinging from the external hooks under their bellies. Like a great gaggle of geese, the 46s choppered toward the combat base. The A-4s arrived at the same time.

The first four A-4s roared in with explosive and napalm bombs, pounding known enemy positions. Two more followed with CS tear gas, and two delivered smoke to blind and choke the enemy as the choppers

....

A CH-46 helicopter delivers supplies to hill 881S during a Supergaggle operation. **OPPOSITE:** Dabney (left) and his men on the radio on Hill 881S.

approached the hilltops. Then, as they descended with their 4,000-pound loads, the final four A-4s strafed suspected enemy positions with 20mm cannon fire, rockets, and bombs.

"The system essentially involved, for one minute, suppressing the antiaircraft fire on the hill," said Capt Dabney. "You could get . . . coming in echelons of four or five at once, ten helicopter loads in.[9]

"Upward of twenty 46s would make the resupply in one, simultaneous super-lift. They flew at high altitude past the Khe Sanh Combat Base to the hills, then went in daisy-chain fashion, one after another. They would saturate the LZ with enough supplies to last several days."[10]

"After the fixed-wing went in, we started in on our run, picking up very short separation between aircraft," said Capt Andrew Adams about a resupply run to 881S. "They planned on fitting two in the zone at a time. We came down from 6,000 feet at 120 knots: 2000-feet-per-minute descent. We had to descend to the west and then whip back in to the right to get into the zone. As we descended, a cloud moved over the target area and the only thing we could see was the bottom of the hill and the side of it. As number one entered the cloud, he was receiving .50-caliber fire. The rest of us followed the leader and went right in behind him. After we got into the cloud, we had to pick out our various LZs. This was done quite rapidly to get out of the zone as quickly as possible."[11]

As the aircraft swarmed in the confined air space around Khe Sanh, the chances for midair collisions were enormous. The pilots also knew that some of the low-hanging clouds contained 3,000-foot mountains.

"During a flight back from Khe Sanh to Quang Tri, I came closer to being wiped out, in one swipe, than during any of my other close calls in Vietnam," said Capt C. G. "Jug" Gerard, who flew a Huey helicopter with VMO-6.

"We were just comfortably cruising home at 5,000 feet, and 500 feet above a solid layer of cloud cover. The sun was setting behind us and it was a beautiful, placid setting at the end of a hectic day. Then, *BOOM*, a Marine VMCJ RF-4 [an attack aircraft] punches right up in front of us, through the clouds, going straight up! It was less than 100 feet in front of us. They never saw us. They passed so close, I could see both crewmen looking away. I could see the details: the green-and-orange pattern on the backs and tops of their hard hats; every word on the side of their aircraft, as well as the afterburner cones from the tail pipes.

"Almost immediately, we passed through the turbulence from the jet, which pitched and rolled us out of control. I fought to regain control of my aircraft, and in just seconds, all was quiet and calm again. Our helicopter was unscathed, but my flight suit sustained major damage in certain areas."[12]

At 1245 on February 21, the NVA prepped the 37th ARVN Ranger Battalion with three hundred fifty rounds of mixed artillery, mortars, and rocket fire. They followed the barrage with a probe of the line, but after a brief firefight, they withdrew. This type of probe was a technique the NVA had used against the French to find weak points in the line prior to its main attack. Once they found a weak point, they usually dug trenches to get their assaulting units close to the jump-off point.

There were only five clear days in February. The 23rd was not one of them as Gen Earle Wheeler's aircraft touched down in Saigon for his visit to Gen Westmoreland. The Chairman of the Joint Chiefs of Staff was there to make his own evaluation of the Khe Sanh/Tet situation so he could report to President Johnson who had "some hard decisions" to make.[13]

Gen Westmoreland found Wheeler a "tired man . . . near the point of exhaustion." The doomsday reporting irked Wheeler, who said that the press had painted the Tet Offensive as "the worst calamity since Bull Run."[14] To make matters worse, and to add to Wheeler's depression, the NVA chose February 23 to unleash its biggest bombardment yet of the siege on Khe Sanh. Enemy gunners pounded the base with more than 1,300 rounds of rocket, mortar, and artillery fire, killing ten men and destroying 1,620 rounds of 90mm and 106mm

A reconnaissance team from Company B, 3rd Reconnaissance Battalion gathers on the combat base airstrip. **OPPOSITE:** Identification papers found on the body of a dead NVA soldier.

ammunition. When the smoke cleared, aerial observers noticed fresh diggings in the area to the south of the base. Closer scrutiny identified them as infantry approach trenches.[15]

But Gen Westmoreland was optimistic; he was ready to exploit the enemy's Tet defeat and heavy losses. The Communists had not pulled off their vaunted "general uprising." In fact, there was growing evidence that the enemy soldiers had not only been defeated, but they had also been rejected by the population in the south.

"The day of my enlistment . . . is the most glorious day of my life," wrote one soldier from the NVA 324th Division. "I left behind me the old mothers, children, brothers, sisters, and comrades who smiled, thinking of the day I would come back after annihilating the U.S. aggressors."[16]

But the euphoria of that soldier was diminished by the realities of war and the battlefield around Khe Sanh. His diary reflected the change.

"For three months we walked and walked, but nowhere were we welcomed as we had been told. Nowhere did people welcome us with open arms. We expected, out of nine million people, some would come to welcome us since we were from the North."[17]

Another soldier detailed the hardships of the trek to the south.

"When we went through the woods, we only ate rice and salt. Many couldn't endure such a regimen, caught malaria, and couldn't walk. First they carried them on stretchers, but little by little, they left them behind. They were left in the bush and died. In my company, there were twenty who died in such a way. We were demoralized."[18]

The rain of steel in the Khe Sanh battle area was more reason for NVA soldiers to be demoralized. Captured NVA documents revealed terrible casualties on the attackers. After five weeks in the attack at Khe Sanh, the 1st Battalion, 9th Regiment of the NVA 304th Division had only 283 remaining soldiers to fight. Sixty-four had died, 83 had been wounded, and 85 had deserted. Several days later, there were 18 more casualties, and 61 more deserters had further reduced the ranks to 204.

Bad news spread quickly among the enemy. Three hundred men of Infiltration Doan [Group] 926 deserted as soon as they reached Khe Sanh.[19]

Gen Westmoreland wanted to press his advantage with offensive operations, including severing the Ho Chi Minh Trail network and raiding sanctuaries in Laos.[20] He wanted to destroy the enemy's ability to supply the war in the south, and to proceed with the offensive operations. Gen Wheeler listened and carried Westmoreland's troop request back to President Johnson.

Despite continuing bombardment, the NVA approach trenches crept forward each day. The trenches began just northeast of Hill 471 and paralleled the access road to the base from Route 9. They then crossed the road and zigzagged along a tree line and terminated by the garbage dump, close to the southern defensive wire. A second parallel trench system approached the Khe Sanh lines from the southeast, from Route 9. The network of those trenches ended close to the lines manned by the 37th ARVN Rangers and farther to the northeast by the eastern end of the runway.

In addition to the trenches, the Marine hilltop outposts reported digging. On Hill 861A, Capt Earle Breeding's men reported tunneling into the side of the hill, less than 20 meters (65 feet) from the defensive wire on the steep, northwestern face of the hill.

Forward air controller Capt Charles Rushforth, flying COVEY 252, watched the trenches creep forward within 300 meters (330 yards) of the combat base.

"I saw more high-speed trenches right up to the southern perimeter of the base," he said. "I saw guys in the trenches—two hundred plus. Who's friendly? I buzzed them, and the guys in the field waved; the others in the trenches, just 500 meters [about 550 yards] away, sat. We zipped over them and started to pull the turn. Then the whole world opened up. The ground troops yelled on their radios, 'Hey, COVEY, get out of there! They're really hosing you down!'"[21]

> # I SPOTTED THREE NVA, AND WE OPENED UP ON THEM BUT WE COULDN'T FIND THEM AGAIN. WE STARTED FOLLOWING, AND AS WE GOT UP ALONG THE ROAD, THEY OPENED UP ON US WITH AK-47S AND CHICOM GRENADES.

On the morning of February 25 the Marines tasked a patrol to make a diamond-shaped sweep from the wire to the south, along the garbage dump road. The patrol's mission was to recon the area and locate an enemy mortar that had been attacking the Marines. Two squads (1st and 3rd) from the 3rd Platoon of Company B—reinforced with headquarters' personnel, a mortar FO, 3.5-inch rockets, and two machine guns—would make the patrol, a total of forty-seven men.

"There were three checkpoints," said Capt Kenneth Pipes, commanding Company B, "and beyond the third checkpoint they were to re-enter our lines in the vicinity of the 1st Platoon, which was standing by as a reaction force in case 3rd platoon ran into some problems. The patrol was to depart 0800 and return 1000."[22]

2Lt Donald Jacques was in command, under strict order to remain within sight of the defensive wire and on the patrol route. Unknown to him, his route would take him between the two NVA trench systems.

"Our mission was to locate an 82mm mortar position," said HM3 Frank Calzia, the platoon corpsman. "We moved out at 0800 and proceeded through the trash pit. We noted a trench had been dug by the NVA, and the trench half-encircled the trash pit and went down the face of a small hill, across a river, and up the face of another small hill, and then around it and out of sight. We proceeded down this trench for 30 meters (about 33 yards), then decided to move out and continue our patrol as planned."[23]

"On the first advance, we saw 82mm mortar positions," said PFC Calvin Bright, a rifleman in LCpl Thrasher's fire team, "and as we advanced through the trench line we noticed there was a trench dug all the way from the ridgeline to the trash pit, 2 to 3 feet deep and

a foot wide. We reached the top of the ridge, and there was a large tree line, and as we advanced along the edge of the tree line, I spotted three NVA, and we opened up on them but we couldn't find them again. We started following, and as we got up along the road, they opened up on us with AK-47s and ChiCom grenades.

"Our fire team was over to the left, and our point man was hit almost immediately. I was pretty well out in the open. There was a road that led right to the village, down in the valley, and I was right beside the trench line. I jumped in it and was pretty well concealed. The trench was L-shaped—it ran 15 to 20 meters [16 to 22 yards], and turned to the right. Directly to the right there was thick shrubbery and they had a machine-gun nest right there.

"At first, we succeeded in having fire superiority over the enemy. Then all of a sudden they had rein-forcements that came up, and they gained superiority over us, and that's when the lieutenant told us to break contact and pull back. Our fire team leader was hit, and I tried to cover him as much as possible. We were pulling back by fire and maneuver, and we went down the valley, through the rice paddy, over the stream, and up the other side of the ridge. And there was no cover at all, and we were getting sniper fire."*[24]

PFC Alexander Tretiakoff started the firefight staring the enemy in the face.

"I was standing face-to-face with this one NVA, and I wanted to shoot him, but my rifle wouldn't shoot. I took the magazine out and threw it away, and put another one in. To my right was a lance corporal and PFC McKenzie, and McKenzie was shot. The lieutenant crawled up to him, and took his weapon, and the

---

*For their heroic action, PFC Calvin Bright and HM3 Frank Calzia were awarded the Bronze Star.

....

An NVA spider hole found on patrol near Hill 881S.

enemy was firing from my right and from my left. And then the NVA got heavy automatic-weapons and machine-gun fire on us. Lieutenant Jacques told us to pull back."[25]

"I noticed that the third squad had been wiped out," said HM3 Frank Calzia. "There was no one left. The lieutenant decided to pull back because of heavy casualties. We couldn't take all the bodies with us, so we pulled back and just took the wounded. We had to move very slowly because of the wounded man. When we got across the open plain, down into the rice paddy, we started getting small-arms sniper fire from in the tree line, so the lieutenant said we had to make it up to the tree line near the road. Right at the tree line, the lieutenant was mortally wounded. So from there it was left to the patrol to struggle back to the perimeter, carrying the wounded and the lieutenant's body."[26]

"When we started to pull back across the road, I looked around, and I was the only man that was left," said PFC Kenneth R. Totten Jr. "The lieutenant was talking on the radio, and he was hit three times by sniper fire."*[27]

"I was on the left flank," said LCpl Thrasher, "and when we pulled back, there were only two of us, me

*PFC Kenneth Totten was later killed, on March 30, 1968.

PFC Calvin Bright (right) and another Marine emerge from the ambush, February 25, 1968.

and PFC Bright. Frank Calzia was with us too. We were located approximately 1,300 meters [1,400 yards], on the tree line, from our perimeter. The trail was very thick and bushy; there were a few trees. The trench line was dug into the shrubs, and you couldn't see it."[28]

The NVA had opened up on the patrol just as they crossed the road and moved in the vicinity of the hidden trenches. HM3 Frank Calzia recognized they had walked into an ambush.

"I came over the trench line, and I saw someone, and I yelled to our gunnery sergeant, 'Mac, they're in the back of us.' He took Cpl Claire's squad and everything happened within seconds. Then Jerry Dodson got hit, and I ran over to him. He'd caught a round through his left eye and it came out the side of his head, but he was still conscious."

Calzia recognized the severity of the wound, but reached for his medical bag anyway, and prepared a dressing for the bleeding PFC Dodson. But Dodson obviously also knew the severity of his wound.

"There was nothing I could do," said Calzia, "but I put a dressing on him and he told me, 'Doc, make sure I've got my weapon.' I gave it to him and I laid a couple of clips [of ammunition] by him."

The NVA fire ripped into the Marine patrol, and the next barrage of grenades knocked Calzia to the ground, and he lay there, stunned by the concussion.

"The grenade had just gone off, and I was stunned, and Lt Jacques came by and said, 'We gotta get out of here. Get out the best way you can. We're getting wiped out.' And I just started crawling; I left my rifle; I just had my .45 with me. I looked over and he stood up for some ungodly reason, and that's when he got it. I crawled over to him. He'd caught it right across both femoral arteries, and he was dead within minutes."[29]

The patrol had wandered far off their plotted course, and had been lured into a deadly ambush. The Marines at the combat base were helpless to assist, and could only offer fire support.

"The platoon commander [Jacques] started withdrawing what he could," said Capt Pipes. "As the 1st platoon moved into position to offer supporting fire, they in turn were pinned down. I called for close artillery support, 81 and 60 mortars, 90mm-gun tanks, firing .50-calibers. The 1st Platoon broke contact and pulled closer to our lines, and dispatched a squad to assist returning members. The patrol took heavy enemy mortars, automatic-weapons and small-arms fire. The platoon leader, 2Lt Jacques, returning as part of the rear guard, was hit and killed in action from bleeding on the way back into the perimeter."[30]

First Lieutenant Thomas O'Toole, flying overhead, had a bird's-eye view of this terrible battlefield.

"There were fifteen Marines in the trench trying to make it back. I thought they were taking fire, because the rear man was shooting to the rear. We went back up to the area of the bunker complex, and in the middle of a field surrounded on all sides by the trenches, there appeared to be fifteen to twenty Marine bodies. We turned around, and I did identify them because of the flak jackets and helmets. Three men lay together as if they had been a machine-gun crew. One man was bandaged on the chest, while another lay beside him as if he were a corpsman.

"We came around again. This time, a figure among the bodies stood up and fired at us and with that the entire trench line opened up, and we received three hits on the aircraft. What obviously happened was the point had walked into this open area, and was annihilated, and the rest were trying to make their way back to the perimeter. We also found a bunker complex off the eastern end of the runway."[31]

The casualties in the Jacques patrol were horrific—one killed, twenty-five missing and presumed dead, and twenty-one wounded.

The patrol became known as the "Ghost Patrol," because the men never came back. The Marines, faithful to an old tradition never to leave a comrade behind, prepared to charge out to their stricken comrades. It took a direct order from Gen Tompkins to restrain them. But that restraining order shattered their morale and left them haunted by the specter of the Ghost Patrol, whose lifeless bodies could be seen every day strewn on the battlefield.

The Americans reacted to the increased incoming and the advancing high-speed trenches with typical fury. FAC controllers circled the sky like eagles looking for any sign of the enemy, and when they found a sign, they directed devastating thunder on the target. The thirteen hundred–round NVA bombardment of the base on the 23rd was not one-sided.

"I really got excited about those rocket positions," said Capt Rushforth. "I saw the smoke in the trees, and then the *whoosh*, and the dust. The F-100s really did the job. They bombed and strafed for twenty-five minutes; really zapped them.

"It was like an endless chain of fighters, rolling in high, glinting in the sun, down through the clouds and blue, disappearing as the trees blended the camouflage, and the target erupted; then, *zoom*, up through the clouds and around again. The last plane pulled off to the right, buzzed Hill 881S, then pulled straight up in an arching right turn. What a bunch of hot shots!"[32]

But resupply difficulties still threatened the Marines. The continuous parachute drops were not enough. Ammunition was running low. The runway had been closed to C-130 traffic since the fiery crash on February 10, but on the 26th and 29th, despite the ever-present enemy gunners, it reopened to receive fourteen 130s carrying emergency loads.

Captain David S. Harmon and his crew of the 314th Tactical Airlift Wing, flying from CCK (Chin Chon Kong) Airbase in Taiwan, flew one of the first missions.

On the 26th, Capt Harmon approached Khe Sanh from the east, in the low overcast. He watched through his window as the tiny runway seemed to approach him, and made ready to "plant" his aircraft, with its vital cargo, and roll out to the near taxiway. The NVA gunners trained their weapons on the slow, rock-steady target as it approached.

"There were people shooting at us all the time," said Harmon. "We could see gunfire coming right at us off on the east end. We're sitting there at 130 knots, gear and flaps down, flying straight in to the runway. Believe me, your heart's in your mouth. There's nothing you can do except sit and take it."

Harmon made the hard landing, roared down the runway, careened off the first taxiway to the unload area, and dropped his cargo, never stopping the aircraft.

"This Marine was flagging me into the ramp, and the next thing I knew, the whole world erupted in front of me. A very large rocket or mortar went off, right on the pilot's side. A crater 6 to 8 feet across and 3 feet deep was there. The airplane rocked back real hard and I thought the damage had to be substantial; but all we had were mortar fragments, and everything kept running. The smoke cleared, and there was the Marine, poking his nose out around this CONEX container, with his hands in a waving motion, saying, 'Get that mortar magnet out of here.'"[33]

Harmon regained the runway, pushed the throttles full forward, and his aircraft lumbered down the runway and into the air. He was thankful to be airborne again and out of Khe Sanh, hopefully never to return. But three days later he was ordered to fly a second mission.

"It was the 29th of February, leap year day. We were less than enthusiastic; because our greeting on the 26th left no doubt in my mind that we really were mortar magnets. We checked out two flak vests—one to wear, and one to sit on, and took off at 1140. We were on final approach, and there was a C-123 on the runway, and we had to pull up and go around. We had taken a lot of hits, and had quite a bit of battle damage."

Harmon knew that with the battle damage, he could abort the mission and return to base with no questions asked, but he polled his crew and they all said, "Let's go back in." They knew the Marines needed the ammunition. The big four-engine plane made a second approach.

"So we swung the airplane around and came back in, took some more fire, and some more hits, popped our load off, and right back out the other way. We were mortared, took some shrapnel hits and some more hits after takeoff. We had a wing fire which burned itself out, and I could not get the elevators past neutral, and we had to manage the pitch of the airplane with flaps and power-land it."

When Harmon finally brought his battered aircraft to a stop on the runway at Da Nang, the maintenance crew gathered around and surveyed the damage. There were 104 holes in the C-130, but the ammunition was now in the Marines' hands, and just in time.*

*Capt Harmon and his crew were each awarded the Distinguished Flying Cross.

A mortar round explodes near a C-123 taxiing on the combat base airstrip.

CHAPTER 11
SMASHING THE RING

Col Lownds looks at a map in the combat base command bunker.

TIMELINE	APRIL 24, 1967	MAY 13, 1967	DECEMBER 1967	JANUARY 21, 1968	JANUARY 31, 1968
	Hill Fights begin at Khe Sanh	Hill Fights end. Marines fought off elements of the 325C NVA Division in a two-week battle that cost the enemy 824 KIA. 168 Marines were killed and 443 wounded in the struggle.	General Westmoreland decides to reinforce Khe Sanh in the face of enemy buildup.	NVA attack hill 861 and bombard combat base exploding ammo dump, and attack Khe Sanh village. Siege begins.	NVA launch countrywide Tet Offensive.

The command bunker was small, crowded, and smoky. Col Lownds had a bunk there, as did the executive officer and the operations officer. At the far end of the command bunker, isolated from the rest by their Top Secret work, Capt Harry Biag and Maj Jerry Hudson (26th Marines intelligence officer) plotted all intelligence information on a tactical map.

"One of the very basic intelligence plotting methods is a pin map," said Maj Hudson. "We'd put little red dots and yellow dots where we knew there was something happening."

Intelligence information came from many sources: The electronic sensors, aerial sightings, artillery-target coordinates, radio intercepts, and even the enemy's own incoming artillery contributed to the library. Crater analyses often revealed the azimuth and range of the NVA guns, and every shred of information from hundreds of reports and sightings every day painted Hudson and Biag's pin map with red and yellow dots.

"When we started to fire on these conglomerations of dots on the map, we started having things happen," said Hudson. "Suddenly all of their radios would start talking, and we'd get secondary explosions, and we might even get return fire . . . so we knew we were having success."[1]

"One night . . . we did a good crater analysis," said LtCol Louis Rann, XO of 26th Marines, "and ran [a back azimuth] on the map, and said there was only one valley they could shoot from; so we scheduled an Arc Light, and ran it in there, and all hell broke loose—secondary explosions for about two hours. At eleven o'clock the NVA came on the air, wanting a personnel report. This poor battalion commander was almost crying. He said, 'Goddamn it, we got hit by an Arc Light, and all hell is breaking loose here and you want a personnel report! I don't even know what I've got left.'"[2]

LtCol Rann was able to eavesdrop on the enemy through one of those quirks of luck that happens in battle. Many Marines had big Panasonic portable radios that kept them in touch with the outside world through Armed Forces Radio Service or even Radio Hanoi. They called these radios "boom boxes" or "ghetto blasters." One night at 2300, while tuning the radio in the command bunker, the Marines picked up a Vietnamese voice instead of music. Unknowingly, they had tuned in to the NVA artillery fire-direction network.

DISK 2, TRACKS 19-21: The Siege is lifted.

FEBRUARY 5-8, 1968	FEBRUARY 23, 1968	FEBRUARY 29, 1968	APRIL 14, 1968	JUNE 19-JULY 5, 1968
NVA attack Hill 861 Alpha, Lang Vei, and Hill 64.	Enemy gunners bombard base with more than 1,300 rounds in heaviest attack.	NVA launch regimental size attack against base.	Marines break out of siege and attack and seize Hill 881N.	Khe Sanh Combat Base is destroyed and abandoned by American forces.

"The guys were listening to it," said Rann, "and we had a *Chieu Hoi* [a former NVA soldier] come up and say, 'Hey, man, they're going to shoot at us tonight, from one o'clock to three o'clock. They've got orders to shoot five hundred rounds.' So we started to listen every night at eleven o'clock."

While most radios could not pick up the enemy communications, anyone who had one of the big Panasonics could. The intelligence people were worried about giving away the secret, and cautioned the soldiers not to listen in, but Rann put an end to their super cautiousness. "Bullshit, we're all going to listen in."[3]

The seismic sensors were the big responders to enemy activity.

"When you get activity at sensor A, and ten minutes later you get activity at sensor B, and ten minutes later at sensor C, it doesn't take long to assimilate that whatever's there is moving in that direction," said Maj Hudson. "Then you add speed [and rhythm] to that, and it's troops walking, troops running, a vehicle, or a herd of elephants. Sometimes we'd be getting all this crap while we were getting incoming, and we'd have a pretty good idea they were running, putting in mortars, and then leaving.

"We'd gotten a lot of activity between Lang Vei and the Hill [471] two nights in a row, and we really shot at it during the evening. The next day, we put an AO out there who said that there was something big going on. He'd seen two big bunkers that had been enlarged. The next time he flew by, there were two antiaircraft guns in these holes."[4]

Shortly after sunset on February 29, the sensors told Col Lownds that the NVA were on the move. This time it appeared that an enemy regiment was on the march for an attack on the base.[5]

"Early in the evening the sensors near the Laotian border on our side started going like crazy," said Col Lownds, "and then the next series went like crazy, and about that time the artillery people came in and said to me, 'Colonel, the sensors are going crazy.'

"I said, 'Let's not be too eager, but start laying plans along that road where we want to get them. I would just as soon hit them all along the road, but I want to make sure that I'm not wasting ammunition.'"[6]

The killing fields would be along Route 9 and on the access road as it came up to the base and on the secondary, parallel road that led to the trash pit on the southeastern perimeter. It was along these routes that the NVA had previously moved in their attempts to overrun Lang Vei and Outpost Alpha. This was also where Lt Jacques's Ghost Patrol had met with disaster.

"So, the sensors started building me a trail," said Col Lownds. "I had a pretty darn good idea where the assembly area was going to be, so I said, 'There'll be one battalion that's going to have an assembly area here, and another's going to have an assembly area here. When they get down to Khe Sanh village, there's a bridge down there. Start pounding the bridge. They'll have trouble going around that, so we'll start there.'"[7]

On Col Lownds' order, the FSCC sprang into action. Examining the target areas he had pinpointed on the map, Biag began to pencil-in his rectangular boxes, overlapping them to cover the anticipated enemy approach along Route 9 and up the access roads to the eastern edge of the combat base. And as Biag plotted, the Marines slipped their massive fire plan into gear, and the wheels of artillery- and air-support began to turn. To bring maximum devastation, Lownds intended to employ every fire technique at his disposal

against the approaching enemy: Time-on-target fires by massed batteries, artillery boxes, rolling barrages, and massive air strikes were plotted to fill Capt Biag's boxes.

They would also employ the Mini Arc Light and the Micro Arc Light: two brainchildren of Capts Kent O. Steen and Harry Biag that replicated the devastation of the Arc Light when B-52s were not available. Steen was the assistant fire support coordinator, and his Mini Arc Light attacked a 500- by 1,000-meter (approximately 550- by 1,100-yard) box.

Steen had been at Khe Sanh since the beginning, and during his twelve-hour shifts in the FSCC, he was never idle.

"I went on watch at 6 p.m.," he said, "and got off at 6 a.m. All I did was sit there and plot schemes."[8] He was an excellent artillery officer, and worked out all the mathematics on artillery missions. His Mini Arc Light was a magnificent scheme.

The Army's 175mm batteries at Camp Carrol covered half of the block with sixty rounds, while the Marine batteries of 1/13 blanketed the second half with two-hundred mixed rounds of 155mm,

Snipers look out into the fog from atop a bunker on the combat base perimeter.

105mm, and 4.2-inch-mortar fire. The final hammer stroke came from the sky, with a radar-guided strike by two A-6 Intruders, each unleashing twenty-eight 500-pound bombs. Steen calculated the numbers so that the entire artillery and air package crashed in the target block in one massive explosion.

The artillery was fired first, and as the rounds were in midair, speeding to the target, the two A-6s rippled their loads. On the ground, the shock effect was shattering. Tons of exploding steel shredded and pulverized the target block. Steen's Micro Arc Light was just as deadly, but targeted only a 500-square-meter (approximately 500-square-yard) target.[9]

Col Lownds reacted to the flood of sensor information, and after ordering the FSCC to target the NVA on their approach routes, called Gen Tompkins at 3rd Division Headquarters. Lownds told the general he felt that this was the night of maximum effort by the enemy, and he wanted to bring in the B-52s, and he wanted them at exact spots along the enemy approach path. Tompkins went straight up the line with the B-52 request but reported back to Lownds that the B-52s were already airborne heading for other, preplanned targets, and higher headquarters did not want to divert. Lownds was furious.

"I really don't care if they've left or not," said Lownds. "Let's be a little flexible and get them. Gen Westmoreland interceded on our behalf and got us the Arc Lights where we wanted them."[10]

The land around Khe Sanh erupted in the explosions of the sustained fire from all supporting arms, and within two hours of Lownds' request, the B-52s arrived to shake the earth with their massive strikes. Artillery brought its massed fires in a continuous drumbeat, and the A-6s filled Capt Biag's boxes with plummeting bombs.

At 2130, the first NVA ground attack hit the wire in front of the 37th ARVN Rangers. A battalion of the 304th NVA Division approached the perimeter under withering fire from the Rangers massed in their trenches and under continuous pounding from aircraft and artillery. The assault hit the outer wire, failed to breach it, and fell back.

The second assault surged forward two hours later, at 2330, and it too recoiled. A third feeble attack at 0315 did not even reach the outer wire. The advancing 304th forces had struggled through the massed air and artillery strike, and had collapsed. Small-arms fire and Khe Sanh's own supporting arms had further

thinned their ranks, and before daylight, the survivors pulled back.

At dawn the Rangers examined the area to their front. Body parts were everywhere; seventy-eight dead soldiers were massed in the assault trenches they had dug to approach the base. Those trenches had become their shallow graves.

"Out in front of the ARVN looked like a slaughterhouse," said LtCol Louis Rann. "That was the damnedest mess you ever saw out there. Bodies were all torn up."[11]

Moyers S. Shore described the battlefield in his excellent monograph *The Battle for Khe Sanh*: "Some were in a kneeling position as if they had been killed just before going over the top. Many had been peppered by artillery airbursts and were covered with small holes. Crude devices made from bamboo strips and laced with blocks of TNT lay beside many of the bodies. These were obviously to be used as bangalore torpedoes, but the sappers never got a chance. The slaughter along the perimeter, however, was nothing compared to the losses sustained by the NVA reserves."[12]

Montagnard tribesmen reported hundreds of bodies along the trails leading to the base.

"I have always felt that that night [February 29] was the key to the defense of Khe Sanh," said Col Lownds.

....

An aircraft delivers a napalm strike to a ridgeline near the combat base. **OPPOSITE:** Capt Kent Steen stands next to a jeep during the 26th Marines's preparations to leave Khe Sanh after the siege was lifted.

"I think the most amazing part is that with the Arc Lights and with the artillery, we broke the back of what was happening because of the sensors, because of the ability for strategic bombing; it was accurate as hell. The main defense of Khe Sanh was done without the enemy ever closing to the wire."[13]

Two weeks later, intelligence would report the withdrawal of major NVA forces from the Khe Sanh area.

The drama that unfolded on the night of February 29 was not reflected in the headline news or TV commentaries. In fact, reporters seemed oblivious to what was going on and were content with filing stories perpetuating the seductive but unrealistic Dien Bien Phu comparison. On February 29, Walter Cronkite filed this report on *CBS Evening News*, just hours before the Marines blocked and crushed the NVA attack along Route 9.

"Since its usefulness as a roadblock and a forward base has been so vastly diminished, Khe Sanh now is mostly a symbol; but of what?"[14]

An ABC reporter, ignoring the fact that only one C-130 aircraft had ever been shot down at Khe Sanh, filed this melodramatic report with the C-130 in the background.

"The big C-130s sometimes make it; sometimes they don't. Here's one that's just been hit by incoming rockets."[15]

A stern-faced Murray Frompson from CBS looked into the camera and proclaimed his sense of doom at Khe Sanh.

"They're getting ready to smack us hard. If the airfield is knocked out and the weather stays bad, we're in trouble. This is one place the Americans cannot claim they have the initiative in Vietnam. Here the North Vietnamese decide who lives, and who dies . . . every day; which planes land, and which ones don't; and sooner or later, they will make the move that will seal the fate of Khe Sanh."[16]

Perhaps the reason for this disembodied reporting was the very distance the press had placed itself from the battlefield. While a few reporters were at the base, most were not—Walter Cronkite never visited. Those that did flew in occasionally, like the moth drawn to the flame, and many reported the terror of their flight, ignoring the fact that Gen Tompkins flew in almost every day.

A Marine displays a Newsweek quote on his flak jacket for an AP photographer, February 21, 1968. **OPPOSITE:** A CBS film crew looks for a story in the fog at the combat base.

When they visited Khe Sanh, the most television friendly spot from which to broadcast was with the destroyed C-130 in the background. Then the reporter flew off to more comfortable surroundings and covered the war from there. None of them witnessed Capt Biag's "vulgar free-for-all" or even cared to imagine its effects.

Except for David Douglas Duncan, a former Marine and still photographer for *Life*, and David Powell, a freelance UPI photographer, no reporters ever visited the outpost hills. They covered the battle and got their visual images from the base, which was the command and support center. That was tantamount to covering the actions on the beaches of Normandy while stationed on the command ship in the English Channel.

Peter Braestrup, the chief of the *Washington Post* Saigon Bureau, took issue with shabby reporting that pandered to sensationalism rather than facts.

"There were only four American planes shot down during the siege,"* he said, "but they were all easy to photograph, and they looked terrific on film; and TV journalists could fly into Khe Sanh, do a stand-upper in front of a wrecked aircraft, and say things like, 'Here we have a graveyard of twisted airplanes.'

"You could have a CBS correspondent say, '*The sense of doom*,' in front of the same graveyard of airplanes—the same four airplanes that were shot down.

"You could have a CBS correspondent stand up and say . . . 'The North Vietnamese determine who lives or dies at Khe Sanh.' Obviously if the North Vietnamese would have had their druthers, there would have been nobody left alive at Khe Sanh.

"The whole thing was a television melodrama, and it was predictable . . . sure-fire, and they exploited it to the hilt."[17]

While the month of February had provided only five clear days, in the month of March there were only five days that hampered air operations. Attack aircraft, previously limited by the ever-present *crachin*, now found clear skies, and they stacked up over the battle area like circling vultures, waiting for the order to attack. The hours available for the NVA to dig trenches under cloud cover greatly diminished, and their

*One C-130, and three of the smaller C-123s.

troop movements during daylight were brought to a virtual standstill. Each round of enemy fire, previously hidden by clouds, now left a telltale flash, or smoke, or arching streak to attract the eyes of the FACs.

Capt Charles Rushforth, COVEY 252, was orbiting over Hills 861 and 861A, enjoying the almost unlimited visibility and working with the Marine air coordinators on the hills. He had already hit several enemy automatic-weapons and bunker complexes, and had destroyed two mortars.

"The weather was clear, and I could see so far that I almost got disoriented," he said. "Fighters were hitting all over the place—their patterns cutting right through my area. Three flights were stacked up waiting. Man, it was crowded."[18]

Then Rushforth's radio crackled from his contact on 861A.

"COVEY 252, this is Echo 1-4. How about hitting the gully between the two hills [861 and 861A]. We think they are digging under us."

Rushforth piloted his small aircraft to fly down the axis of the ridgeline that connected the two Marine strongpoints. He observed that hardly one hundred meters (about 110 yards) separated the two hilltops. It would be a very delicate operation, but he felt it could be done. It would require great flying and bombing skills, but only the attacking pilots themselves could approve the mission.

The attacking flight was WHALE 34, four Marine F-4B Phantoms from VMFA-122 at Da Nang. They circled above, awaiting orders. Rushforth briefed them on the proposed strike and its difficulties. There was not the least hesitation from WHALE leader.

"WHALE lead, Roger, I can do it," responded Capt Robert Dougal.

Rushforth then polled the other three pilots.

"Don't be afraid to back out. This is ticklish. Anyone feel uneasy about it?"

The other Marines' answers were again short. "Two – negative." "Three – negative." "Four – negative."

Capt Dougal's fellow attack pilots were Capt Cahill, Bergman, and Burghart, and they were rigged for combat.

"We were told to orbit for ten minutes while controllers got ahold of ground troops and asked where they wanted the bombs," said Dougal. "Two aircraft carried 750-pound bombs, and the two others had four 750-bombs and six packs of rockets."

Rushforth decided on one bomb from each man on the first pass, and the aircraft roared in on the target line, wings glinting in the sun. One by one, they made the bomb run while the hilltop defenders looked skyward from trenches away from the impact area.

"On my fifth pass, I dropped one 750-pound bomb," said Dougal. "It was on target, and the controller cleared the rest of the flight to drop the other ordnance. The bombs came within 20 meters (65 feet) of friendly troops, and we got two large secondary explosions, and three medium secondary explosions."[19]

The other jets roared in on the small gully target: Cahill first, then Bergman, then Burghart, each fixated on their sites. The bombs fell from the underbodies of the aircrafts and drifted to the ground as the shrieking jets pulled out with afterburners on fire. The small stretch of land between 861 and 861A exploded and disappeared, providing a spectacular show to the onlooking infantry. Cheers followed each pass, and shouts erupted when the bombs detonated secondary explosions.

Like unrelenting eagles, the four Phantoms struck again and again. Finally, out of bombs, they roared from the battlefield, becoming only tiny specks in the distance.

"It was fantastic," said Rushforth. "Five secondary explosions, two huge ones, and one after the fighters had left for home. It blew trees and crap all over the place."[20]

Rushforth wrote a letter of commendation for the pilots of WHALE 34. He concluded, "It is a great pleasure to work with men of this caliber."

The aerial assault continued around the clock. On March 15, Marine intelligence reported that the 325C NVA Division Headquarters had retreated toward Laos, along with elements of two of its attacking regiments. The 304th Division had also withdrawn to the southwest, perhaps to attempt to refit and to put some distance between itself and the murderous supporting arms fire.

The following day in Washington, President Lyndon Johnson told his staff that he was not supporting a bombing halt recommended by McNamara.

"Let's get one thing clear," Johnson said. "I'm telling you now; I am not going to stop the bombing. Now I don't want to hear any more about it."[21]

The following day, he addressed the National Farm Union and again reasserted his tough, Alamo-like stance.

"Make no mistake about it . . . we are going to win."[22]

Johnson saw himself as standing tall against the NVA and Ho Chi Minh. He was not a leader who would cut and run. Four months earlier he had seen Secretary McNamara wobble on his Vietnam commitment. Johnson didn't like that, and since November, McNamara had become a lame-duck Secretary of Defense. He had told the president that the only job he really wanted was to be president of the World Bank. Johnson paved the way for that appointment, but sensed that McNamara's request proved that the secretary was in over his head.

An aerial view of Hills 861 (left) and 861-A.

"Two months before he left, he felt he was a murderer, and didn't know how to extricate himself," the president observed. "I never felt like a murderer; that's the difference. Someone had to call Hitler, and someone had to call Ho. After a while, the pressure got so great that Bob couldn't sleep at night. I was afraid he might have a nervous breakdown."[23]

But while McNamara might have been at the end of his rope and wilting at the decisive moment of the war, the Marines were not. In fact, they were planning their first offensive operation to drive the enemy from positions close to the combat base perimeter. A company-size combat patrol would attack down the access road, by the trash pit, to the area where the ghost patrol had met its demise.

Their mission was to drive any NVA forces that had bellied-up to their positions back toward Route 9, and at the same time to recover the remains of their lost comrades. At last the Marines of Company B would get the chance to exorcise the demons that had haunted them for a month.

Although the NVA had pulled some of their forces off the line, their artillery still harassed the base every day with more than a hundred rounds. March 23 was an exception. A massive bombardment struck the combat base with more than eleven hundred rounds, much of it from heavy artillery in Laos.

So the patrol was meticulously planned, with maximum fire support, once again employing rolling and shifting artillery boxes that would sweep the land like a giant plow. Artillery and air would create the massive rolling barrage, and Capt Pipes and his Marines would attack within this moving box, following 75 meters (about 80 yards) behind the exploding wall.

On March 30, shortly after 0730, Company B stepped across the line.

"By first light we had deployed behind our line of departure," said Capt Kenneth Pipes. "First Lieutenant Dillon of the 2nd Platoon secured the first objective, and we paused to link up, and then jumped off from Objective One, toward our final objective. We immediately came under extremely heavy RPG, 82mm and 60mm mortar fire, as well as heavy automatic weapons and small arms."[24]

"We found the enemy well dug in in trenches and well-fortified bunkers, and they had heavy small-arms fire, automatic-weapons fire and mortars," said Cpl Edward I. Prendergast, the 60mm mortar section leader.

"Cpl Kenneth A. Korkow captured an NVA mortar, brought it up in front of the assaulting units, and fired, 50 meters [55 yards] away from his position, with three high-explosive rounds, knocking out the position and allowing the assaulting unit to make their way to the trench line.

"After firing all of our 60mm mortar rounds . . . our fourteen men turned into infantrymen and fell in to different fire teams and squads, and helped out as much as they could. The enemy didn't have to peer up over the top of the trench to see us. He just fired the mortar at a high elevation, and had many rounds available. We had to assault one trench at a time."[25]

The 3rd Platoon became pinned down by heavy fire from the entrenched NVA. But one of the squad leaders, Cpl Samuel Boone Jr., shouted to his fire teams, and ordered them to attack in rushes. Not waiting for the men to move, Boone jumped to his feet and led the way.

"Boone immediately charged the enemy positions and proceeded to destroy the positions and kill many of the enemy before being joined by his men,"[26] said Sgt William M. Simpkins.

"Boone led this assault himself," concurred LCpl Lonnie W. Morrison. "He assaulted position after position, and destroyed and killed the enemy within. Marines who had been hesitant to join the assault became inspired, and assaulted the remaining positions with great enthusiasm. The enemy hit the company with a heavy mortar barrage, and we received orders to break contact. Cpl Boone provided covering fire so that the casualties could be taken from the field."[*27]

The 1st Platoon attacked on the right flank, as the company hammered forward. There were many bunkers, trenches, and fighting holes. The barrage had rolled over the enemy positions, but the bunkers had offered some protection. As the line of Marines moved forward, one of the squads enveloped an enemy trench.

"The squad enveloped and got on line," said squad leader LCpl Michael H. McCauley, "and came upon a trench where NVA were shooting AK-47s and numerous other small arms at the rest of the company. We cleared the trench line, killing fourteen NVA, including one officer. We continued up the trench and they started dropping mortars all around us and it was too much. I was wounded by a mortar round, and picked up some of the dead and wounded men, and brought them back in. Lieutenant Weise pulled the rest of our patrol back."[28]

The incoming was terrific. PFC Frank C. Tanner fired his M-79 grenade launcher to try and suppress the fire, and described the enemy incoming as "a holocaust of mortars and rockets."[29]

*Cpl Samuel Boone Jr. received the Silver Star for his heroism.

Marines pause for a moment on hill 861 during the Easter Egg Hunt.

The NVA gunners hit Company B with more than one hundred rounds of mortar fire and scored a direct hit on the company CP, killing the forward observers and their radio operator and wounding Capt Pipes. But he pressed on, despite his wounds, and directed all the supporting-arms fire.

"The impetus of the attack never slackened," said Pipes. "All the young Marines had been waiting several weeks for an opportunity to recover their comrades. From the point of initial contact until we reached our final objective, 600 meters [about 660 yards] away, they covered the ground in twenty to twenty-five minutes.'"[30]

But the firefight with the NVA was not that quickly over; it lasted over four hours and, when it was concluded, nine Marines had been killed and another forty wounded. But the Marines had shattered the enemy force. One hundred fifteen NVA soldiers lay dead. During the fight, Marine radios monitored the enemy commander frantically calling for reinforcements that never came. Finally his radio was silent.

Recovery of the bodies of the Ghost Patrol was almost nonexistent. For over a month they had lain in the open, while numerous air strikes and artillery had pulverized the area. A few remains were collected under hostile fire, and a detailed examination of the battlefield was precluded by the ferocity of the firefight.[31]

It was over. Capt Pipes's attack was the first offensive operation and marked the breakout. The fighting would go on for more than a month, and the Marines would suffer similar casualties in attacking Hills 471 and 689; the remnants of the NVA force continued to lob artillery and mortars at the base; but it was over.

On April 1, Army and Marine forces attacked from the east along Route 9, and Operation Pegasus swept past Khe Sanh toward A Shau Valley. Engineers began the job of restoring Route 9 from Ca Lu to Khe Sanh, and opened the road on April 11, two days after the airfield opened to receive unlimited supplies.

Perhaps the final stroke went to the Marines who started the whole thing on 881S. On April 14, in an attack they dubbed "the Easter Egg Hunt," the 3rd Battalion, under the command of LtCol John C. Studt, stormed up the slopes of 881N to kick the enemy off and end the fight that had begun on January 20.

The Marines assembled their well-rehearsed orchestra of supporting arms to precede the attack. Added were the new instruments of the Army's 1st Air Cavalry Division's 155mm guns and 8-inch batteries.

The aircraft came in with their bombs, rockets, and napalm, and the Marines on 881S chipped in with their own mortars, artillery, and machine guns. Ingeniously they lined up the battalion's eight 106mm recoilless rifles to fire broadsides into the opposing hill. Hill 881S became a stationary battleship.

The enemy defenders on 881N were overwhelmed. "The men of 3/26 stormed up the hill, swarmed over the crest, and killed anyone who stood in their way," said Moyers S. Shore II.[32] Six Marines were killed in the attack that left 106 enemy bodies strewn on the hilltop.

But the victorious Marines were not through. In keeping with their great tradition, they planted the flag on

---

*Capt Pipes received the Silver Star for his heroism.

top of 881N, with Capt Bill Dabney in attendance. Col Bruce Meyers, who had relieved Col Lownds, was also there.

"I watched a jungle-utility-clad Marine shinny up a shrapnel-torn tree whose limbs had been sheared [by] the intensive prep fires, and affix the Stars and Stripes," said Meyers.[33] Press and television reporters saw none of this.

The month of March brought about a transformation in President Johnson. Following his disappointment in McNamara's lack of will, and the president's later proclamations on March 16 and 17 to stand firm and continue the bombing, he sank into a quagmire of his own. During the last two weeks of the month, Johnson's staff and advisors, including his new secretary of defense, Clark Clifford, a proclaimed "hawk," persuaded him to try to get out of Vietnam.

With the enemy crushed at Khe Sanh and reeling from losses in their failed Tet Offensive, and with Gen Westmoreland poised to clean out the DMZ and sever the NVA supply lines in Laos, Johnson quit. Incredibly, he announced another bombing pause, and on March 31 declared that he would not seek reelection and would concentrate the remainder of his term seeking peace.

Colonel Travis had surrendered.

A platoon of Army Cavalrymen sweep toward Khe Sanh during Operation Pegasus, April 5, 1968.

EPILOGUE

....

The Marines eventually left Khe Sanh, opting to cover the area from two advanced firebases instead. When they did, they completely bulldozed the base so there would be no recognizable features. No NVA cameramen would be taking pictures of NVA soldiers planting a flag on the base, as had flashed around the world at Dien Bien Phu in 1954.

Many people asked, "Who won?" The Marines, and their interservice teammates, were the obvious victors on the battlefield, but there were many losers.

Lyndon Johnson's presidency was shattered, and he became the lamest of ducks. His latest bombing restriction assured the NVA no meaningful effective action would thwart their continued invasion of South Vietnam for at least a year. As commander in chief, he abandoned the war, the soldiers who fought for him, and the South Vietnamese people, who would later flee for U.S. shores as refugees, and came to be known as "boat people." In a moment of bizarre reasoning, he stated he had lost the confidence of news reporter Walter Cronkite, and therefore lost the American people.

In October, just before the election, in an attempt to swing the election to Hubert Humphrey, Johnson declared a total bombing halt of the North, thereby handicapping any new administration, and gave the North Vietnamese a gift they could hardly have imagined. His boastful self-comparisons to Texas Rangers and Alamo defenders proved hollow. His harsh criticism of Secretary McNamara's failure to stay the course preceded his own quitting.

Secretary of Defense Robert McNamara had firmly tied the albatross of the United States' ultimate failure around his own neck. His attempts at strategy and tactics were absurd and violated all the principles of war. His micromanaging and handicapping of the military fulfilled the 1947 nightmare of Senator Millard Tydings, who envisioned tremendous harm to the military with a "martinet," or "dumbbell," as Secretary of National Defense. McNamara had continued to send men into battle in a war he later admitted he felt he could not win, and, instead of resigning on principle, he continued on and, at the decisive moment, abandoned his president.

General Westmoreland was not a politician, and after he had crushed the enemy's fiercest attack, politics denied him the follow-up he sought. He was hard-pressed to understand President Johnson's squeamishness and inability to recognize that this was the turning point in the conflict.

"The objective of that war was to bring the enemy to the conference table," he said, "but by virtue of vocal attitudes, forged by antiwar groups, the Army was never allowed to do the job . . . the political leadership lost their nerve. Walter Cronkite had a lot to do with that. After Tet . . . he stayed in Saigon in the Caravelle Hotel, and said to give it up. LBJ said, 'Once I lost Cronkite, I lost the American people.' That's frightening.

Here's a guy who is a script reader, who has more clout with the American people than the president."[1]

Gen Giap was the biggest loser, and his actions were those of a desperate man. He had planned his grand strategy long before the American buildup in the north, and then ignored the danger of the buildup to his plan. He believed his own propaganda, and nowhere did anyone rally to his predicted "general uprising." His forces were shattered by the events of 1967–68, including Tet and Khe Sanh. After Khe Sanh, he ran for the peace table in Paris to gain time to refurbish and refit.

In an interview with the famous Italian journalist Oriana Fallaci in 1969, he actually denied any involvement with Tet and Khe Sanh, passing it off to the Viet Cong who were nowhere present at Khe Sanh. These were not the words of a victorious general. No commanding general, in the history of warfare, has ever denied his involvement with victory. Only in defeat do they shy away from the spotlight, and Giap held himself well out of the spotlight. By distancing himself he effectively answered the question, "Who won on the battlefield?"

Giap's strategy had been to get the Americans out. To do that, he planned to shock the South Vietnamese government by seizing the two northern provinces while simultaneously inflicting a major defeat on the Americans. Lieutenant Tonc had revealed part of the plan, and the Marines had reacted.

Giap tried to seize the high ground to have unlimited observation, lay siege to the base, and bombard and starve it into submission. His tactics imitated those he had successfully employed at Dien Bien Phu, but there the comparison ended. Presuming a general uprising with the Tet Offensive, and a successful fight at Khe Sanh, his armored attack was to be the punch to finally break through to sweep on toward Hue. He would then control Quang Tri and Thua Thien provinces—two-fifths of South Vietnam.

But Giap lost. He never anticipated a reinforced Marine regiment would be dug in on the plateau and hilltops; he never thought the Americans could keep Khe Sanh supplied without Route 9; he failed to take the outpost hills, and failed to understand the massive supporting fires the Americans could unleash against him, although he had seen it at Con Thien. There was no general uprising, and the inflexibility of his outdated plan forced his battalions to follow rigid timetables and hurl themselves futilely against the wire.

Early on, Capt Mizra M. Biag had figured Giap out. Counting on the inflexibility of Giap's plan and his slavish commitment to it, Biag designed killing fields to swallow his soldiers. Unfortunately, Capt Biag never got the accolades he deserved. After Khe Sanh, he was assigned to Thailand. In 1971, with his wife and daughter, he perished in a hotel fire in Bangkok.

The men who fought at Khe Sanh were both the big winners and the big losers. They met Giap's forces and virtually annihilated them, only to have their efforts ignored by their president, the press, the television reporters, and the American people. Their great victory at Khe Sanh and during Tet was spun into defeat and stalemate. This book is an attempt to set things straight, and is dedicated to all who fought in our nation's longest, most controversial war, and never lost a battle.

ACKNOWLEDGMENTS

On behalf of Dr. Douglas Brinkley and myself, I would like to thank some of the many people who have made this wonderful book possible. When I first started research in 1978, the idea that this story would ever be told seemed remote. The only other person doing any research on Khe Sanh was Chaplain Ray Stubbe, chaplain of Khe Sanh, who was present for the entire battle of 1968.

I was with intelligence at III Marine Amphibious Force Headquarters during those early months of 1968 and flew into the combat base on two occasions—hardly a courageous feat in view of the constant exposure to the enemy of the men at the base, but I was privy to many of the classified aspects of the battle, especially the aerial bombardment of Operation Niagara and the intelligence reports revealing the destruction of the NVA forces at Khe Sanh and the despair of their soldiers. I also knew that what was being presented and reported in the mainstream press and on television was indeed distorted.

As years went by, declassified documents added light to complete the story of the Vietnam War's most remembered battle in a war of unremembered names. I joined with Chaplain Stubbe and began an independent, individual research of the veterans who fought there both in 1967 during the Hill Fights, and in 1968 during the encirclement. During those years of research, Kathi Jones, now a historian with the U.S. Air Force, ably assisted me.

Stubbe and I became friends and in the end shared our research, and that archive is the basis for this book. But an archive does not translate into a story, and the idea for the book rests with Andy Mayer, co-president of becker&mayer!, who approached Doug Brinkley and me after we had written *Voices of Valor: D-Day, June 6, 1944*. He thought the time had come for a book about Vietnam, and Doug and I agreed. We knew the excellence of the becker&mayer! team and were anxious to work with them again. Shayna Ian, who did a splendid job on photo research and selection for the D-Day book, has managed to outdo herself here. Kate Hall has crafted the selection for the accompanying new CDs bringing us the voices of the men who were on the battlefield, and Stephen Lang's excellent narration continues in the spirit of *Voices of Valor*. Sheila Kamuda, the project manager, and Sheila Hackler, the production coordinator, have expertly overseen the entire assembly of this unique work, and Todd Bates's book design makes it compelling.

Conor Risch has done a remarkable job editing the manuscript, has survived the task of wading through interminable military jargon and usage, units and nomenclature, strategy and tactics, and has succinctly arranged this story to be a page-turner.

We are also very fortunate to be working for a second time with the people at Bulfinch Press. Editorial Director Michael Sand has offered ideas and enthusiasm for this story every step of the way.

Publisher Jill Cohen and Associate Publisher Karen Murgulo recognized the importance of this story and believed in our ability to tell it, and Publicity Director Matthew Ballast has again devoted great effort to helping us reach our audience.

Finally, special thanks to Gerard McCavera, an historian and friend indeed, who graciously read, and re-read the manuscript, and encouraged and delighted in every word.

Ronald Drez

Ronald J. Drez (standing, third from right) Commander of Company H, 2nd Battalion, 5th Marines, with some of his men in Vietnam, 1968.

GLOSSARY

1, the: Military term for battalion or brigade level personnel administration.

175mm Self-propelled Gun: The M-107 was a long-range, tracked artillery piece that could fire 174-pound rounds 32,000 meters and had a crew of ten artillerymen.

2, the: Military term for battalion or brigade level intelligence section.

3, the: Military term for battalion or brigade level training section.

4, the: Military term for battalion or brigade level supply and logistics section.

50: 50mm mortar tube.

60: 60mm mortar tube.

81: 81mm mortar tube.

A-6: Abbreviation of A-6A Intruder, the all-weather bomber used by the U.S. Navy for tactical ground support at Khe Sanh and throughout South Vietnam.

A-7: Navy single engine all-weather light attack aircraft equipped with advanced radar and navigational systems that allowed night and foul weather operations.

actual: Military term for the commanding officer.

ADSID: Air Delivered Seismic Intrusion Devices were sensors dropped from planes to monitor enemy troop movements. The battery-powered ADSIDs lodged in the ground, detected vibrations, and sent signals to remote monitoring stations.

AK-47: Soviet-designed assault rifle used by the NVA and Viet Cong.

AO: Areas of Operation were established to reduce the chance of firing on other friendly units.

AOC: Air Operations Center, a command center established to coordinate air operations of U.S. Air Force and South Vietnamese Air Force. AOC was also an acronym for Army Operations Center, located first in Saigon and later in Long Binh.

Arc Light: Code name for air strikes flown by B-52 bombers.

APC: The M-113 armored personnel carrier.

artillery: Artillery pieces used in Vietnam were defined by type and size. The diameter of a weapon's barrel was designated in millimeters or inches, i.e. 81mm mortar or 105mm howitzer. *See also* Mortar *and* Howitzer.

arty: Military slang for artillery.

ARVN: Army of the Republic of Vietnam.

AW: Automatic weapons.

B-40: *see* rocket propelled grenade.

B-52: The Boeing-built bombers flew out of Guam, Okinawa, Japan, and Thailand. They could fly at 55,000 feet at a speed of 660mph, and accurately deliver 500- and 750-pound bombs on targets as close to American troops as 1000 meters.

bangalore torpedo: Devices consisting of a series of explosive tubes connected together; used to blow holes in barbed wire defenses.

BAR: Browning Automatic Rifles were World War II vintage .30 caliber light machine guns.

BAS: Battalion Aid Station, a small medical aid station located in the field at battalion headquarters.

boat people: Name given to Vietnamese refugees who fled South Vietnam after the Communist takeover in 1975.

B & S Ration: Marines operating in the field were given a ration of beer and soda.

C-123: Twin-engine propeller plane used by the Air Force for transport.

C-130: Four engine, turbo propeller plane was the primary aircraft used for transport by American forces in South Vientam.

C-Rations: Combat rations, individual meals issued to troops in the field.

CAC: Combined Action Company, a combined Marine/South Vietnamese force used to provide security to hamlets such as Khe Sanh Village. Also called a Combined Action Platoon.

Cam Lo: Marine base camp located along Route 9 14kms west of Dong Ha in Quang Tri Province.

Cam Ranh Bay: Seaport in South Vietnam was a large logistics center for U.S. forces in South Vietnam.

Camp Carroll: Marine fire base located along Route 9 22kms west of Quang Tri. The Army 175mm artillery guns located there provided support for the Marines at Khe Sanh.

Camp Evans: Located 22 kms northwest of Hue, the camp was occupied by elements of 3rd Marine Division.

CAP: Combined Action Platoon, *see* CAC.

CCK Air Base: Located in Taiwan, the U.S. used this air base, also called the ROC (Republic of China) air base.

CH-46: Twin engine transport helicopter used by Marines.

character: Radio discipline used to announce the transmittal of letters.

Charlie Med: Khe Sanh headquarters of C Company, 3rd Medical Battalion.

ChiCom: Abbreviation of Chinese Communist used to reference military equipment manufactured in China, i.e. ChiCom Grenade, which was used by the NVA and VC and had an explosive head attached to a wooden handle.

Chieu Hoi: Vietnamese for "open arms," this program guaranteed amnesty to NVA and VC soldiers who wished to defect.

CIDG: Civilian Irregular Defense Group units were created from montagnard tribesmen, and were trained and led by U.S. Special Forces A-Teams.

CINCPAC: Commander in Chief, Pacific, the command center for all U.S. military operations in the Pacific Command Area.

Cluster Bomb Unit: Also called CBUs, these single bomb units broke apart over a target dispersing hundreds of smaller bombs.

COC: Command of Camp was the administrative headquarters for large U.S. base camps such as Khe Sanh Combat Base.

Con Thien: Series of low hills located just south of the DMZ, the northernmost Marine outpost in South Vietnam.

concertina wire: Coiled barbed wire used in defensive positions.

CONEX container: Large corregated metal shipping container used for supply storage and transport.

CP: Command post, units of platoon size and larger established these command centers for their operations.

crachin: This French slang term meant "spit," probably derived from the verb *cracher*, "to spit."

CS gas: tear gas, a chemical irritant used to smoke enemy soldiers out of bunkers, tunnels and trenches, was delivered via hand grenade or artillery shell.

Da Nang: Port city in Quang Nam Province that was headquarters for U.S. Marines and was a major airfield for Marine, Navy, and Air Forces.

DMZ: Demilitarized Zone, a five-mile wide demarcation line running along the 17th parallel that was supposed to be clear of military forces.

Duster: M-42 Dusters, tanks with twin 40mm antiaircraft guns, were used in Vietnam against enemy troops and fortifications.

DZ: Drop zone, a designated area used for delivery of parachuted troops or supplies.

F-4: McDonnell Douglas—made twin engine, all weather tactical fighter bomber, also called the Phantom.

FAC: Forward Air Controller, an airborne observer who coordinated aircraft and artillery attacks against ground targets.

FDC: Fire Direction Center, the command center for artillery support of units in the field.

flak jacket: Sleeveless armored vest designed to stop shrapnel wounds to the chest, back, and stomach.

FO: Forward Observer, an artillery officer who accompanied units in the field and directed supporting fire for those units.

foxhole: A fighting position big enough for one or several individuals, dug into the ground.

FSCC: Fire Support Coordination Center, a command center for planning artillery and strategic air strikes.

Gio Linh: A Marine outpost just 4kms south of the DMZ.

Green Berets: Nickname for U.S. Army Special Forces.

Gs: Term used for the effect of gravity on pilots.

H & I: Harassing and Interdiction fires were random artillery fires at preselected targets meant to disrupt enemy activity.

H & S Company: Headquarters and supply service group of a Marine battalion.

HE: High Explosive artillery and mortar rounds.

hootch: Living and sleeping shelter, usually a bunker or small building.

howitzer: The 105mm and 155mm howitzer were towed and self-propelled artillery pieces used at Khe Sanh.

I Corps: The northernmost tactical zone in South Vietnam.

John Wayne crackers: Marine term for crackers or biscuits found in C-Rations.

Jolly Green: Also called Jolly Green Giant, the CH-3E helicopter was used by the Air Force for rescue and troop movement operations.

JP-4: High performance, kerosene-based jet fuel.

Khe Sanh Shuffle: Name Marines gave to the quick dashes from bunker to bunker that were made during the siege.

KIA: Killed In Action.

LAAW: M-72 light anti-tank assault weapons were one-shot, shoulder-fired disposable rocket launchers.

Lang Vei: Site of the Special Forces CIDG camp west of Khe Sanh near the Laotian border.

LP: Listening post, see **OP**.

LZ: Landing zone, generally associated with insertion and extraction of troops by helicopter.

M-14: Standard U.S. infantry rifle until 1967.

M-16: Replaced the M-14 as the standard infantry rifle in 1967.

M-79: U.S. single shot 40mm grenade launcher.

MACV: Military Assistance Command, Vietnam was the advisory command to the armed forces of South Vietnam. General William Westmoreland was the second of four MACV commanders.

medevac: Medical evacuation helicopter flights.

Micro Arc Light: see **Mini Arc Light**

Mini Arc Light: An artillery barrage in which several artillery pieces fire at interlocking target zones in a coordinated effort.

Montagnards: Aboriginal tribes of the Central Highlands mountain range in Laos and South Vietnam. The Bru tribe inhabited the area around Khe Sanh. Many Montagnards fought in CIDG forces.

mortar: Small, portable artillery pieces named for the diameter of their tube. In Vietnam U.S. and ARVN forces used 60mm, 81mm, and 4.2-inch mortars. The NVA and VC used 50mm, 60mm, 82mm, and 120mm mortars.

mortar magnet: Nickname for C-130 aircraft that resupplied Khe Sanh Combat Base during the siege.

Mu Gia Pass: Mountain Pass in Quang Binh Province of North Vietnam that was used by NVA forces to move matériel into South Vietnam.

Nakhon Phanom: Royal Thai Air Base used as an Air Force computer center processing intelligence information. Nicknamed "Naked Fanny" by Air Force pilots.

napalm: Naphthenic-Palmitic Acid, a gasoline mixture delivered by bomb that would ignite on impact, cling to anything in its blast radius, and suffocate victims by consuming oxygen as it burned.

NLF: National Liberation Front, the political arm of the Communist party in South Vietnam whose primary aim was the reunification of Vietnam.

NVA: North Vietnamese Army, also called the People's Army of North Vietnam.

Ontos: M-50A1 Ontoses were tracked vehicles armed with six 106mm recoilless rifles used for convoy security and base defense.

OP: Observation post, a station set up in front of the unit as early warning of enemy attack. Also called a listening post (LP).

Operation Dyemarker: Operation begun in April 1967 to build a barrier across the south side of the DMZ to stop NVA infiltration into South Vietnam. Also called McNamara's Line after Secretary of Defense Robert S. McNamara.

Operation Hastings: Joint operations by the 1st, 4th, and 5th Marine divisions and ARVN forces in July 1966.

Operation Neutralize: A 49-day concentrated air effort started in September 1967 to eliminate NVA long-range guns operating north of the DMZ that were disrupting the Marine's construction of the McNamara Line, especially at Con Thien.

Operation Niagara: Joint U.S. Air Force, Navy, and Marine air campaign to destroy NVA elements built up around Khe Sanh Combat Base.

Operation Pegasus: The combined effort of elements of the 1st Air Cavalry Division, 1st and 3rd Marine regiments, Navy SEABEES, Army 11th Engineers and ARVN 3rd Airborne to open Route 9 and lift the siege of Khe Sanh. The operation began on April 1, 1968, and ended April 11.

Operation Rolling Thunder: Code name for U.S. bombing campaign against the NVA that ran from February 1965 to November 1968.

People Sniffer: An experimental personnel detector used by U.S. forces that was attached to helicopters and meant to detect high concentrations of ammonia content resulting from human excrement and sweat.

Phantom: see **F-4**.

PRC: Abbreviation for People's Republic of China often used to describe Communist manufactured weapons, such as PRC mines, which were flat-topped anti-vehicle and anti-personnel mines used by the NVA.

quad-.50s: The M-55 quad featured two .50 caliber machine guns that were mounted on a truck bed.

R & R: A break from combat for rest and relaxation.

RF: Regional Force, South Vietnamese militia forces.

RIO: Radar intercept officers were Navy air officers who rode in the backseat of F-4s and operated radar and weapons systems.

RPG: Rocket propelled grenades were Soviet-made, single shot, shoulder-fired antitank weapons used by the NVA.

Skyraider: A-1 Skyraiders were single engine, propeller planes used for close air support of ground troops.

SLAM: Acronym for Seek-Locate-Annihilate-and-Monitor, a tactic of concentrating B-52 bomber, naval bombardment and artillery fires on a target. SLAM was first used in Operation Neutralize.

Spooky: AC-47 gunship with electronically operated Gatling guns and a large supply of aerial flares.

Spunky Hanson: Call sign for the Army Special Forces Camp at Lang Vei.

Supergaggle: Nickname for the coordinated delivery of supplies to the hill outposts around Khe Sanh that utilized the combined efforts of Marine helicopters and Air Force fighter/bombers.

teamhouse: combination dayroom, kitchen, storage area at U.S. Special Forces camps where off-duty personnel gathered.

Tet: The Chinese New Year, an annual celebration of Buddha's birthday at the end of January.

Tet Offensive: The country-wide offensive launched by the NVA and VC during the Tet holiday in 1968. NVA and VC forces were defeated in their attempt to seize South Vietnam and cause a general uprising among South Vietnamese citizens. More than 32,000 NVA and VC soldiers were KIA during the offensive, while only 2,100 U.S./ARVN soldiers were KIA.

TOC: U.S. Tactical Operations Centers were responsible for coordinating the actions of combat units assigned to the center. Also called Combat Operations Centers (COC).

TPQ Missions: Radar-controlled bombing missions performed by Marine fighter-bombers in which an aircraft would fly to a designated site and then a guidance system on the ground would automatically direct the aircraft to release it's ordinance.

TPQ-10: Portable radar system used to guide aircraft on resupply or bombing operations in poor weather conditions.

tube: Slang for artillery piece.

VC: Viet Cong, an abbreviation of Vietnamese Communists, the military arm of the NLF.

VMCJ: Marine Air Squadron Designation assigned to reconnaissance photograph and electronic warfare aircraft.

VMA: Marine Air Squadron Designation assigned to A-4 and all-weather (AW) attack A-6s.

VMO-6: VMO was the Marine Air Squadron designation for observation aircraft.

VT: Variable Time Fuse ammunition was set so the rounds would explode over the target in an airburst that maximized the damage radius.

Willie Peter: Slang for U.S. white phosphorous hand grenades, the contents of which burned when exposed to the air.

NOTES

The following abbreviations are used throughout these source notes:

AAR: After Action Report
CHECO: Contemporary Historical Examination of Current Operations
ComC: Command Chronologies
FMFPAC: Fleet Marine Force Pacific
Hist&MusDiv: History and Museum Division
HQMC: Headquarters, Marine Corps
HQPACAF: Headquarters Pacific, Air Force
HQ USMACV: Headquarters, US Marine Corps, Vietnam
JCS: Joint Cheifs of Staff
MACV: Marine Corps, Vietnam
MCHC: Marine Corps History Collection
OHC: Oral History Collection
SITREPS: Situation Reports
SSM: Surface-to-surface Missle
USMACV: US Marine Corps, Vietnam
USNCB: United States Naval Construction Battalion

CHAPTER 1: THE ROAD TO THE SHOWDOWN

1. III Marine Amphibious Force and 3rd MarDiv ComdC, Jan-Jun 67 (Hist&MusDiv, HQMC, Washington, D.C.).
2. New York Times, 8 Mar 65, p. 1
3. Gen William C. Westmoreland, A Soldier Reports (Garden City, N.J.: Doubleday & Co., 1976), p. 199. Hereafter Westmoreland, A Soldier Reports.
4. Ibid., p. 256.
5. Jack Shulimsom, U. S. Marines in Vietnam: An Expanding War 1966 (Hist&MusDiv, HQMC, Washington, D.C., 1982), p. 158.
6. Ibid., p. 175-76.
7. Department of Defense, United States Vietnam Relations, 1945-1967, bk 5, sec. IV-C-6, V. I, 52 (Washington, D.C.: Government Printing Office, 1971), p. 52.
8. Ibid., p. 83.
9. BrigGen Lowell E. English intvw, 1974, Tape 402 (OHC, MCHC, Washington, D.C.).
10. Maj Gary Telfer and LtCol Lane Rogers, V. Keith Fleming Jr., U. S. Marines in Vietnam: Fighting the North Vietnamese 1967 (Washington, D.C.: Hist&MusDiv, HQMC, 1983), p. 9. Hereafter Telfer et al., U.S. Marines in Vietnam.
11. Cap Joseph G. Roman intvw, 28 Jan 67, Tape 367 (OHC, MCHC, Washington, D.C.).
12. Sgt Donald E. Harper intvw, 28 Feb 67, Tape 567 (OHC, MCHC, Washington, D.C.).
13. SSgt Dennis W. Ritchie, 8 May 67, Tape 995 (OHC, MCHC, Washington, D.C.).
14. 2Lt Thomas G. King intvw, 8 May 67, Tape 994 (OHC, MCHC, Washington, D.C.).
15. Capt Bayliss L. Spivey intvw, 12 May 67, Tape 950 (OHC, MCHC, Washington, D.C.).
16. LCpl Larry W. Umstead intvw, 11 Jun 67, Tape 1126 (OHC, MCHC, Washington, D.C.).
17. Bob Maras intvw with Peter Rollins, no date.
18. LCpl Larry W. Umstead intvw, 11 Jun 67, Tape 1127 (OHC, MCHC, Washington, D.C.).
19. LCpl Terrence Walsh intvw, 11 Jun 67, Tape 1125 (OHC, MCHC, Washington, D.C.).
20. Telfer et al., U.S. Marines in Vietnam, p. 44.
21. William Steptoe intvw with Ray Stubbe, Oct 88.
22. PFC Anthony C. Bruno, 12 May 67, Tape 996 (OHC, MCHC, Washington, D.C.).
23. 2Lt Terrence M. Weber intvw, 12 May 67, Tape 996 (OHC, MCHC, Washington, D.C.).
24. PFC Steven D. Lopez intvw, 10 May 67, Tape 1115 (OHC, MCHC, Washington, D.C.).

CHAPTER 2: BOMBING AND THE BARRIER

1. U.S. Congress, Senate, 14 Mar 85, Congressional Record, p. S 2,987.
2. Ibid., S 2,985-87.
3. Lyndon Baines Johnson, The Vantage Point: Perspectives of the Presidency 1963-1969 (New York: Holt, Rinehart, and Winston, 1971), p. 235. Hereafter Johnson, The Vantage Point.
4. Ibid., p. 578.
5. As quoted in James David Barber, The Presidential Character: Predicting Performance in the White House (Englewood Cliffs, N.J.: Prentice Hall, 1977), p. 132. Hereafter Barber, The Presidential Character.
6. As quoted in Hugh Sidey, A Very Personal Presidency: Lyndon Johnson in the White House (New York: Atheneum, 1968), p. 220. Hereafter Sidey, A Very Personal Presidency.
7. Ibid., p. 22.
8. Lyndon B. Johnson intvw with Senate Armed Services Committee Chairman Richard Russell, 26 Jul 65, Conversation #8399 (C-Span's LBJ White House Archives).
9. 26th Marines summary of action on hill 950, 7 Jun 67 (Hist&MusDiv, Washington, D.C.)
10. Sgt Richard W. Baskins intvw, 23 Jun 67, Tape 1196 (OHC, MCHC, Washington, D.C.). Hereafter Baskins intvw.
11. John Prados and Ray W. Stubbe, Valley of Decision: The Siege of Khe Sanh (New York: Houghton Mifflin Co., 1991), p. 129. Hereafter Prados and Stubbe, Valley of Decision.
12. Baskins intvw.
13. MajGen Rathvon McCall Tompkins intvw, 13 Apr 73 (OHC, MCHC, Washington, D.C.), p. 73.
14. MajGen Raymond G. Davis intvw, 1977 (OHC, MCHC, Washington, D.C.), p. 83.
15. Cushman remarks to Ronald Drez as quoted in Telfer et al., U.S. Marines in Vietnam, p. 91n.
16. MajGen Louis Metzger debriefing, 22 Jan 68 (Hist&MusDiv, HQMC, Washington, D.C.)
17. Telfer et al., Fighting the North Vietnamese, p. 94.
18. U. S. Congress, Senate, Preparedness Subcommittee of the Armed Services Committee, Air War Against North Vietnam, 90th Congress, 1st session, 1977, p. 8. Hereafter Senate, Air War Against North Vietnam.
19. Ibid., p. 14.
20. Ibid., p. 15.
21. Ibid., p. 13.
22. Ibid., p. 461.
23. Ibid., p. 53.
24. Ibid., p. 136.
25. Ibid., p. 96.
26. Ibid., pp. 118 & 461.
27. Ibid., p. 14.
28. Ibid., p. 133.
29. Ibid., p. 209.
30. Ibid., pp. 88-89.
31. Ibid., p. 304.
32. Ibid., p. 317.
33. Ibid., p. 319.
34. Ibid., p. 287.
35. Ibid.
36. Ibid., pp. 298-99.
37. Ibid., p. 369.
38. Kim Willenson, The Bad War: An Oral History of the Vietnam War (New York: New American Library - NAL Books, 1987), pp. 48-49.
39. Senate, Air War Against North Vietnam, p. 348.
40. U.S. Congress, Senate, Armed Services Committee, p. S 758, National Defense Establishment: Unification of the Armed Services, 80th Congress, 1st session, 1947, pp. 302-3.
41. Ibid., p. 270.
42. W.W. Rostow, The Diffusion of Power: An Essay in Recent History (New York: The McMillan Company, 1972), pp. 460-61. Hereafter Rostow, The Diffusion of Power.

CHAPTER 3: RUNNING THE GAUNTLET: ROUTE 9 TO KHE SANH

1. Col John W. Ripley memoir, 1 Mar 78, Eisenhower Center.
2. Telfer et al., Fighting the North Vietnamese, p. 129.
3. Ibid., p. 130.
4. Westmoreland, A Soldier Reports, p. 266.
5. Westmoreland, A Soldier Reports, p. 268.
6. Johnson, The Vantage Point, p. 371.
7. Westmoreland, A Soldier Reports, p. 157.
8. Johnson, The Vantage Point, p. 372.
9. Ibid.
10. Quoted in Sidey, A Very Personal Presidency, p. 240.
11. Doris Kearns, Lyndon Johnson and the American Dream (New York: Harper & Row Publishers, 1976), p. 321. Hereafter Kearns, American Dream.
12. Peter Braestrup, Big Story (Garden City, N.J.: Anchor Press/Doubleday, 1978), p. 54.
13. Johnson, The Vantage Point, p. 379; Westmoreland, A Soldier Reports, p. 314.

CHAPTER 4: THE INTRUDERS AND THE LISTENING POST

1. With the commitment of the 26th and 27th Marines of the 5th Division to Vietnam, the 28th Marines became the only Marine reserve regiment left in the United States. It was located at Camp Pendleton, California.
2. Commander USNCB Pacific Annual Report, 2 Jan 68.
3. Chaplain Ray Stubbe diary, p. 684. Hereafter Stubbe diary.
4. Ibid., p. 704.
5. Adm U.S.G. Sharp and Gen W.C. Westmoreland, Report on the War in Vietnam (as of 30 June 1968), (Washington, D.C.: Government Printing Office, 1969), p. 41.
6. Westmoreland, A Soldier Reports, p. 413.
7. As quoted in Eric Hammel, Khe Sanh: Siege in the Clouds (New York: Crown Publishers Inc., 1989), p. 41. Hereafter Hammel, Siege.
8. Ibid., pp. 13-14.
9. PFC Charles Thornton Jr. memoir, Jan 88, Eisenhower Center. Hereafter Thornton memoir.
10. Hammel, Siege, p. 14.
11. Nile Buffington intvw with Ronald Drez, 13 Mar 90. Hereafter Buffington intvw.
12. Thornton memoir.
13. Buffington intvw.
14. Stubbe diary, p. 723.
15. Buffington intvw.
16. Capt Moyers S. Shore II, USMC, The Battle for Khe Sanh (Washington, D.C.: Historical Branch, G-3 Division, HQMC, 1969), pp. 30-31. Hereafter Shore, The Battle for Khe Sanh.
17. Westmoreland, A Soldier Reports, pp. 446-47.
18. Bernard C. Nalty, Air Power and the Fight for Khe Sanh (Washington D.C.: Office of Air Force History, USAF, 1973), p. 14. Hereafter Nalty, Air Power.
19. As quoted in Robert A. Devine, Since 1945: Politics and Diplomacy in Recent American History, 2nd ed. (New York: John Wiley & Sons, 1979), p. 166.
20. As quoted in Hugh Sidey, "The Presidency: A Long Way from Spring," Time, 9 Feb 68, p. 16. Hereafter Sidey, "The Presidency: A Long Way from Spring."
21. Quoted in Hugh Sidey, "Deep Go the Roots of the Alamo," Life, 31 May 68, p. 32B.
22. Vaughn Davis Bornet, The Presidency of Lyndon B. Johnson (Lawrence, Kansas: University Press of Kansas, 1983), p. 272.
23. Col William H. Dabney intvw, 20 May 82 (Hist&MusDiv, HQMC, Washington, D.C.). Hereafter Dabney intvw.
24. Schuminson, Blasiol, Smith, and Dawson, The U.S. Marines in Vietnam: The Defining Year, 1968 (Hist&MusDivision, HQMC, Washington D.C., 1997), p. 271.
25. Ibid., pp. 29-31.

CHAPTER 5: HILL 881N: THE OPENING ATTACK

1. MACV Document, Vietnam Lessons Learned #69, Khe Sanh: Analysis of Enemy Positions and Evaluation of the Effectiveness of Weapons Systems Against Enemy Fortification, 8 Jul 68, Eisenhower Center.
2. Jack Corbett intvw, 22 Feb 89, Eisenhower Center. Hereafter Corbett intvw.
3. Capt Mizra M. Biag letter to Col F.C. Caldwell, 23 Dec 68. Hereafter Biag comments.
4. U.S. Congress, Senate, Electronic Battlefield Subcommittee of the Preparedness Investigating Subcommittee of the Armed Services Committee, Investigation into Electronic Battlefield Program, 91st Congress, 2nd session, 1969, p. 91. Hereafter Senate, Investigation into Electronic Battlefield Program.
5. Nalty, Air Power, p. 14.
6. Shore, The Battle for Khe Sanh, p. 32.
7. As quoted in Hammel, Siege, p. 44.
8. Hammel, Siege, p. 35.
9. Col William Dabney statement to Brindley's Navy Cross citation, 21 Jan 68. Hereafter Dabney statement.
10. RFC Kenneth D. Brewer statement to Brindley's Navy Cross citation, 21 Jan 68. Hereafter Brewer statement.
11. Dabney statement.
12. Brewer statement.
13. Dabney statement.
14. Maj Matthew Caulfield statement to Thomas' Navy Cross citation, 21 Jan 68.
15. Dabney intvw.

CHAPTER 6: THE ENEMY STRIKES

1. Hammel, Siege, p. 56.
2. Ibid., p. 57.
3. Ibid., p. 58.
4. Shore, The Battle for Khe Sanh, pp. 39 & 48; Westmoreland, A Soldier Reports, p. 416.
5. Jacob Van Staaveren, History of Task Force Alpha – 1 October 1967 - 30 April 1968 (Air Force Archives, 1969), p. 50.
6. As quoted in Hammel, Siege, p. 60.
7. Ibid.
8. Ibid., pp. 60-61.
9. Ibid.
10. Ibid., p. 61.
11. 2Lt Linn Oehling intvw, 22 Jan 68, Tape 2589 (OHC, MCHC, Washington, D.C.).
12. PFC John Lewis intvw, 22 Jan 68, Tape 2589 (OHC, MCHC, Washington, D.C.).
13. PFC Michael R. James, intvw, 22 Jan 68, Tape 2589 (OHC, MCHC, Washington, D.C.).
14. GySgt Bernard Goddard, "Vietnam 1967-1968," (taped letters of Bernard Goddard), Goddard Design.
15. 1Lt Jerry N. Saulsbury intvw, Tape 2776 (OHC, MCHC, Washington, D.C.).
16. GySgt Mykle Stahl intvw, 22 Jan 68, Tape 2589 (OHC, MCHC, Washington, D.C.).
17. LCpl Billy R. Moffett intvw, 22 Jan 68, Tape 2589 (OHC, MCHC, Washington, D.C.).
18. As quoted in Khe Sanh Veterans' Newsletter, Summer 1993.
19. Ibid.
20. As quoted in Hammel, Siege, pp. 67-71.
21. Ibid., pp. 71-72.
22. As quoted in Hammel, Siege, p. 174.
23. As quoted in Khe Sanh Veterans' Newsletter,

Spring 1992.
24. Ibid.
25. Ibid.
26. Corbett intvw.
27. Department of Defense film, *The Battle for Khe Sanh*, 1969. Hereafter DOD film.
28. Cap William J. O'Connor intvw, 13 Feb 68, Tape 2536 (OHC, MCHC, Washington, D.C.). Hereafter O'Connor intvw.
29. 1Lt William L. Eberhardt Jr. intvw, 13 Feb 68, Tape 2536 (OHC, MCHC, Washington, D.C.).
30. Sgt Ronnie D. Whitenight intvw, 13 Feb 68, Tape 2536 (OHC, MCHC, Washington, D.C.).
31. O'Connor intvw.
32. DOD film.
33. Ibid.
34. Shore, *The Battle for Khe Sanh*, p. 43.
35. Quoted in Hammel, *Siege*, p. 87.
36. Corbett intvw.
37. DOD film.
38. Ibid.

CHAPTER 7: THE ENCIRCLEMENT
1. Tom Stamper intvw with Ray Stubbe, 20 May 90.
2. John R. Roberts intvw with Ray Stubbe, 13 Sept 89.
3. Ibid.
4. Bruce Clark intvw with Ray Stubbe, 15 Oct 88.
5. John Balanco intvw with Ray Stubbe, 30 May 92.
6. Maj Darrell L. Guttormson intvw, 22 Jan 68, OHC.
7. Cap Ronald M. D'Amora intvw, 23 Jan 68, Tape 2406 (OHC, MCHC, Washington, D.C.). Hereafter D'Amora intvw.
8. FMFPAC Operations of U.S. Marine Forces Vietnam, Jan 68, p. 61.
9. D'Amora intvw.
10. Maj Jerry Hudson letter to HQMC, 2 Jan 69.
11. Bruce Pollica and Joe R. Rickey, *Monograph of 834 Air Division Tactical Airlift Support for Khe Sanh, 21 Jan - 8 Apr 68*, no date, pp. 4-6.
12. CHECO Report, *Khe Sanh (Operation Niagara) 22 Jan-31 Mar 69*, HQPACAF, 13 Sep 68.
13. Shore, *The Battle for Khe Sanh*, p. 45.
14. Robert Brewer intvw with John Wright, 5 Feb 89; Robert Brewer intvw with Ronald Drez, 5 May 88.
15. As quoted in Gloria Emerson, "A Major at Khe Sanh Recalls 1968," *New York Times*, 21 Feb 70, p. 3.
16. John R. Roberts intvw with Ray Stubbe, 13 Sept 89.
17. Bruce B.G. Clark intvw with Ray Stubbe, 17 May 89.
18. LtCol Harry T. Hagaman intvw, 2 Mar 68, Tape 2548 (OHC, MCHC, Washington, D.C.).
19. As quoted in Shulimson et al., *U.S. Marines in Vietnam: The Defining Year, 1968* (HQMC, Washington, D.C., 1997), p. 266.
20. Capt Earle G. Breeding intvw with Ronald Drez, 30 Jun 88.
21. Charles P. Rushforth III intvw with Ronald Drez, 9 Apr 88. Hereafter Rushforth intvw, 9 Apr 88.
22. Ibid.
23. Ibid.
24. 26th Marines twice reported the five-tank information: once at 0604, and again at 1130. 26th Marines SITREPS #338 (240604Z/JAN68); #339 (241130Z/JAN68).
25. Rushforth intvw, 9 Apr 88.
26. MajGen Rathvon McCall Tompkins, comments on draft manuscript of Cap Moyers S. Shore II's *The Battle for Khe Sanh*.

CHAPTER 8: EMBRACED BY THE ENEMY
1. Earle Breeding intvw with Ronald Drez, 30 Jun

88. Hereafter Breeding intvw.
2. Shore, *The Battle for Khe Sanh*, p. 51.
3. Biag comments.
4. "The Battle of Bunker's Bunker," *Time*, 9 Feb 68, p. 23.
5. As quoted in Johnson, *The Vantage Point*, p. 381.
6. Ibid.
7. Peter Braestrup, *The Big Story* (New York: Anchor Press/Doubleday, 1978), p. 262. Hereafter Braestrup, *Big Story*.
8. As quoted in Sidey, "The Presidency: A Long Way from Spring," p. 16.
9. JCS memo to President Johnson, Subject: "Situation at Khe Sanh," 29 Jan 68 (Johnson Library).
10. Westmoreland, *A Soldier Reports*, pp. 425-31.
11. Defense Intelligence Agency Bulletin, 26 Jan 68.
12. Rostow, *The Diffusion of Power*, pp. 85-90.
13. Herbert Y. Schandler, *The Unmaking of a President: Lyndon Johnson and Vietnam* (Princeton, N.J.: Princeton University Press, 1977), p. 69.
14. Robert Karwoski intvw with Ronald Drez, 1987. Hereafter Karwoski intvw.
15. As quoted in Westmoreland, *A Soldier Reports*, p. 447.
16. Karwoski intvw.
17. Nalty, *Air Power*, p. 86.
18. Braestrup, *Big Story*, p. 262.
19. Dr. Harvey DeMaagd intvw with Duon Rose, Jul 89.
20. Jeff Bodenweiser intvw with Ronald Drez, 23 Aug 88.
21. Breeding intvw.
22. Cpl Eugene J. Franklin intvw, 24-26 Apr 68, Tape 2775 (OHC, HQMC, Washington, D.C.)
23. PFC Newton D. Lyle intvw, 24-26 Apr 68; Tape 2775 (OHC, HQMC, Washington, D.C.). Hereafter Lyle intvw.
24. Ibid.
25. Tom Eichler intvw with Ronald Drez, 30 Jun 88. Hereafter Eichler intvw.
26. Donald Shanley intvw with Ronald Drez, 14 Apr 89.
27. Eichler intvw.
28. Breeding intvw.
29. Biag comments.
30. Lyle intvw.

CHAPTER 9: THE ATTACK FROM THE WEST: LANG VEI AND OUTPOST ALPHA
1. Prados and Stubbe, *Valley of Decision*, p. 317.
2. 5th Special Forces Group (Airborne), 1st Special Forces Group AAR for Battle of Lang Vei, 24 Jan-7 Feb 68. Hereafter AAR, 24 Jan-7 Feb 68.
3. Ibid.
4. Ibid.
5. Ibid.
6. Ibid.
7. Ibid
8. Ibid.
9. Ibid.
10. Ibid.
11. Ibid.
12. Ibid.
13. Ibid.
14. Ibid.
15. Ibid.
16. Ibid.
17. Ibid.
18. Ibid.
19. Ibid.
20. Ibid.
21. Ibid.
22. Ibid.
23. Ibid.

24. Ibid.
25. Rushforth intvw, 9 Apr 88.
26. AAR, 24 Jan-7 Feb 68.
27. George Einhorn intvw with Ray Stubbe, 9 Mar 92. Hereafter Einhorn intvw.
28. David Ford intvw with Ray Stubbe, 22 Jan 92. Hereafter Ford intvw.
29. Arnold Alderette intvw with Ray Stubbe, 9 Mar 92. Hereafter Alderette intvw.
30. 2Lt Francis Brian Lovely Jr. intvw, 5 May 68, Tape 2802 (OHC, HQMC, Washington, D.C.).
31. As quoted in Einhorn intvw.
32. Alderette intvw.
33. Seavy-Cioffi Silver Star citation, 2002.
34. Alderette intvw.
35. Ford intvw.
36. Einhorn intvw.
37. Kearns, *American Dream*, p. 271.
38. As quoted in Braestrup, *Big Story*, p. 261.
39. As quoted in "The Dusty Agony of Khe Sanh," *Newsweek*, 18 Mar 68
40. Michael Herr, *Dispatches* (New York: Alfred A. Knopf, 1978), p. 144.
41. Dabney intvw.
42. Biag comments.

CHAPTER 10: VULGAR FREE-FOR-ALL
1. Joint General Staff, Ministry of National Defense, "Study of VC Documents," 27 Apr 68, No. 111/68 (Eisenhower Center). Hereafter Ministry of National Defense, "Study of VC Documents."
2. HQ USMACV Research Analysis Study, ST67-013, "The NVA Soldier in South Vietnam." Hereafter HQ USMAVC Study, "The NVA Soldier in South Vietnam."
3. As quoted in Shore, *The Battle for Khe Sanh*, p. 101.
4. Douglas Spitler intvw with Ronald Drez, 23 Aug 88.
5. Ibid.
6. Tom O'Toole intvw with Ray Stubbe, 30 Jun 91.
7. Dabney intvw.
8. As quoted in Shore, *The Battle for Khe Sanh*, p. 83.
9. Dabney intvw.
10. Ibid.
11. Cap Andrew B. Adams intvw, 4 Mar 68, Tape 2555 (OHC, MCHC, Washington, D.C.).
12. C.G. Gerard, "One Pilot's Perspective of Khe Sanh," *The Khe Sanh Veteran Newsletter*, Fall 1992.
13. As quoted in Westmoreland, *A Soldier Reports*, p. 465.
14. Ibid.
15. Shore, *The Battle for Khe Sanh*, p. 186.
16. HQ USMACV Study, "The NVA Soldier in South Vietnam," pp. 40-43.
17. Ibid.
18. Ibid.
19. Ministry of National Defense, "Study of VC Documents."
20. Westmoreland, *A Soldier Reports*, pp. 466-67.
21. Capt Charles P. Rushforth III memoir, 30 Apr 88. Hereafter Rushforth mem., 30 Apr 88.
22. Capt Kenneth Pipes intvw, 8-13 Mar 68, Tape 2621 (OHC, MCHC, Washington, D.C.). Hereafter Pipes intvw, 8-13 Mar 68.
23. HM3 Frank Calzia intvw, 8-13 Mar 68, Tape 2621 (OHC, MCHC, Washington, D.C.). Hereafter Calzia intvw.
24. PFC Calvin E. Bright intvw, 8-13 Mar 68, Tape 2681 (OHC, MCHC, Washington, D.C.).
25. PFC Alexander Tretiakoff intvw, 8-13 Mar 68, Tape 2681 (OHC, MCHC, Washington, D.C.).
26. Calzia intvw.

27. PFC Kenneth R. Totten, Jr. intvw, 8-13 Mar 68, Tape 2681 (OHC, MCHC, Washington, D.C.).
28. LCpl Doss B. Thrasher intvw, 8-13 Mar 68, Tape 2681 (OHC, MCHC, Washington, D.C.).
29. Calzia intvw.
30. Pipes intvw, 8-13 Mar 68.
31. 1stLt Thomas O'Toole statement, 25 Feb 68 (Eisenhower Center).
32. Rushforth intvw, 30 Apr 88.
33. LtCol David Harmon intvw with Kathi Jones, 21 Jun 93.

CHAPTER 11: SMASHING THE RING
1. Jerry Hudson intvw with Kathi Jones, 4 May 90.
2. LtCol Louis Rann intvw with Ronald Drez, 30 Aug 88. Hereafter Rann intvw.
3. Ibid.
4. Ibid.
5. Senate, *Investigation into Electronic Battlefield Program*, p. 87.
6. DOD film.
7. Ibid.
8. Col Kent O. W. Steen intvw with Ray Stubbe, 28 Jul 91.
9. Shore, *The Battle for Khe Sanh*, pp. 109-10.
10. DOD film.
11. Rann intvw.
12. Shore, *The Battle for Khe Sanh*, pp. 124-25.
13. DOD film.
14. Walter Cronkite, "CBS Evening News," 29 Feb 68.
15. "ABC Evening News," 14 Feb 68.
16. Murray Frompson, "CBS Evening News," 29 Feb 68.
17. As quoted in Peter C. Rollins et al., *Television's Vietnam: The Impact of Visual Images* (Department of English, Oklahoma State University).
18. Rushforth intvw, 30 Apr 88.
19. Cap Robert J. Dougal intvw, 10 Apr 68, Tape 2664 (OHC, MCHC, Washington, D.C.).
20. Rushforth intvw, 30 Apr 88.
21. As quoted in Barber, *The Presidential Character*, p. 41.
22. As quoted in Kearns, *American Dream*, p. 339.
23. Ibid., p. 321.
24. Cap Kenneth W. Pipes intvw, 21 May 68, Tape 2810 (OHC, MCHC, Washington, D.C.). Hereafter Pipes intvw, 21 May 68.
25. Cpl Edward I. Prendergast intvw, 21 May 68, Tape 2810 (OHC, MCHC, Washington, D.C.).
26. Sgt William M. Simpkins statement to SSM Citation for Cpl Samuel Boone Jr., 6 Sep 68.
27. LCpl Lonnie W. Morrison statement to SSM Citation for Cpl Samuel Boone Jr., 6 Sep 68.
28. LCpl Michael H. McCauley intvw, 21 May 68, Tape 2810 (OHC, MCHC, Washington, D.C.).
29. PFC Frank C. Tanner intvw, 21 May 68, Tape 2810 (OHC, MCHC, Washington, D.C.).
30. Pipes intvw, 21 May 68.
31. The Marines recovered partial remains that they identified as nine of the men. None could be individually identified. Those remains were combined with the remains of nine sailors who had died in a separate incident. All were interred in a mass grave in St. Louis. PFC Ronald Ridgeway was listed as one of the eighteen men buried there, but in 1973, Ridgeway returned home from prison in Hanoi.
32. Shore, *The Battle for Khe Sanh*, p. 142.
33. As quoted in Shore, *The Battle for Khe Sanh*, p. 143.

EPILOGUE
1. Gen William Westmoreland intvw with Ronald Drez, 4 Nov 88.

PHOTO CREDITS

The Vietnam War was the first American war in which many of the soldiers carried personal cameras. In creating this book we received photographs from a number of Khe Sanh veterans, and we would like to thank them for documenting their experiences and sharing their photographs with us. Thank you also to the family members of Khe Sanh veterans for their photograph contributions.